MILFORD PUBLIC LIBRARY
330 FAMILY DRIVE
MILFORD, MI 48381

S0-AIF-223

DISCARD

RECEIVED

JUL 01 2007.

1607

1607
Jamestown and the New World

Compiled by Dennis Montgomery

with the staff of the Colonial Williamsburg Foundation

Principal photography by David M. Doody

Colonial Williamsburg

THE COLONIAL WILLIAMSBURG FOUNDATION   Williamsburg, Virginia

in association with

ROWMAN & LITTLEFIELD PUBLISHERS, INC.   Lanham · Boulder · New York · Toronto · Oxford

© 2007 by The Colonial Williamsburg Foundation
All rights reserved. Published 2007

20 19 18 17 16 15 14 13 12 11 10 09 08 07   1 2 3 4 5 6

Library of Congress Cataloging-in-Publication Data
1607 : Jamestown and the New World / compiled by Dennis Montgomery with the staff of the Colonial Williamsburg Foundation ;
principal photography by David M. Doody.
        p. cm.
    Includes index.
    ISBN-13: 978-0-87935-232-5 (pbk. : alk. paper)
    ISBN-10: 0-87935-232-9 (pbk. : alk. paper)
    ISBN-13: 978-0-7425-5837-3 (hardcover : alk. paper)
    ISBN-10: 0-7425-5837-1 (hardcover : alk. paper)
    [etc.]
    1. Jamestown (Va.)—History—17th century. 2. Virginia—
History—Colonial period, ca. 1600–1775. 3. Powhatan Indians—
Virginia—Jamestown—History—17th century. 4. Frontier
and pioneer life—Virginia—Jamestown. 5. Jamestown Island
(Va.)—Antiquities. I. Montgomery, Dennis. II. Colonial
Williamsburg Foundation. III. Title.

    F234.J3A15 2007
    973.2'1—dc22   2006037700

ISBN-10: 0-7425-5837-1 (R&L: hardcover)
ISBN-13: 978-0-7425-5837-3 (R&L: hardcover)
ISBN-10: 0-7425-5838-X (R&L: pbk.)
ISBN-13: 978-0-7425-5838-0 (R&L: pbk.)
ISBN-10: 0-87935-232-9 (CWF: pbk.)
ISBN-13: 978-0-87935-232-5 (CWF: pbk.)

Designed by Bessas & Ackerman
Printed in Singapore

The chapters in this book appear in a slightly different
form in Colonial Williamsburg, the journal of the
Colonial Williamsburg Foundation, in issues published
between 1990 and 2007.

Please note the spelling of "Sir Walter Ralegh."
The style of Colonial Williamsburg is to spell
the adventurer's surname as he and his father spelled it.

Frontispiece: A Jamestown colonist portrayed by Fred Schlopp.
Cover and jacket: Nova Virginiae Tabula, published by William Blaeu
after John Smith, Amsterdam, 1635-90/The Colonial Williamsburg
Foundation.

Published by The Colonial Williamsburg Foundation,
PO Box 1776, Williamsburg, VA 23187-1776
in association with Rowman & Littlefield Publishers, Inc.,
4501 Forbes Blvd., Suite 200, Lanham, MD 20706

www.colonialwilliamsburg.org
www.rowmanlittlefield.com

Colonial Williamsburg is a registered trade name
of The Colonial Williamsburg Foundation,
a not-for-profit educational institution.

Image Credits
Architect of the Capitol: 42 bottom, 43, 65 bottom. APVA Preser-
vation Virginia: 73, 74. Beinecke Library, Yale: 184 left and right.
Bermuda Historical Monuments Trust: 87. Bridgeman Art Library:
76 bottom. Brigham Young University Museum of Art: 66. The
Colonial Williamsburg Foundation: 5, 9 bottom (gift of Abby
Aldrich Rockefeller), 17, 19 top (gift of Preston Davie), 19 bottom
(gift of Sir Harold Harmsworth), 21 (gift of John T. and Gretchen
Howell), 24, 30 top, 33 top, 33 bottom (gift of Anne Kondrup
Gray), 42 top, 46, 65, 67 bottom (gift of Abby Aldrich Rockefeller), 102, 112, 127, 147, 172, 173, 174. Corbis-Bettman: 105 left and
right. David Rumsey Collection: 88 right. Dave Doody/The Colonial Williamsburg Foundation: frontispiece, 2, 14 top and bottom,
22, 26, 36, 39, 40 left and right, 48, 50, 57, 60, 69 top and bottom,
71 top, 72, 76 top, 77, 79, 80, 95, 97, 98, 101, 104, 110, 111, 113, 116,
117, 119 top, 120 left and right, 121 left and right, 124, 129, 132 top,
135, 136, 145, 146, 150, 164 left and right, 166 left and right, 167, 169,
176 bottom, 181, 186 top and bottom, 191, 192, 193, 194, 196, 200,
203, 204, 205, 206, 207. Keith Archibald Forbes: 92. Free Library
of Philadelphia: 85. Granger Collection: 89. Tom Green/The Colonial Williamsburg Foundation: 106, 119 bottom, 163. Huntington
Library: 58, 141. Jamestown-Yorktown Foundation: 4, 60. Thierry
Legault: 183. Library of Congress: 11, 67 top. Hans Lorenz/The
Colonial Williamsburg Foundation: 102. National Maritime
Museum: 132 bottom. National Park Service, Colonial National
Historical Park: 197. National Portrait Gallery, Smithsonian Insti-
tution: 59. New Line Cinema: 71 bottom, 139. New York Public
Library: 90. Ivor Noël Hume: 54, 55. Richard Schlecht/National
Geographic Image Collection: 175. Society of Antiquaries, London:
182 left and right. University of Virginia Library: 25, 30 bottom.
Utah State Historical Society: 83 bottom. Virginia Historical Soci-
ety: 78. Virginia State Library and Archives: 8, 9 top. Wellcome
Library: 191. Suzanne Wescoat: 149. Vernon Wooten/The Colonial
Williamsburg Foundation: 176 top.

Contents

Foreword

In accepting the invitation to write this brief foreword, I anticipated, of course, that the task would enlarge my knowledge of the founding of Jamestown. What has surprised me, however, is how reading the following essays has brought me to face a fascinating question, one usually ignored by historians: Which was the more meaningful event for American history—the settlement at Jamestown in 1607 or the Pilgrims' landing that took place at Plymouth Rock thirteen years later?

These essays, all of them published in the journal *Colonial Williamsburg,* need not draw every reader into debating this question. The book most assuredly can be read comfortably with pleasure and with profit. If, however, there are persons eager to pit New England Pilgrims against Virginia Cavaliers, I suggest they begin their reading by turning first to James Axtell's provocative essay "Historical Rivalry." I found this chapter to be very helpful, particularly once I decided that I should, after all, seek to compare the importance of the Jamestown settlement with that begun at Plymouth.

I say "after all" for it startled me a bit to find myself setting out to determine just how Jamestown's story ought to compete for standing in history's long view. Until then, I had chosen to ignore any comparison. My indifference probably grew from the luxury, so to speak, of wearing two hats. Many years ago and after writing several biographies about individuals beloved in either Massachusetts or Virginia, I found myself elected a cultural laureate of Virginia as well as a fellow of the Pilgrim Society. Thus adopted by both commonwealths, I decided it was the better part of valor to keep clear of any debate between champions of Jamestown and of Plymouth.

But now, after reading the essays in this volume, I have concluded that the event of four centuries ago at Jamestown has a significance for history beyond the establishment of other English colonies in North America. Jamestown's primacy is due not merely to its being the first permanent English settlement on this continent.

Rather, it is because the purpose behind the founding of the colony at Jamestown became the basic characteristic of the American nation, its people, and its culture.

By no means do I wish to disregard the motive bringing the Pilgrims to New England. Their desire to escape the Anglican Church, which they deemed spiritually unclean, was the start of a "holier than thou" attitude that has dogged the American outlook, both secular and denominational, over the centuries. Yet, despite this so-called Puritan heritage, the sweep of American history has been shaped more by the worldly, profit-seeking materialism that lay behind the establishment of Jamestown.

This viewpoint may seem almost irreverent when confronted by the legend arising from the *Mayflower*'s voyage and the landing of its Pilgrim passengers. After all, these immigrants were reputedly filled with the Holy Spirit as they began their claim to a divinely inspired errand into the wilderness. Well, despite the beguiling simplifications that have prevailed in the Pilgrims' history, I believe that, in portraying so convincingly how dreams of wealth brought Englishmen to Jamestown, the essays in this book actually help us see how this motive would remain for over 400 years the chief force fueling American history. In time, it even conquered the Pilgrim world, where individual economic success was established by congregations as proof of being one of God's chosen and basis for full membership in society.

True, this materialist drive has often evoked the baser side of human nature—or sometimes even worse. As, for instance, when the Native Americans in Virginia and elsewhere were to discover the woe likely to befall those who blocked the way of the Englishman's—or American's—drive for economic success. But, of course, there was much more to the story than greed after the three English vessels sailed into the Chesapeake Bay in April 1607. One of the admirable features of these essays is that, while they do not shield us from the sordid and even horrid behavior of which we humans are capable, they still include edifying accounts of what mankind can pause to do even while seeking security and wealth.

For instance, while Jamestown was the source from which culture in the Old World and the New was infected by the malignant passion for tobacco, it was also the birthplace of government by popular legislature—this occurring in 1619, one year before the *Mayflower* set sail. Alas, however, only three years after these representatives had assembled, many of them were slain during an Indian assault on the Jamestown neighborhood. This massacre, by the way, discouraged only for a moment the drive for profit that had led the Virginia Company in London to establish Jamestown.

In these stories of courage, greed, and perseverance that began in 1607, there was no lack of colorful personalities, both English and Native American. If nothing else, these essays depict a panorama of saints and scoundrels. It is a scene that should appeal to all readers, whether they seek the significance of Jamestown in history or simply some captivating tales of how human endeavor, in the face of often overpowering difficulty, founded the first permanent English settlement in North America.

So, let me detain the reader no longer from returning to 1607.

Paul C. Nagel

Preface

That Americans confound Plymouth for Jamestown as the site of England's first permanent New World settlement or confuse the contributions of the Massachusetts Pilgrims with the achievements of the Virginia colonists is not the fault of *Colonial Williamsburg,* the popular history journal of the Colonial Williamsburg Foundation. The magazine has been sharing with its readers Jamestown's claims to primacy since Parke Rouse's article about the nation's first Thanksgiving—not the one in the Bay State—appeared in the autumn 1986 issue.

A score or so of contributors since have narrated for the journal audience chapters from the history of the village the Virginia Company of London founded beside the River James in 1607. That, by the way, more than a decade before the *Mayflower* fetched up on the shores of the Bay State. Across the magazine's pages, writers have traced the steps of such early Virginia luminaries as King James, Powhatan, Pocahontas, planter John Rolfe, and Captain John Smith—as well as such lesser lights as Opechancanough, physician John Pott, spy Don Diego de Molina, and Captain John Martin.

But why? Why does a magazine named for the restoration of an eighteenth-century Virginia town spend so much ink on a vanished seventeenth-century settlement? What has Jamestown to do with Williamsburg?

Everything.

Jamestown was the closest thing the colony had to a city for almost a century. Among its outposts was Middle Plantation, a scattering of cottages down a horse path at the central point of a miles-long fence. The fence, which began close to Jamestown and ended near what became Yorktown, was supposed to keep the Indians out and the cattle in.

For ninety-two years, Jamestown was Virginia's capital—until 1699, when the government christened the horse path "Duke of Gloucester Street," renamed Middle Plantation for King William, and moved in mace, General Assembly, and quill pens. Williamsburg, capital for eighty-one years, was, in a sense, built on Jamestown's foundations. The cornerstone of the republican government raised at its Capitol in 1776 was the meeting of English America's first representative assembly at Jamestown in 1619. The culture that furnished the classrooms of the College of William and Mary and the drawing rooms of the Governor's Palace found its first solid American footings at Jamestown. So did Williamsburg's capitalism, its Indian policies, its commerce and trades, its Anglican religion, its devotion to Anglo-Saxon law, and its reliance on African slavery.

The stories in this book, collected for the 400th anniversary of Jamestown's founding, tell of the first Americans and of America's first settlers, of Jamestown's rise, and fall, and rediscovery.

And nary a Pilgrim in sight.

In a Peninsula on the North side of this river

are the English Planted in a place

by them called James Towne,

in honour of the Kings most excellent Majestie.

CAPTAINE JOHN SMITH

The Generall Historie of Virginia, New-England,

and the Summer Isles (London, 1624)

Shadows on the Land

The Powhatan Indians

ALLAN C. FISHER JR.

What were they like, the original masters of the dense forests, the lovely rivers, the sunlit Chesapeake in the coastal lands of what we now call Virginia? Were they mere brutish savages? Or people with a culture and proud heritage of their own? Did they just exist? Or did they live in knowing harmony with their Eden? What happened when proud Indian met haughty Englishman in the dawn time of our nation?

Repeatedly the foremost priests, who talked to the gods and whose insights none dared question, had warned of it. From out of the Chesapeake Bay would arise a nation that would destroy the empire of the mightiest of all rulers, Powhatan, feared master of more than thirty tribes. And the people also heard and pondered a second prophecy: They would fight three battles against the invaders of their lands, and the last battle would leave them broken and subject to the aliens.

Bitter, bloody prophecies—and both came to pass. The prolonged confrontation in Tidewater Virginia between the Indians known collectively as Powhatans and the land-hungry English settlers who first came "from the Chesapeake" in their great winged canoes almost four centuries ago could end in only one way, defeat and capitulation for the original Americans and the loss of their vast hunting grounds. Guns and numbers, not some star-crossed destiny, determined the outcome. The invaders carried fearsome thundersticks that spat fire and death, and each year more and more came in an overwhelming flood. Women and children on both sides, not just the combatants, died in

Former Pamunkey chief Tecumseh Cook, 91, standing on what the tribe believes is the burial mound of Powhatan, points to a landmark he uses in locating the grave site.

clashes of a ferocity that gave no quarter and asked none. Unhappily but predictably, this pattern of confrontation continued across a vast continent for almost three centuries and in a thousand encounters: Tippecanoe and the Trail of Tears, Custer's Last Stand and the massacre at Wounded Knee, the 1,700-mile fighting trek of Chief Joseph and the surrender of proud Geronimo.

Festering wounds, these, in the national psyche and the reason some contemporary historians at times take sides and condemn or defend either the Powhatans or the Jamestown colonists for their excesses and for not setting an enduring example of brotherly concern. Indeed at times both adversaries tried to live amicably. But no judgments from the moral vantage point of the late twentieth century seem warranted. They were what they were, Indians and English alike, warlike peoples. To the Indians tribal warfare had been a way of life for untold centuries, and the English in their latest of many wars had vanquished the Spaniards. Settlers would include many old soldiers as keen for throat cutting as any brave. Converting the Indians to Christianity and the English economy did not prove successful as means of bridging differences. Above all, two vastly different cultures grated upon one another with no real hope of accommodation.

The English founded Jamestown, their first tenuous toehold in Virginia, on May 13, 1607, and what we know of the Powhatans of that time we learn from only a handful of chroniclers. William Strachey, the colony's official secretary, tells us of the two dire prophecies:

> Not long since yt was that his [Powhatan's] Priests told him, how that from the Chesapeacke Bay a Nation should arise, which would disolue and give end to his Empier, for which not many years since, perplex't with this divelish Oracle, and divers understandings thereof, according to auncyent and gentile Custome, he destroyed and put to the sword all such who might lye under any doubtful construction of the said prophesie.

Strachey added that this slaughter resulted in the annihilation of the "Chessiopeians," or Chesapeakes, who lived on the bay's shores. In that same passage, Strachey wrote:

> Some of the inhabitants againe, haue not spared to giue vs to vnderstand, how they have a second Prophesy likewise

amongst them, that twice they should give overthrow and dishearten the Attempters, and such Straungers as should envade their Territoryes, or labour to settle plantations amongst them, but the third time they themselues should fall into their Subjection and vnder their Conquest.

The secretary then speculated that "their apprehension may fully touch at vs" and had "bredd straung fears amonst them."

That master of derring-do, Captain John Smith, who wrote copiously about Virginia, recorded such a fear. During one of many forays to explore and trade, Smith and his men suffered an ambush near the falls of the Rappahannock River and captured an attacker. Smith asked him "why they came that way to attack us, that came to them in peace, and to seek their loves; he answered, they heard we were a people come from under the world, to take their world from them." None other than the mighty Powhatan himself voiced a similar concern to Smith during one of their several meetings: "Many doe informe me, your comming hither is not for trade, but to invade my people, and possesse my Country."

Were Virginia's Indians predestined to drain the cup of prophecy to its bitter dregs? Or did Indian experience, not prescience, bring about their qualms? Spaniards sailed into the Chesapeake Bay at least twice in the 1560s and 1570s. They attempted to establish a mission, which the Indians sacked. In retaliation Spanish soldiers killed a number of natives and took others for sale as slaves. Sir Walter Ralegh dispatched several expeditions to the area south of the bay, including an attempt at settlement by the Lost Colony on Roanoke Island in 1587. Powhatan once taunted Smith by claiming braves of his empire killed those earlier colonists.

The Jamestown colonists got a bloody foretaste of what they could expect from the Indians on their very first day ashore, April 26, 1607. A landing party at the mouth of the James River encountered warriors creeping up on them. The Indians charged and were driven off, but not before two Englishmen were wounded. Thus began years of guerrilla warfare mixed with friendly contacts, of vicious ambuscades, mass attacks, and ruthless reprisals, and times of wary and exhausted peace. In their written records the English invariably referred to the Indians as "salvages." Few settlers saw, or cared, that their adversaries fought not just for their land but for their way of life, an ancient culture surprisingly complex and in many ways worthy of respect.

Before Chesapeake Bay existed, Paleo-Indians inhabited the area. Their handiwork, chipped stone points for spears and arrows found with charred mammal bones that could be carbon-dated, take Indian ancestry back about 10,000 years to the late Pleistocene period. Folsom points of that remote era and Clovis points some 2,000–3,000 years earlier have been found in Virginia. Many a Virginia farmer cherishes a treasure trove of arrowheads and spear points turned up by the plow or found on eroded riverfront beaches.

Historians place the Powhatans in the Late Woodland period of development. They were not so advanced technologically as the Incas and Aztecs decimated by the Spanish, but they lived in permanent settlements, farmed as well as hunted, believed in a benevolent God, a devil, and a paradise, erected warm houses and sacred temples, and lived under an effective government admired by Smith. He wrote, "Although the countrie people be very barbarous; yet have they amongst them such government as their Magistrats for good commanding, and their people for du[e] subjection and obeying, excell many places that would be counted very civill."

Powhatan, their great chief, inherited the overlordship of half a dozen tribes and, by threat and conquest, added to his empire until it included most of the Virginia coastal plain. Smith estimated the population at about 9,000, including 2,385 warriors. But historians believe Smith did not include some tribes. Overall population estimates run as high as 14,000, with more than 3,000 warriors. The first Jamestown settlers numbered only 104 men and at times must have felt like luckless waifs who had stumbled into a lair of bears.

These Virginia Indians spoke several dialects of the Algonquian language, but they could understand one another. Smith seems to have picked up their speech quickly; he was their prisoner for a time and traveled extensively among them. Early accounts contain references to individual colonists sent to live in friendly villages expressly to learn the language.

The once-mighty Algonquian-speaking Indians of Powhatan's empire overspread Tidewater Virginia, as shown in John Smith's map of 1612. Powhatan's domain had vanished by the mid-seventeenth century.

Upon becoming supreme chief, Powhatan took the name of his home village; his given name was Wahunsonacock, and he ruled as an absolute despot with power of life and death over anyone. He exacted "eight parts of ten tribute of all comodities which their country yeldeth." Each tribe lived in fealty to Powhatan's representative, the *werowance*, who led them in war and the hunt and collected the emperor's tribute. Early chroniclers do not record an additional tribal chief called the *cockarouse*, first reported in 1705. He seems to have been an administrative officer, judge, and head of the tribal council. Strachey, writing about the Chickahominy

Indians, mentions a tribal elder called the *cawcawwassoughs,* which may have been the same functionary. In many important matters, such as ceremonies, celebrations, judgments, even decisions for war, the priests took dominant roles.

As their usual attire, women wore aprons of deerskin or woven grasses, and the men loincloths, often leather but sometimes, if their hunting had been luckless, mere grass and leaves held around their middles with belts. The belts also supported bags reminiscent of the Scotsman's sporran; they contained personal belongings such as pipe and tobacco.

Outer garments of animal skins, mostly deer, bear, or wolf, with the hair on for winter wear and without hair in summer, also were worn. But many Indians ("the better sort," in a condescending reference often used by settlers) dressed in deerskin mantles, usually fringed and decorated with beads and paints. Fur cloaks and leather leggings warmed them in winter. Curiously, early accounts contain no mention of moccasins.

In accessorizing their apparel the Powhatans showed a flamboyant improvisation. Both sexes kept three holes in each earlobe, where they commonly wore anything they valued, often pieces of copper. Smith records,

> Some of their men weare in these holes, a small green and yellow coloured snake, neare half a yard in length, which crawling and lapping herself about his neck oftentimes familiarly would kiss his lips. Others wore a dead rat tied by the taile. . . . Many have the whole skin of a Hawke or some strange foule, stuffed with wings abroad. . . . Some the hand of their enemie dryed.

On another occasion Smith met a warrior with the ears of a bear attached to his shoulders, the bear's nose, teeth, and a paw hanging down his chest. Another man dangled from his neck the head of a wolf, plus a tobacco pipe three-quarters of a yard long and elaborately carved with bird and animal figures.

One suspects this finery, if that's the right word, was not everyday attire but worn to impress Smith. Or, as Smith himself put it, "He is the most gallant who is the most monstrous to behold." Yet warriors often painted themselves elaborately, and some even wore loincloths with painted designs. With the license for adornment that has always been accorded their sex, many women not only painted themselves but tattooed faces, hands, breasts, and shoulders "with divers workes, as beasts, serpents."

Women acted as barbers for both sexes, using the sharp edges of two shells to abrade hair on the head until it parted; they plucked body hair with tweezers made of mussel shells. Married women wore their hair long and braided. The front and sides of young girls' heads were shaved, but they too had braids in back. Men's heads were shaved on the right side to prevent their hair from

The print "Habit of a Nobleman of Virginia," dating from about 1760, evokes the earlier work of Theodore de Bry and Roanoke governor John White.

becoming entangled in bow strings, but they retained a crown of hair like a cockscomb atop the head and let hair grow long on the left side.

Since they lacked metal axes, the Indians felled the huge trees only with great effort by hacking and burning the roots, and they did not shape logs for houses. But their dwellings were comfortable. Colonists found them warm in winter and cool in summer, though smoky. Women built them, using as framework green saplings set in the ground in rows, bent over, and lashed together at the tops with strips of bark and fibrous roots. They covered the framework with large slabs of bark or woven grass mats. Multiple layers kept interiors warm in winter; in summer layers could be peeled off. Fires for warmth and cooking burned in the centers of these structures, with a small hole in the roof for smoke to escape. Family members slept on mats, sometimes atop platforms. During prolonged hunts women accompanied the men and built for them smaller versions of their houses.

Indeed, endless labor seemed the lot of women. They planted and harvested corn, beans, peas, squash, pumpkin, tobacco, and sunflowers grown for seeds in garden plots assigned each family. They dressed skins and made clothing, gathered wood, tended fires, bore most of the burdens, made the family's pottery and wooden plates and platters, grass mats, baskets, and mortars, prepared the food, and, of course, raised their children. The men undertook any task beyond the physical capability of their women, such as felling a great tree, making a dugout canoe or a fishing weir, preparation of garden spaces, and hunting and fighting.

A warrior courted a maiden with presents and paid her family a bride price. He promised to be a good provider and either built or bought their initial home. A brief clasping of hands before parents and friends sealed the bargain. The tribes practiced polygamy but only among the *werowances* and other great men. Powhatan, for example, had more than 100 wives. Some historians say married couples lived together with a swanlike fidelity; others believe infidelity was acceptable for men but not for married women—unless with the husband's permission; still other authorities contend both men and women were promiscuous. Perhaps all these practices occurred, not unlike people today.

Although most women worked like slaves, they did live in a matrilineal society; inheritance came through the female line. For example, by ancient tribal custom Powhatan's sons could not inherit his mantle. The line of succession would go to his brothers, the eldest first, then to his sisters, and after them to the sons and daughters of the eldest sister. There were female tribal rulers who owed their positions to the deaths of brothers. Powhatan died in April 1618 and was briefly succeeded by a lame brother, Opitchapan. But he soon disappeared, some say retired, in favor of a second brother, the warlord Opechancanough, a bitter enemy of the English.

Smith wrote, "There is yet in Virginia no place discovered to be so savage in which they have not a religion." Indeed the Powhatans were deeply religious. They believed in a benign god, Quioquascacke, who took the appearance of a Great Hare and showered good things indiscriminately upon all. He never harmed anyone and so never had to be placated. But the god Okee, the evil spirit in their pantheon, demanded fearful deference and ceremonial offerings of food, tobacco, and treasure. Gods also bestrode the four winds and hurled the lightning. Before each passage upon the water in times of storm, the Indians cast offerings of tobacco into the waves.

They not only believed in an afterlife but reincarnation as well. After death they walked down a pleasant trail lined with all sorts of wild fruits, stopped for rest and refreshment at the home of a female goddess, and continued on to a reunion with their parents in a happy hunting ground, a place of abundant food and dancing. Strachey tells us they became "ould there as the body did on earth, and then yt shall dissolue and dye, and come into a womans womb againe, and so be a new borne into the world." But this afterlife was not for everyone. According to Smith, Strachey, and other early settlers, only the *werowances* and priests enjoyed life after death. Common people did not. Later observers do not record any such distinction. Everyone passed on to a pleasant afterlife, if deserving. The bad existed in a stinking, hot lake.

When ordinary people died, they were wrapped in skins and mats and buried with offerings of food and jewelry. But sometimes bodies were placed upon scaffolds above ground, and, when the flesh had rotted from the bones, the remains were freshly wrapped and kept in the home. The bodies of their *werowances* received similar but more elaborate interment. First they were disemboweled, then bones were

dried upon hurdles till they bee verie dry, and so about the most of their jointes and necke they hang bracelets or chaines of copper, perle, and such like, as they used to weare: their inwards they stuffe with copper beads and cover with a skin, hatchets, and such trash. Then lappe them very carefully in white skins, and so rowle them in mats for their winding sheetes. And in the tombe, which is an arch made of mats, they lay them orderly. What remaineth of this kind of wealth their kings have, they set at their feet in baskets.

Priests constructed these tombs within temples, so sacred that none dared enter but *werowances* and priests. Temples were built in the manner of houses but larger. The entrance always faced east. Within, at the other end of the temple, priests maintained a sort of altar of shelves containing wrapped bones guarded by carved effigies. Under the altar, in a vault in the ground, they kept an image of their Okee, described by Smith (although he probably never saw one) as "illfavoredly carved, all black dressed, with chaynes of perle." In other words, Okee looked as menacing and fearful as some artist-priest could devise.

Priests wore cloaks of skin or feathers; they tied one end about a shoulder but left the other shoulder and arm bare. Unlike warriors, the priests shaved all the hair on their heads except the crests or crowns and a border of hair above the forehead. The Indian priesthood included conjurers, as the settlers called them, the tribal medicine men who employed sacred rituals and a wide array of herbal remedies to treat and purge the sick. With some success they healed wounds from the bottom up, using a powder from crushed roots or juice made from herbs. If battle slashes became infected, they cut into them and drained them by suction. Compound fractures were beyond their ministrations, as were deep body wounds from bullets. The English, instead of loading their muskets with a single ball, sometimes used a number of smaller pistol balls, and these could inflict horrible multiple wounds. Settlers often made Indians flee simply by leveling, but not firing, a musket.

Today's steam-bath users would have appreciated the Indians' sweat lodges. In them the sick might be placed, and the medicine men would throw water on red-hot coals. Well persons also enjoyed these steam baths; six or eight would gather in a lodge at one time, and occasionally the priest would throw cold water on them to keep them from fainting. Such forerunners of the hot tub were always built beside a river or creek, and after a prolonged sweat the Indians dashed outside and jumped into the water.

Obviously the Powhatan culture had evolved well beyond simple hunter-gatherer practices. They lived comfortably, ate well, had a stratified society and a common religion, enjoyed the relative serenity of stable government, and were plagued only by intertribal warfare. Much of their successful way of life they owed to a moderate climate and a bountiful land.

Then came the aliens, who at first sight of Virginia marveled at what seemed an Eden. George Percy, one of the settlers who stepped ashore for the first reconnaissance, told of "faire meddowes and goodly tall Trees, with such Fresh-waters running through the woods, as I was almost ravished at the first sight thereof." On another day he commented upon

> excellent ground full of Flowers of divers kinds and colours, and as goodly trees as I have seene, as Cedar, Cipresse, and other kindes; going a little further we came into a little plat of ground full of fine and beautifull strawberries, foure times bigger and better than ours in England.

They marveled at the great size of trees, many with vines on them as big as a man's thigh. They saw wild fruits and nuts, animals, many kinds of birds, and turkey nests with eggs.

But they soon found that this demi-Eden could also be a kind of hell. They built their little town and fort on a marshy point of land in the James River, selected because good water depth permitted ships to tie up at the shoreline and because the fort could be easily defended not just against Indians but any marauding Spanish. Yet throughout Jamestown's history, it proved to be a pestilential place. Strachey described the air as "unwholesome and sticky" and said the peninsula "hath no fresh water springs serving the Towne, but what we draw from a Well sixe or seven fathom deepe fed by the brackish river oozing into it, from whence I verily beleeve, the chief causes have proceeded of many diseases and sicknesses." Throughout that first summer colonists were felled and died of "Fluxes and Agues."

Thus began a strange two years, what seemed to be a "feeling out" period for both Indians and settlers: skirmishes and attacks by the Indians, followed by words of friendship and gifts of food. Powhatan knew that not only were many of the Englishmen sick but most of the gentlemen among them would not work or plant crops.

A determined attack in overwhelming force could have exterminated them.

There seems little doubt that almost from the beginning Powhatan wanted the intruders out of his domain, but he greatly feared their guns, particularly their cannon. And with reason. On May 26, 1607, while a party of exploration led by Captain Christopher Newport and Smith was being feted by Powhatans far up the James, hundreds of braves attacked the incomplete fortifications at Jamestown. They killed two colonists and wounded more than a dozen, but ship's cannon and musket fire took a severe toll on the Indians and drove them off. They launched a second attack on May 29 but were again broken and scattered with no loss of settlers.

Both sides then seemed to draw back and consider what to do next. The Virginia Company of London, sponsors of the colonists, had given them orders, backed by stiff penalties, to treat the Indians fairly and kindly and make friends of them. But Jamestown twice had been attacked, and anyone setting foot outside the fort was in danger of becoming a target for arrows. To explore and obtain food, Smith organized and trained a group of what we might call commandos, and in 1607–09 they ranged Tidewater Virginia by boat with virtual impunity. During this period Smith also compiled his famous map that showed with a surprising degree of accuracy the Chesapeake and its rivers. Some Indians traded with Smith, providing corn in turn for beads, hatchets, and iron pots; other Powhatans, seemingly under orders from the great chief, refused to trade, but Smith often forced them to do so at gunpoint.

The year 1607 had a very curious denouement. In *taquitock,* "the time of the falling of the leaves," ill and hungry colonists received a huge gift of food from Powhatan, and several Indian chiefs called upon them bearing food. In December Captain Smith, now widely known and feared by the Indians, fell prisoner while hunting with only two of his men, both of whom were killed.

Here begins the stuff of legend. Smith was taken before various tribes and not only treated well but feted. In return he amazed his captors with a compass, and he gave them lessons in geography and the movement of heavenly bodies. Finally they took him to Powhatan, who had a reputation for bashing in the brains of pris-

oners, throwing them alive into fires, and flaying them alive while severing their limbs. Even the steel-nerved Smith must have been beset by fears. The emperor lounged upon a platform, surrounded by his courtiers and favorite wives. Years later, in calm retrospect, Smith described him in these words:

> He is a goodly old man, not yet shrincking, though he has been patient of many necessityes and attempts of his fortune to make his name and famely great, he is supposed to be little less than 80 [historians say about 60 at the time Smith was kidnapped] yeares old of a tall stature, and clean lymbes, of a sad aspect, round fat visag'd with gray haires, but plain and thin hanging vpon his broad shoulders, some few haires vpon his chynne and so on his vpper lip.

Earlier Smith had experienced priests conducting strange ceremonies with kernels of corn. Now Powhatan conferred at length with his advisers and priests. Then, according to the famous account Smith published seventeen years later, he was placed upon a stone to have his head bashed in. But Powhatan's favorite daughter, Pocahontas, about thirteen, threw herself protectively on him. Powhatan relented, and some of his men took Smith to the fort.

◀ ▶ Forever linked in legend, Pocahontas and John Smith played pivotal roles in early Virginia. The princess is said to have saved the bearded captain from Powhatan's wrath—as depicted in the 1874 lithograph (below). Smith, whose portrait derives from an engraving by Simon van de Passe, was captivated by Pocahontas—"the only Nonpareil"—and might have won her had not an injury forced him to return to England. She instead was kidnapped by the English and later converted to Christianity. Her marriage to John Rolfe brought an abatement to hostilities between Indians and colonists. Her portrait by William L. Sheppard is a copy of an earlier version that derived from a 1616 engraving by Simon Van de Passe.

In earlier versions of his captivity published in London, Smith made no mention of the threat of being clubbed to death or of Pocahontas. Was Smith lying? Or did he have some reason for withholding for a time the role of Pocahontas? She died in England before Smith's story appeared, but her husband John Rolfe never denied it. Some believe the ceremony, with or without the princess, made Smith a *werowance*. In *The Proceedings of the English Colony in Virginia* (1612), an account of the colony's affairs, it is recorded that at the time of Smith's return from captivity some settlers charged that he intended to marry Pocahontas and make himself king of the Powhatans. *The Proceedings* also state that the young girl often visited Smith at the fort, bringing him food and once coming at night to warn of a guileful plot by her father.

It's not difficult to imagine Pocahontas, whose name meant "Playful One" in some translations, "Bright Waters" in others, being attracted to the dashing captain. And Smith? He found her a comely wench. He wrote of Powhatan's much-loved daughter that she, "for feature, countenance, and proportion, much exceedeth any of the rest of his people: but for wit and Spirit, the only Nonpareil of his Country." If Smith had not returned to England in 1609 because of a severe leg injury from an accidental explosion of gunpowder, perhaps he, not Rolfe, might have wooed and married the Indian princess. The union brought some years of peace to the two antagonists, a possibility that was not lost upon leaders of both sides.

During 1608–09 Smith renewed his explorations and marauding ventures. He often found tribal representatives lined along the riverbanks to trade him food. He and his men always kept their guns close at hand. Some Indian leaders, including Powhatan, would entertain Smith and his men but asked them to put their guns aside and come empty-handed, as friends would. The English never did.

Smith himself recorded an eloquent plea by Powhatan:

My people dare not come to bring you corne, seeing you thus armed with your men. . . . What will it availe you to take that . . . you may quietly have with love, or to destroy them that provide you food? What can you get by war, when we can hide our provisions and flie to the woodes, whereby you must famish, by wronging us your friends?

But Smith was not moved. A friendly Indian chief had told him Powhatan and his men would fall upon the Englishmen and kill them if they did not have their guns. Moreover, Smith had experienced Powhatan's guile. While feasting with Opechancanough in the war chief's home, Smith became aware that scores of warriors, arrows notched in their bows, had surrounded the place. Smith had with him only two of his hard-bitten crew; the rest had remained nearby with their boat. But the captain stuck his pistol in Opechancanough's ribs, and the Englishmen marched the surprised chief to the boat. No one dared raise a finger against them. Before sailing away, Smith coolly held Opechancanough ransom for many baskets of corn.

Historians find the period 1607–09 a confusing one. No doubt Smith did too. Powhatan wanted the English to help him conquer his enemies to the west in Virginia's Piedmont, and they promised to help but never did. This promise may explain why Powhatan suffered the English as much as he seemed to at times. He even permitted them to stage a coronation for him as emperor, though he had long been one without any sanction from the English. During part of this period Smith was subordinate to Captain Newport, a ship commander, whose sailors, in league with some colonists, traded guns to the Indians. Newport himself traded swords for food. Undisciplined garrisons stationed downstream and upstream of Jamestown needlessly provoked the Indians, who killed many of the English.

Smith eventually became governor, stopped the arms trading, disciplined the settlers, made the malingerers work, and succeeded in feeding his people by his bold forays along the rivers. Indeed, many Indians seemed to accept him not only as a *werowance* but a man with a charmed life, a demigod. To enforce his will, he took two tribal chiefs as hostages, keeping one of them in chains. Powhatan went into hiding for five years. Historians variously have painted Smith as a brutal despot and the savior of the colony. No one questions that for sheer courage, he stands tall in the history books.

But because of his accident, Smith left for England on a supply ship in October 1609. The feared *werowance*

Opechancanough, a fearsome warrior, devised the infamous attack in 1622, when more than 300 Virginia colonists, caught off guard, were slaughtered. This work was published in Theodore de Bry's *Grands Voyages*, 1626–27.

of the aliens no longer ranged the rivers, and his ship was hardly out of sight before the Indians "all revolted and did spoile and murther all they incountered."

A survivor of the following winter, which came to be known as the Starving Time, wrote: "Now we all found the losse of Captaine Smith, yea his greatest malingerers could now curse his losse: as for corne, provision and contribution from the Salvages we had nothing but mortall wounds, with clubs and arrowes." Holed up in their fort at Jamestown, the colonists ate all their animals, then roots, herbs, acorns, and berries. "Nay, so great was our famine, that a Salvage we slew, and buried, the poorer sort tooke him up againe and eat him, and so did divers one another boyled and stewed with roots and herbs: And one amongst the rest did kill his

wife, powdered [salted] her, and had eaten part of her before it was knowne, for which hee was executed."

Not just famine but disease killed the colonists faster than they could be buried. They complained of dysentery and fever, but it is believed that typhoid, influenza, malaria, pneumonia, yellow fever, beriberi, scurvy, smallpox, and a host of other diseases, even plague, may have ravaged them. Sixty-five percent of the besieged garrison died.

When a relief ship arrived in May, breaking the siege, the commander decided to take all the survivors, some sixty emaciated scarecrows, back to England. They actually abandoned Jamestown and set sail down the James, only to meet a small boat from three relief ships with more colonists. So they turned back and reclaimed their ghost town. Powhatan had come within hours of ridding his land of its usurpers. The Indians would never come that close again.

Upon learning of the debacle at Jamestown, the Virginia Company adopted a mailed-fist approach. Over the next four years it sent hundreds of former soldiers with able commanders to the colony. Killing and burning, they struck grievous blows against many tribes. The Indians retaliated whenever and wherever they could, including another unsuccessful attack on Jamestown. The English, with the connivance of a *werowance*, kidnapped Pocahontas and kept her a prisoner at Jamestown for two years. Her father would not ransom her. But there she met John Rolfe, and their marriage in 1614 brought an exhausted halt to the first of several Anglo-Powhatan wars.

During the next eight years of relative peace, the Indians watched uneasily as more and more settlers came into Virginia. Their outposts spread up and down the James. The colonists paid for land in baubles, tools, and utensils valued by the natives, but the two sides held very different concepts of land ownership and use. To the Indians, land, except for family garden plots, was communal for hunting and gathering. It took them some time to realize that once they accepted payment they could not set foot on the land, which often was fenced and used for grazing animals or raising a kind of tobacco introduced by John Rolfe—a mild and sweet tasting tobacco that became an enduring favorite in England and the wealth of an expanding colony.

Opechancanough, who had succeeded Powhatan, was a more decisive and bitter antagonist for the English than his brother had ever been. He decided upon a ruthless and well-planned attempt to destroy the invaders. On March 22, 1622, Indians pretending to be friendly callers appeared at each plantation, mingled with the colonists, then upon a signal seized whatever came to hand, including the colonists' own weapons, and slaughtered them. Most accounts say 347 died. The plan failed at Jamestown, thanks to a warning by young Chanco, a friendly Indian.

London reacted with a grim determination virtually to exterminate the "salvages." They lifted all restraints on the colonists—never well observed—and troops conducted raids on Indian villages, putting them to the torch and killing their inhabitants, including women and children, seizing food and laying waste to crops. That went on each summer for years, and the Indians retaliated bravely, attacking Jamestown's blockhouse, where they killed twenty men, and wiping out luckless groups of explorers, farmers, and soldiers.

In 1624 King James I withdrew the Virginia Company's charter. The company had not found gold and silver to plunder, and it had become nearly bankrupt, thanks largely to mismanagement and the expense of fighting Indian wars. Now the Indians faced a royal colony backed by all the resources and pride of a mighty nation.

Another exhausted peace of sorts came about. It lasted until 1644. Then Opechancanough, so old and lame he had to be carried into battle but still dangerous as a rattlesnake, led his braves to the plantations on April 17, 1644, with the same plot as in 1622: pretended friendship, sudden slaughter. Again the English proved gullible and trusting, and again they died like animals in an abattoir, this time from 300 to 500, accounts vary. And once more the English retaliated with indiscriminate slaughter and the torch.

They captured Opechancanough, and a guard dispatched the implacable old warrior with a shot in the back. At the time of this second massacre the English numbered 8,000. They had become much too strong for the Indians to oust, and in 1644 they forced Necotowance, successor to Opechancanough, to sign a peace treaty. The Indians agreed to abandon all land between the York and James Rivers from the falls to the Chesapeake. They acknowledged the overlordship of the English king and took upon themselves a token tribute: "Twenty beaver skins at the goeing away of the geese yearely."

By restricting the Indians to lands north of the York, the settlers acknowledged for the first time these original Americans had need of territory of their own free of colonization. Of course that didn't last, as it almost never did in reservations granted the Indians. Human tides washed away solemn promises.

A 1646 entry in the records of the colony's assembly seemed to chortle in triumph. It said the Indians were "so routed and dispersed that they are no longer a nation, and we now suffer only from robbery by a few starved outlaws." Powhatan and his legatees had fought and lost the three battles foretold by the priests.

But both sides had to endure a few more alarums and excursions. In 1655 or 1656 some 600 mountain Indians, probably driven from their ancestral lands by other tribes, settled near the present site of Richmond. Militiamen and 100 Pamunkey (Powhatan's own tribe), bound by treaty to fight intruders if the English so demanded, moved against the brash newcomers but suffered a defeat that killed the Pamunkey chief and nearly all his men. But the victors soon fled Virginia, as did other Indians.

Then ensued Bacon's Rebellion, a bloody internecine squabble among the colonists themselves that involved the Indians. In 1675 and 1676 two Maryland tribes and one in southwestern Virginia pillaged Virginia frontiers. A popular planter, Nathaniel Bacon, demanded help from Governor William Berkeley. When he didn't get it, he raised his own army, moved against the Indians without permission, and killed hundreds. Emboldened by success and backed by fanatic followers, Bacon marched on Jamestown, got his commission from Berkeley at gunpoint, and set out against the Pamunkey, thought to be responsible for raids along the York River. Bacon's force killed some warriors and took forty-five prisoners; the rest fled in panic into the depths of Dragon Swamp. He then seized everything the Pamunkey owned.

Unjust and high-handed government by Berkeley, not just Indian depredations, brought about Bacon's Rebellion. It ended with Bacon's natural death in 1676 at the height of his power—but not before he had twice forced Berkeley to flee to the Eastern Shore and had burned Jamestown.

In 1677 the colonial government decided yet another treaty should be concluded with the Powhatans. Chiefs of ten tribes met with their conquerors at Middle Plantation, later the site of Williamsburg, and put their marks on papers that mostly reaffirmed earlier treaties, including the Indians' right to lands north of the York.

By 1705 the Powhatan empire had been reduced to six tribes with about 1,170 members. Not just warfare decimated those who once bestrode the tidewater lands. European diseases for which they had no immunities, principally smallpox and tuberculosis, also took a fearful

toll. Whiskey and rum, all too often the curse of Indians to this day, demoralized a once prideful people.

However, from the beginning of the confrontation there were men in London and colonists in Virginia of good will, particularly toward Indian children. King James I in 1617 allowed his clergy to raise money for the education of children, native and English, in Virginia; and the Virginia Company reserved more than 10,000 acres at Henrico, an outpost near the falls of the James, for a university. Within that large area, 1,000 acres were set aside for a residential school for Indians. But that plan died when the company lost its charter. Its leaders had thought the conversion of Pocahontas to Christianity while a captive at Jamestown would make easy the conversion of other Indians. It did not. London's reaching out to the New World often seemed based upon good intentions that could not survive Virginia's maelstroms.

The College of William and Mary, chartered in 1693, established an Indian school about 1700, which sputtered along, seldom very effectively and often without any students, until nearly the outbreak of the Revolutionary War. At times it had to depend upon buying children or accepting children taken as hostages. Graduates who were supposed to become missionaries among their people quickly reverted to old ways. Indeed hundreds of colonists captured and adopted by the Powhatans often preferred the Indian way of life and, if recaptured, wanted to be returned.

Secure in their triumph, which freed them to indulge pangs of conscience, the colonial assembly as early as 1649 began passing laws to assure and protect rights of Indians. Legislators forbade the casual killing of Indians and the kidnapping of their children; colonists could no longer keep Indian children in their homes, where their fate often was little better than slavery. Native Americans were given the protection of English law.

Today scattered remnants of Powhatan tribes still live in Virginia and belong to the Virginia State Council of Indians. Only two tribes, the Mattaponi and the Pamunkey, still retain portions of once sprawling reservations, both in King William County. The Pamunkey hold 1,200 acres, the Mattaponi about 100 acres, and they retain their rights under a treaty of 1677 with the colony of Virginia. For that reason the State of Virginia, not the

▲ Chief William Miles, in traditional head-dress of turkey feathers, stands amid a corn-field on the Pamunkey Reservation.

▶ Mattaponi Chief Webster Custalow, out-side his reservation's small museum, has "had visions ever since I was a young man."

Federal Government, recognizes the reservations. Each year at Thanksgiving the Pamunkey and the Mattaponi keep a treaty obligation by presenting the Governor of Virginia with game, usually venison, or fish.

Each reservation has only forty-five to fifty permanent residents, but both maintain a small museum and craft shop. The Powhatans today live mostly as scattered peoples, their Indian blood diluted by that of other races, their features commonplace in the great melting pot. How do surviving Powhatans feel about the fate of their ancestors? Often bitter. Oliver L. Perry, Sr., emeritus chief of the Nansemond Tribe, who lectures on Indian affairs, puts it bluntly.

> From the Indian perspective, their history is a study of pain, grief, bitterness, tragedy, injustice, removal from ancestral homelands, loss of language and culture. In the long run the Indians inevitably would be overrun and dispossessed. The constant flow of people from Europe against a stagnant population assured loss of land. But there could have been a much better result. The English should have had a better and more sympathetic understanding of the peoples here, as did the French to the north. All the hostilities and atrocities were not unavoidable. Where were the convinced Christians?

And one might ask, where were the moderate Indians who might have stayed the treacherous hand of Opechancanough?

It's all remote history now, matters for academics to debate. But the great emperor Powhatan's priests saw the outcome from the very beginning. Their people would indeed drain the cup of prophecy to its bitter dregs.

Virginia's Father

King James I

BRUCE P. LENMAN

There is no doubt Sir Walter Ralegh invented the name Virginia. Ralegh, as he and his father spelled their name, initiated the attempts to establish an English colony in North America in territory that imperial Spain regarded as part of its empire and described sweepingly as Florida. Ralegh's first and abortive colony in 1585 was essentially a privateer base. His second attempt in 1587 was a serious effort to establish a permanent settlement, though it failed. In between the attempts, Ralegh received such marks of favor from Queen Elizabeth as knighthood and permission to call the newly settled land Virginia in her honor, for she never married and was "the Virgin Queen." This had the virtue of making an end of the linguistic muddle over names into which Ralegh knew he and his colonists had fallen because of ignorance of the local Algonquian language. The English had been using absurd terms like "Wingandacoia," whose origin was native, but whose meaning is still obscure.

Ralegh has no role in the continuous history of the plantation that grew to become the Old Dominion of Virginia. His colonists, including the holding party his cousin Sir Richard Grenville left on Roanoke Island in 1586, were all active in what is now North Carolina. He planned latterly to move the second group of colonists to somewhere on Chesapeake Bay, but they disappeared before it could be done. Though the later Virginia Company of London tried to find survivors and to take advantage of their hard-won experience, they failed, which accounts for some disastrous decisions in the early history of colonial Virginia.

The Father of Virginia was not the handsome English courtier Ralegh. It was the monarch who, under heavy Spanish pressure, had Ralegh's head cut off in 1619—King James VI

Portrayed here by John de Critz or Marcus Gheerhardt the Younger, James I appears to have inherited few of his father Henry Stuart's good looks.

of Scotland and, from 1603, James I of England and Ireland. He was not handsome.

The son of Mary, Queen of Scots and her second husband, Henry Stuart, Lord Darnley, James had more brains than his parents put together, but none of their startlingly good looks. Mary and Darnley were tall, with long, elegant legs. James had short, bowed legs. He was most comfortable on a horse. He would walk supporting himself on the shoulders of two courtiers. His homely face often wore an apprehensive look, and his personal manners were gross. He could not help having a too-large tongue that made him slobber when he ate or drank, but his personal hygiene was based on an aversion to water that confined washing to the tips of his fingers. Before Fidel Castro, James was a contender for the position of longest-winded politician ever. He harangued his English Parliament for hours. Unusually for a king, he was a voluminous writer, so we know exactly what he felt relations between himself and his subjects ought to be.

In a 1597 pamphlet, *The True Lawe of Free Monarchies*, James said the reciprocal relationship between a rightful and righteous king and his dutiful subjects was based on the king being "a naturall Father to all his Liegis." James meant this seriously, as he did when he said, "The proper office of a King towardes his subiectes agrees with the office of the head towards the bodie." To James, royal authority was fatherly, and a people only constituted a body politic by virtue of submission to their ruler.

By 1603, Elizabeth, the once glamorous Gloriana, had become an unpopular old woman with a reputation for meanness. Most Englishmen welcomed the ascension of an open-handed adult male ruler. There was a great surge in patriarchal theories of politics, arguing that the male head of household was the model of all righteous authority.

James was clear that after 1607 he was the father of all Virginians and the head of the body politic they belonged to, which was England. The word "colony" was not used as much as the term "plantation," because Virginia was England planted in America.

After 1603, James ruled three realms. Multiple dominions were common in Europe. United under one monarch, the individual kingdoms kept their identities in a sensible compromise between unity and autonomy. Their laws and customs were the guarantors of their traditional liberties. James most unusually wanted his ascension to the English throne to be followed by an incorporating union between England and Scotland.

Modestly, he called on his first English Parliament in 1604 to pass on "the blessings, which God hath in my person bestowed upon you all," by legislating for such a union. His believed he was the husband of his kingdoms, inflicting on the English legislature at Westminster embarrassingly explicit, disorganized addresses about the difficulties of sleeping with two wives in one bed. He admitted, disarmingly, that he seldom had time beforehand to think about the content of speeches.

Nobody really wanted his union. In Westminster a future treasurer of the Virginia Company, Sir Edwin Sandys, who said that he thought the proposal unnecessary, led the opposition. By 1607, when Virginia was being born, the Jacobean Anglo-Scottish union was in its final death throes at Westminster, a situation that James deemed an insult to him, and to God.

His fallback position was to encourage parallel developments in politics and religion in the three kingdoms and the intermarriage of their aristocracies to decrease national antagonisms. Parallel developments included colonies.

Irish colonies were established in the huge delta of the River Amazon. They were responsible to his Irish Privy Council, neighboring colonies to his English one. Toward the end of his reign in 1621, James granted vast territories in what are now the Maritime Provinces of Canada to Sir William Alexander, later Earl of Stirling, to establish a Scottish colony, Nova Scotia. Alexander said that in an age of New England, France, and Spain, Scots would not support attempts to set up overseas plantations "unless . . . they might likewise have a New Scotland."

James said his subjects had a right to settle in the Americas wherever a Christian prince did not already effectively occupy, as distinct from claim, the territory. It was an admirable position, but he did not always stand up for it. The Portuguese, detested by the local tribes, and who had never occupied the area, destroyed the Irish and English Amazon colonies. The only argument they would heed was an effective counterattack, but the king of Portugal between 1580 and 1640 was the Spanish monarch, whom James was desperate to appease. Nothing was done.

The Spaniards normally killed other Europeans they found in the Americas. The birth of Virginia was possible because of the terms on which James had managed to conclude the deadlocked Elizabethan war with Spain in the Treaty of London of 1604. Because Spain needed peace more than England, the principal Spanish negotiator, the Constable of Castile, had reluctantly to agree to drop from the treaty all mention of Spain's exclusive claims in the Americas. That did not mean that Spain accepted the English colony.

Spanish reconnaissance expeditions, scouting the land before military action, were dispatched to the Chesapeake in 1605 and, significantly, also in 1609. The constable hoped to see all the English colonists hanged, but the resources of imperial Spain were strained even by the cost of its most northerly garrison at St. Augustine. Spain's best bet after 1607 was to bully, wheedle, or con King James into abandoning his Virginian "children."

▶ Virginia is named for Elizabeth I, the Virgin Queen, the last of the Tudor monarchs and James I's immediate predecessor.

▼ Sir Walter Ralegh—he never spelled his surname with an "i"—took over from his brother the patent to the Virginia colony and dispatched the first settlers.

This looked possible in 1608, when his vanity and delusions about being the great arbiter of Europe were tickled by insincere Spanish talk about marrying his heir, Prince Henry, to a Spanish princess, or infanta, and making Henry regent of a reunited and reconciled Netherlands. The Dutch in the northern Netherlands had long been in rebellion against their Spanish overlords. The Spaniards, however, overplayed their hand by abusing the crews when they captured English ships bound for Virginia. By 1609, they had so alienated English opinion that it was clear Virginia had become a matter of national prestige for which even England's near-pacifist Scots monarch would have to fight.

That diplomatic shield was vital for Virginia, especially after the crippling Indian uprising in 1622. A critic of the Virginia Company reported in 1623 that he had found "not the least piece of fortification" around its principal settlement, Jamestown. The company said that there were a few cannon and wooden palisades, but the report was probably right in saying one small enemy warship could have flattened the place.

Because he issued his two charters in 1606 and 1609 to the Virginia Company, James I was committed to protecting the settlement. It lay within Elizabethan grants that had reverted to the crown when Ralegh, whom James loathed, was convicted of treason in 1603. It is fair to ask what else James did for Virginia.

He put no assets into it. He was a financial desperado, creating massive deficits by compulsive spending and gifts to favorites like George Villiers, Duke of Buckingham. When the Virginia Company, even after reorganization and the charter of 1609, did not make a profit, James granted it the privilege of running a lottery. This lasted until parliamentary objections to monopolies led to its lapse after 1621.

In 1612, one pessimist said Virginia would probably fail less because of the Spanish ambassador's endless ravings on the subject to James than because of "the extreme beastly idleness of our nation." He said deserters from Virginia slandering the plantation back in England hurt the Old Dominion more than the lottery helped. The colony had nearly died out in the winter of 1609–10. James's ambassador in Madrid, Sir John Digby, reported in 1612 that the Spaniards were moved

to contempt by news of the lottery, and determined somehow to destroy Virginia. The Spanish ambassador in London in late 1612 was urging Philip III of Spain, unrealistically, to strike before the Virginian colony could put down roots.

By 1613, however, a spy with access to Spanish confidential sources obtained proof that most of James's senior counselors were in receipt of Spanish pensions. There was a danger the Jacobean regime might betray Virginia.

James became so worried about the pro-Spanish influence in his council that he concealed from it sensitive communications from his ambassador in Madrid. Yet as late as 1623 he was anxious for a marriage between his heir, Prince Charles, whose elder brother Prince Henry had died in 1612, and a Spanish infanta. Before the negotiation collapsed, Charles and Buckingham briefly placed themselves in the power of Spain by making a foolish and dangerous trip to Madrid.

The Earl of Southampton believed the royal menagerie might help the cause of Virginia. He reported in December 1609, "The King is eager to have one of the Virginia Squirrels that are said to fly." James loved exotic animals. He failed to catch a white hind seen roaming in the Grampian Mountains in Scotland. In 1623, however, Spain got the king's erratic attention by sending an elephant and camels to England.

Native Americans were exotic, though familiar. North American Indians and Eskimos had been brought to London since the reign of Elizabeth's grandfather, Henry VII. In September 1603 a plague-ridden London had seen "Virginians" demonstrate their skill in handling their dugout canoe on the River Thames, sponsored by James's first minister, Lord Salisbury. They may have been Algonquians from the Chesapeake. James was a renaissance humanist scholar, taught by the greatest Latin poet of the day—the Scotsman George Buchanan. Basic to classical and renaissance thought was the distinction between civilization and barbarism. To James, who regarded most Gaelic speakers in Scotland and Ireland as barbarians, North American tribesmen were like barbarous Highland clansmen.

Nevertheless, such people could have leaders whose obvious nobility enabled James to relate to them. Thus in Scotland James wanted the MacGregors, who had no chief to control them, "ruit oute and extirpat." Clan Gordon was no problem. James favored its chief, Lord Huntly, as he did the Earl of Tyrone in Ulster, despite the earl's nine-year war with Elizabeth. The Council of the Virginia Company in London always insisted that there was no king in Virginia save King James, but Powhatan, the paramount Tidewater Indian ruler, was often referred to as an emperor and the normal English translation of Indian terms for chief was "king."

When Christopher Newport came to Virginia with the third reinforcement vessel of 1608 in September, he had with him a copper crown and instructions to seek out Powhatan and crown him with it—which he did in November—making Powhatan "King James his man." James assumed that a pagan ruler should submit to a Christian one, but Powhatan was clearly to be a cooperative regional prince, like Huntly or Tyrone.

In 1616 Powhatan's daughter Pocahontas—converted to Anglicanism and baptized "Rebecca," because in Genesis 25:23 the Lord said of another Rebecca, "Two nations are in thy womb"—came to London with her husband, colonist John Rolfe, and their baby son. Received by the royal court and the citizens of London, she "carried herself as the daughter of a king" and was treated with respect by James and his nobility before her death on the eve of her return to Virginia in early 1617.

James was, on his own terms, benign and liberal. For a few desperate years after 1611, the Virginia Company imposed martial law on its plantation. It dispatched Governor Thomas Dale to discipline the colonists for the sake of their sheer survival. Nevertheless, the royal charters promised the colonists the full freedoms and privileges of Englishmen, which is what they were, and access to the common law, the guardian of those liberties.

Virginia was an Anglican church-state, with the bishop of London an influential member of the company's council, but King James's spirit was ecumenical. His devotion to peace and respect for Christians of a different persuasion—absurdities to most contemporary kings or popes—meant that the reunification of Christendom was his dearest, and most impractical, wish. The Anglican establishment in Virginia in his reign was informal, with no elaborate ritual, and was no persecutor.

Cape Charles, which guards the northern entrance to the Chesapeake, is named for Charles I, son of James I. Charles inherited from his father the failing Virginia venture.

James secured the forfeiture of the charter of the Virginia Company in 1624 because there was no alternative. A takeover in 1618 by a group of gentry and nobles led by Sir Edwin Sandys and the Earl of Southampton failed to make the company solvent, but led to vicious factional fighting. The Indian uprising of 1622 and subsequent retaliatory war destroyed the company's viability. James sent the colonists obsolete armor from the Tower of London, England's chief ordnance store, believing that it would not be obsolete against Powhatan's archers.

When he personally tried to conciliate the company's warring factions, however, the job proved so frustrating that he rebuked Sir Edward Sackville for impudence. James would have liked them to surrender their charter voluntarily, and would have given them a revised one, but company holdouts refused the deal. They tried to raise trouble in the English Parliament,

Modern remembrances of James I, the Jamestown Ferry slides down the James River past Jamestown Island bound for James City County.

denouncing the Spanish ambassador Gondomar, who was no Virginia well-wisher, and his successors for "using their utmost efforts to destroy the plantation." The king said he had the matter in hand and asked the House of Commons not to get involved. It agreed, though suspicious that "by such means any business might be taken out of the hands of Parliament."

When the Court of King's Bench ruled the company's charter forfeit for noncompliance with its terms, rumor said that, "the popular nature of the government having displeased the king," one hundred soldiers would be sent as a garrison. James could not afford the soldiers, and the General Assembly set up in Virginia in 1619 survived. Like James's other legislatures, it met occasionally, when needed. England was a monarchy, normally run by its king, and Virginia, after 1624, by the governor he appointed.

James was initially violently hostile to tobacco, associated with Ralegh. The king's authorship of the anonymous *A Counterblaste to Tobacco* of 1604 was soon common knowledge. What grieved his fatherly humanist heart was that loyal Christian subjects should, on a whim, debase themselves by smoking like what most English perceived to be Devil-worshipping Indian barbarians. He denounced its effect on the health, morals, and finances of the lieges. He realized, when a few years later John Rolfe proved tobacco was the paying cash crop in Virginia, that he could use income from it, negotiating eventually for a third of the company's importation by weight. Businessmen like Sir Arthur Ingram warned the company not to offer cash when James was too broke to make allowances if prices collapsed.

He and the company leaders so misunderstood Virginia's climate they persuaded themselves tobacco cultivation was only a necessary interlude before healthy products like silk, flax, hemp, and wine started to flow from the Chesapeake. They never did.

Gradually, James's name and those of members of his family spread over the map of Virginia. From 1607, there was Jamestown. A manuscript map of 1608 showed King James His River, which by 1635 was on a printed map as the James River. Capes Henry and Charles are named for his sons. A map of 1651, drawn by a woman, Virginia Ferrar, showed Elizabeth City near Point Comfort, named after James's daughter. By 1673, a map showed counties called Henrico and Charles City.

His great favorite, Buckingham, flattered the sentimental James by addressing him as "Dad." Virginia could have had a much worse dad than this shambling Scots eccentric with his great strengths and preposterous weaknesses.

The Virginia Company of London

The Business of Jamestown Was Business

DENNIS MONTGOMERY

Silent Cal Coolidge got off just a handful of utterances memorable enough to make the dictionaries of familiar phrases and popular quotations. Few were longer than: "If you don't say anything, you won't be called on to repeat it." When Coolidge said anything, it could be as succinct as an epigram or as terse as a commandment. One Sunday a newspaper reporter asked him what his minister said during a sermon on sin. Coolidge answered, "He said he was against it."

Coolidge, thirtieth president of the United States, was against taxes, deficit spending, high interest rates, and government regulation. An original supply-side Republican, he was for free enterprise, and he is credited with coining the maxim "the business of America is business." What he really said, January 17, 1925, was: "The chief business of the American people is business." Either way, Coolidge was right.

From its inception, America has been about business. In the dreams of acquisitive fifteenth-, sixteenth-, and seventeenth-century Europeans, the Americas North, Central, and South were reveries of avarice, plunder, and profit—perhaps palliated by some wispy notion like delivering the local Indians, kicking and screaming, to Christianity. But from the outset, the central question of the enterprise called civilizing the New World was how to make a buck, or *real,* or *escudo,* or pound. At the approach of the Great Depression, which Coolidge did so much to foster before announcing, "I do not choose to run for President in 1928," it was still America's leitmotif.

No example of the original urge to market economies in this hemisphere may be so instructive as the first permanent commercial venture in English America: the outfit run by the Treasurer and Company of Adventurers and Planters of the City of

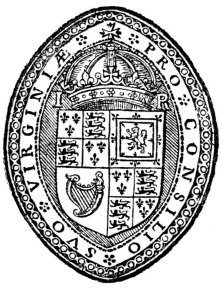

A likeness of King James I and the company's coat of arms were incorporated in the seal granted by the crown to the enterprise.

London for the first colony of Virginia—the Jamestown business.

Historian Wesley Frank Craven, whose 1932 Depression-era volume on the fate of that undertaking is still authoritative, wrote:

> The most common error in writing the history of the Virginia Company has been a failure to understand the fundamental character of that corporation. Whatever else may have entered into the activities of the company, it was primarily a business organization with large sums of capital invested by adventurers whose chief interest lay in the returns expected from their investment.

England was emerging from a seventeen-year depression of its own in 1604. There was again surplus capital for oceangoing employment, and nothing lent itself so readily to the pursuit of transoceanic trade and profits as the joint-stock company.

A variety of trading firm, a joint-stock company was a syndicate of people, and sometimes such organizations as trades guilds and incorporated towns, that pooled resources in dividend schemes, usually called adventures.

The investors called themselves adventurers, though most safely stayed at home. What they adventured was their money, which they thought of as the company's stock. Commonly, the adventure was restricted to one project at a time—a single trading voyage, for example. The company wound up the joint stock when its ship came in, remitting to the adventurer his principle with a proportionate share of the returns.

The first things the English expected to return from Virginia were gold, silver, copper, and jewels. The list grew to include such commodities as clapboard, wainscot, masts, spars, sassafras, bayberries, poccone, galbrand, sarsaparilla root, walnut oil, wine, silk, silkgrass, beaver and otter skins, beaver cod, turpentine, pitch, tar, resin, sturgeon, sturgeon roe, tobacco, wines, glass, hemp, soap ashes, iron, and pearls. But at the outset, it was one of those get-rich-quick deals.

To seventeenth-century entrepreneurs, the joint-stock organization offered the advantages of what today might be denominated a corporation. The joint stock could support projects bigger, more complex, and more lucrative than an adventurer could undertake by himself. The risk of the enterprise was spread over many pocketbooks, so that though the failure of a voyage meant individual loss, it need not mean individual ruin. Though stockholders' meetings allowed adventurers a voice in the company's affairs, policy was confided to a board of trustee-like assistants, and day-to-day direction of the business to officers. The head of the company often was titled "treasurer," the approximate equivalent of today's chairman, president, and chief executive officer.

A charter issued by the crown secured a company's status as a legal entity, setting out its structure, and bestowing a seal, privileges, and duties. With it might come powers to make and enforce contracts, remove his majesty's subjects across the sea, and govern them in their trading posts and settlements, applying insofar as desirable the laws of England. The charter could establish the geographical boundaries of a company's authority and allow it title to the land within, as well as the right to dispose of it. To the Virginia Company, the throne, in the person of James I, gave a block of land fifty miles north and south, and 100 miles east and west, of its initial settlement; a monopoly in its trade; relaxation of imposts for a period of years; and other good and valuable considerations.

In exchange for these indulgences, James required a cut of all the bullion and gems the company discovered and control of the enterprise. It was not at first a regular trading company in that the king adventured neither a farthing nor a flatboat but claimed such powers as appointment of the firm's thirteen-member governing councils at home and abroad and the promulgation of orders. The role of the company and its adventurers consisted mainly of raising funds, underwriting Captain Christopher Newport's voyages to Virginia, superintending the goods shipped back and forth, and minding such profits as came their way. They assumed all the risks and obligations but had not final say in the business.

There was, however, more to the business than unvarnished capitalism. Kingdom and company also looked forward to an expansion of England's dominions and a strategic base in its struggles with Spain; the extension of the Church of England's authority to the Christianization of Native Americans; a port from which to protect the North Atlantic fishery; a place to obtain naval stores and build ships; and a land to which to consign religious dissidents, criminals, the poor, and "waste people"—to use the phrase of the day—and, like as not, recovery of survivors from Sir Walter Ralegh's Lost Colony of 1587. There was, moreover, the prospect of new sources for tax revenues when the enterprise matured, and a new outlet for England's manufactures, as well as the confidently expected discovery of a water route across the continent to the Far East.

Sir Thomas Smythe, perhaps the richest merchant in London at the time, was the company's first chief executive officer and presided over the early Virginia disasters.

Those were more or less the limits of the company's eleemosynary aspirations. The adventurers gave the most charitable of them little more than lip service. But the erection of English forms of church and state on Virginia's shores proved to be the company's most durable contributions to the inroads of social and political progress on the American seaboard.

Of the adventurers Craven wrote, "Their motives were not entirely selfish; their desire to render a public service is unquestionable." Yet, as historian Herbert Levi Osgood said of their company:

> The object of its first undertakers was doubtless to search for minerals and for a route to the southwest, and to secure for trade the materials which were native and peculiar to those regions. . . . To establish a settlement which would become a market for English goods, to advance the shipping, to spread the religion of the kingdom were doubtless motives which

Jamestown's trade with London depended on ships such as the replicas at today's Jamestown Settlement re-creation.

aroused sympathy for the undertaking; but the arguments which brought investment were the opportunities for gain.

In pursuit of those opportunities, the Virginia Company propagandized its homeland, squandered the lives of thousands of Englishmen and Indians, tore through a fortune, and poisoned itself with faction before the king put it out of the agonies of bankruptcy. The business of America began with a bust.

James granted the Virginia Company its first charter, or letters patent, April 10, 1606. The first patentee listed was Sir Thomas Gates, a veteran of the Low Country wars with Spain. The first treasurer was Sir Thomas Smythe, England's wealthiest merchant and, writes a historian, "the most single active figure in English overseas commercial enterprise" from 1587 to 1617.

Subscriptions were limited to a private group of men much like the Sir Thomases who agreed to trade in a joint stock to last five years. The public at large was excluded from the subscription, and the generality of investors had no say in operations, which made it more a semi-joint-stock company.

Jamestown initially was intended to be more a trading post than the capital of an agricultural colony and, though the charter did not require it, was organized as much as a garrison as a depot. There was a hierarchy of admirals, captains, ensigns, and corporals supporting a governor and captain general, his councilors, a trading agent or cape merchant, and others. In exchange for a term of service, at the outset seven years, the ordinary settler was to be sustained from a company store called the magazine, which would supply him with tools, food, drink, and clothes. At the end of his term, a colonist would have his freedom and farmland as a dividend for the adventure of his person. Through the magazine, all the gold and goods the colonists produced would be shipped home for the company to sell.

The Reverend Mr. Richard Hakluyt, England's chief propagandist for colonial endeavors, wrote *Instructions by Way of Advice* suggesting how the colonists conduct themselves upon landing. The 104 men and boys who reached Virginia on April 26, 1607, were to poke about a bit and find a place to fortify for an encampment. Then a contingent of colonists, with some of the forty-odd sailors who had ferried them and their supplies across the Atlantic, was to improve its time reconnoitering the neighborhood and looking around for handy valuables to freight Newport's vessels. Each voyage, even the first, was to make good its costs and something more.

In these expectations, the adventurers were customarily disappointed. There was no gold or silver, nor any jewels but a few misshapen pearls. The first return consisted of clapboard riven from white oak, and of sassafras—a carcinogen mistaken for a specific for syphilis. So much sassafras got into the ships the cargo threatened to be, so to speak, a drug on the London market.

Neither the company nor the colonists appreciated how much time or money it would take to build, support, and maintain a town in the wilderness. Moreover, the crew of second sons, footmen, laborers, and castoffs in which the company invested its hopes were sometimes of low character, too-often mutinous, and always fractious. They deported themselves disgracefully, distinguished themselves by greed, and showed too little regard for their survival.

Thirty-eight lived to see Newport return in January with a few supplies and more fodder to feed Virginia's voracious appetite for Englishmen. Just under two-thirds of the original 104 died in the first seven and a half months, killed by disease, hunger, heat, cold, and Indians. At that rate, without Newport's succor, Jamestown would have consumed them all before the end of April. But the adventurers at home bothered their heads chiefly about the loss of their capital. They blamed the colonists' misfortunes, and Virginia's failures, on the colony's disorder.

Captain John Smith, who contributed as much as anyone to the first-charter disasters, inveigled himself into Virginia's governorship and, for all his bragging self-promotion, was as useless as his predecessors when it came to meeting corporate goals. Later, he wrote:

> Now because I sent not their ships full fraught home with those commodities, they kindly writ to me, if we failed the next returne, they would leave us there as banished men, as if houses and all those commodities did grow naturally, only for us to take at our pleasure, with such tedious Letters, directions, and instructions, and most contrary to that was fitting, we did admire how it was possible such wise men could so torment themselves and us with such strange absurdities and impossibilities . . . all their aime was nothing but present profit.

By 1609, these disappointments had exhausted the enterprise's resources. New investment could not be recruited or cozened, and the Virginia Company was on the brink of collapse. To use today's term, reorganization was the only way out. In Osgood's words: "Failure of the investment to bring in returns of gold and silver and articles of trade, or to accomplish anything in the way of discovery of trade routes to the East Indies during the first three years served to convince both King and undertakers that a change in method of control was essential."

That May 23, the crown granted a second charter to a Virginia Company reconstituted with 650 members, who together subscribed at least £10,000 in a new joint stock. An adventurer's share was now worth 100 acres on the first division in 1616, and 100 more on the second. For a post-1616 adventurer, a dividend was fifty acres, plus fifty more for each person he sent to furnish his holdings. The business grew to 659 individuals and fifty-six companies, but for now it remained a semi-joint-stock company, the generality allowed no vote in its doings. Nevertheless, the restructuring empowered the corporation to regulate its membership and transformed it into a body politic.

The second charter took from the crown and gave to the councils primary authority—the king still had the last word—with exclusive powers for an unlimited term over new lands. It extended Virginia's boundaries to 200 miles north and south of Old Point Comfort at modern Hampton, and from the Atlantic to the Pacific, including all islands within 100 miles of either coast. It also established a common trade until the 1616 distribution and a common magazine until 1620. In Osgood's words, it "erected a commercial company and made it the overlord of a proprietary province."

To take strict order in that province, the reinvigorated company dispatched the first version of its "Articles, Lawes and Orders Diuine, Politique, and Martiall for the Colony in Virginia, or, For the Colony in

Virginia Britannia Lawes Divine, Morall and Martiall." These laws were perhaps the most draconian code ever imposed on an English settlement not a penal colony. They regulated freedoms of conscience, restricted commerce, directed labor, and prescribed the demeanor that the common sort would display toward the better. Many of the statutes imposed corporal or capital punishment. To the mind of more than one settler the code was "a Booke of most Tyrannycall Lawes written in blood."

Smythe remained treasurer, and the company still looked for precious metals and a water route to the Pacific. But the adventurers saw more clearly after three years the possibilities of a plantation colony seconded by tradesmen and small manufactures. To the minds of the managers, what was needed to jump-start Virginia was a quick infusion of hands to farm its lands and take up its work.

To date, the company had consigned 275–320 souls to Jamestown's maw. No more than 109—likely no more than eighty—survived to see the summer of 1609. That July, according to a troublemaking adventurer and settler named Gabriel Archer, "They were in such distresse" that "many were dispersed in the Savages townes, living upon their almes."

In its second charter-enthusiasm, the company dispatched to Virginia, without warning, an armada of ten ships and at least 500 men, women, and children. The fleet sailed into a hurricane and the lead vessel shipwrecked at Bermuda, marooning about 140 colonists until June 1610. One ship turned back, another foundered, drowning twenty, all were scattered, and at least thirty-two people died of disease during the passage. But seven bottoms with perhaps 298 settlers reached Virginia that August—roughly tripling the number of mouths the surprised and famished colony had to feed.

Perhaps 100 Virginia English survived the winter they called the Starving Time. Under Indian siege, sixty hung on at James Fort, some eating the flesh of the dead. About forty survived at Old Point Comfort, mostly on crabs and oysters. Fifty-four stole vessels and ran away for England. Indians ambushed at least forty-seven but sheltered a handful more. Some settlers bolted into the woods and were never heard of again. By the best-case calculation, 58 percent of the Virginia English died for the company's unintelligent fooling.

The managers did their best to keep the truth of their miscalculations and Jamestown's misfortunes from reaching English ears, including the investors'. Bad news discouraged share sales and emptied the pool of prospective colonists. The company had from the outset censored and controlled information from Jamestown, but it could not stop the mouths of runagates—though it later got authority to arrest them. The company could and did, at all events, try to explain away the Virginia horrors with such propaganda tracts as *A True Declaration of the estate of the Colony of Virginia.*

In 1609 alone, it foisted on the gullible four of such mendacities, and Smythe got out another in 1610, *A True and Sincere Declaration of the Purpose and Ends of the Plantation begun in Virginia.* People who might have known better accepted such at face value. Sir Thomas Dale arrived in Virginia the next year to assume the governorship, and, "at his arrival, pulled Capt. Newport's beard, and threatened to hang him, for affirming Sir Tho. Smythe's relation to be true." Captain Smith said, in another context, "And that the adventurers might be thus abused, let no man wonder; for the wisest living is soonest abused, by him that hath a faire tongue and a dissembling heart."

By 1615, the company published nine dissembling declarations in a stream of promotional ballads, books, pamphlets, and sermons that enticed unwary English men and women to their deaths. Typical features of such productions were missionary appeals to piety. The adventurers were spreading the gospel, so worthy an end as to excuse robbing the Indians of their land. The company described itself as "us who by way of merchandizing and trade, do buy of them the pearls of the earth and sell to them the pearls of heaven."

London ministers William Crashaw and William Symonds seconded such pusillanimity from the pulpit, but most adventurers steered clear of investment in anything so dicey as proselytizing. In a sermon to the company in 1610, Crashaw said: "Tell them of getting" £20 for investing £100, and "Oh how they bite at it. Oh how it stirres them. But tell them of planting a church, of converting 10,000 souls to God, they are as senseless as stones." Smith wrote that his employers were "making religion their colour when all their aime was nothing but present profit."

It took the English until 1614, seven years, to convert their first Virginia heathen to Christianity. Had they not kidnapped and confined her, it is doubtful they would have had even that soul to show. Her name was Pocahontas, later the Lady Rebecca, wife of John Rolfe. Two years later, at the end of a public relations tour of England, the church did its last service for the Indian princess by laying her away at Gravesend.

Not all the propaganda in Christendom could alter the facts on the ground there or in Virginia, and, no matter how attractively composed, the company's tracts did little to persuade significant numbers of good-quality people to risk their lives in its service. In 1611, Dale wrote from Jamestown to an investor at home:

> It shall be in vaine to strive any longer to settle a handfull of wretched and untoward people here, and great expectations to be placed over their labours, with waking and jeleous eyes, expecting the return of such retributions and benefites, secrett commodities and ritches, which is as impossible for them to get, either into their possession or knowledge, as it is to poise and weigh the mountains.

The next year, 1612, Smythe secured a third charter, and it transformed the Virginia business into a full-fledged joint-stock company at last. The generality met in monthly company courts and decided Virginia questions by ballot at quarterly courts. Power shifted from the company's council to company committees, and investment was opened to anyone with £12 6s for a share. A blank Bill of Adventure, as the stock certificates were called, sometimes read:

> Whereas _____ paid in ready money to Sir Thomas Smythe, Knight, treasurer for Virginia, the sume of _____ adventure towards the said voyages. It is agreed that for the sume _____ the said _____ shall have ratably according to _____ adventures _____ full part of all such lands, tenements and hereditaments as shall from time to time there be recovered, planted and inhabited, and of all such mines and minerals of gold, silver and other metalls or treasure, pearls, precious stones or any other kind of wares or merchandise, commodities or profitts whatsoever which shall be obtained or gotten in the said voyage according to the porcion of

money by _____ employed to that use in as ample a manner as any other adventurer thereon shall receive for the summe.

By October 1613, the Virginia Company subscribed £30,000 in new adventures. To raise money otherwise, it had sold for £2,000 the Bermudas, which it had claimed in the Starving Time shipwreck and looked to have more economic promise than Virginia. Another £4,000 came from loans, sales of goods, and a new nationwide lottery granted to the company by the king.

But for lack of profits the business still went badly. Between 1613 and 1616, most of the primary joint-stock adventurers gave up on the Virginia Company. Few, as Osgood found, paid in their subscriptions, few shares were sold, and the lottery became the company's primary support. Part of the problem was that England's economy was slumping through the business cycle toward the depression of 1617.

In 1616 the company sold its first subsidiary joint stock, conveying to a group of adventurers the rights to the magazine, heretofore a primary corporate profit center. Such self-cannibalization makes apparent the company's undercapitalization. Smythe's administration already had poured £67,000 into the Virginia Company's failures. It appears that £36,624 had come from eleven years of adventurers and about £29,000 from four years of lotteries. To show for these expenditures, the company had very little.

Sales of subsidiary joint stocks in privately owned plantations—tracts like Smyth's Hundred—began in 1617. What had made these private plantations worth buying was tobacco. John Rolfe, who arrived in 1609, experimentally shipped a cargo of leaf from Virginia to England in 1613, and commercial cargoes followed four years later. Virginia, England's first colony, had discovered the staple that would make it her richest and most populous. Tobacco was so remunerative that, by one account, settlers planted it in Jamestown's streets. After 1618, a ruinous percentage of settlers signed on for subsidiary joint-stock private plantations, farms that diverted investment in the company's larger, backbone projects.

After three charters and eleven years of reeling disappointment, the company's finances were in tatters.

▲ Only tobacco shipments, like that depicted in this nineteenth-century drawing, provided investors with any reliable return on their Virginia investment.

▶ Sir Edwin Sandys, who pursued a vigorous and ill-fated policy of expansion after he captured control of the Virginia Company, sent his brother George (right) to Virginia to help in the effort to diversify the colony's economy.

Historian Richard Davis wrote:

In 1618 it was discovered to the consternation of many stock-holders that almost the entire investment of the common stock in the public estate and property of the company had been allowed to waste away until almost nothing of value remained to show for an investment estimated at £75,000. The first step toward the decline of the company's plantation, or "publique" as it was known, had come in 1614. The seven-year term of service of the oldest inhabitants expired in that year, and there were present for the first time in the colony free laborers.

The time had come to change the company's management and amend its strategic plan.

Sir Edwin Sandys had been a Virginia Company adventurer since 1606, advancing in 1616 to what we would call a director, and becoming Smythe's deputy. Among the sparkplugs of England's public-service-minded country gentry, Sandys had a seat in the House of Commons and used it to check James I's monotonous demands for levies on trade. Sandys was as loyal to the crown as anyone, however, and innocent of the secret democratical tendencies with which twentieth-century historians have attempted to credit him. All he opposed was the burdens the king's policies imposed on commerce. Perhaps the Commons' leading authority on the arcana of imports and exports, he applied his knowledge to Virginia Company affairs.

In Smythe's management Sandys saw three primary faults: declining income from the company's land, the colony's inordinate reliance on tobacco, and the small number of recent immigrants. His solution was to secure Virginia's place in England's trade, supported by a rapid increase in emigration and economic development.

On August 28, 1619, he stood against Smythe for election as treasurer and won—partly because share-holder Sir Robert Rich and his followers supported Sandys, partly because the voting was secret, and partly because Smythe withdrew. John Ferrar was elected Sandys's deputy treasurer.

Sandys exhorted the colonists to turn from tobacco cultivation to the production of silk, wine, potash, flax, hemp, silkgrass, cotton, wool, salt, soap, pitch, tar, walnut oil, masts, planks, and boards. He prodded investors to form more subsidiary joint stocks—for a watermill, salt works, a windmill, a shipyard, a glassworks, an iron-works, and more.

To run these industries, Sandys recruited artisans, and he attempted to restock the company's lands with sharecropper servants. In Sandys's first year were shipped to Virginia 1,261 people, of whom 871 went at company expense. Among them were ninety women dispatched to the female-scarce colony in a subsidiary joint stock as wives for men who would collect them and pay their fares. Another 100 women, like the first shipment's politely called maidens, followed in 1620.

During Smythe's twelve years, the company issued about six patents for private plantations; in less than half that time, Sandys granted forty-four. To administrate the colony more efficiently, Sandys authorized election of burgesses to form a general assembly that met in July 1619—the first representative assembly in English America.

But except for the assembly and the maidens, none of Sandys's development efforts was novel. For example, a glassworks had been tried before and failed, and the idea of rapidly increasing Virginia's store of English was as old as the Starving Time. The company ordered the construction of guesthouses to receive the newcomers this time and sent a new governor to oversee its program, to no especially useful result. Most of the colonists Sandys inherited from Smythe were about as ready to sacrifice self-interest for the greater good as they were to give up planting the only crop that had ever paid them. Nor could Sandys quickly amend the quality of Virginia's human stock. Historian Davis wrote that "this impatience of Sandys for quick results through a rapid increase in population was his greatest blunder and one of the chief causes of his ultimate failure." The people sent were unfit, poorly equipped, and underprovisioned: "Sir Edwin had been informed in private letters of the dangers of sending so many colonists so ill provided, and the impact it had on the old settlers. He not only ignored the warnings but solicited false letters to be presented to the courts that misrepresented conditions in Virginia."

The colony remained as unruly as ever, and as impatient of government. As Rolfe wrote to Sandys in 1620:

I speak on my own experience for these 11 years, I never amongst so few have seen so many falseherted, envious and malitious people (yea amongst some who march in the better rank) nor shall you ever hear of any, the justest Governor here, who shall live free from their scandals and shameless exclamations, if way be given to their reports.

The ironworks, among Sandys's favorite projects, may stand as an example of the manifold mistakes of his program. Directed by John Berkeley, they were set up at Falling Creek just below today's Richmond in 1621 at a cost of £5,000. A bloomery, the works depended on low-grade bog ore, and the total output of its first and only year was a fire shovel and tongs, and a small bar of iron.

Virginia affairs prospered no better in England. Sandys got off to a poor start by antagonizing the still-powerful Smythe and making a to-do over the inadequacy of the company's books. Smythe could produce for his successor no records of lottery income, or goods brought from Virginia, or of disbursements, and the books he did have were indecipherable. No satisfactory accounting was ever made; Smythe said there was £4,000 in the treasury when he left; Sandys said debts totaled £5,000.

At length, Sandys contrived to alienate the Rich faction by accusing Rich of financing piracy—a charge that may have stung the more because it was probably true. Members of the shifting factions began to invite one another to the field of honor. Worse, Sandys's management bothered the king, who insisted someone else be elected treasurer in 1620. Henry Wriothesley, the Earl of Southampton, took the title that June 28, but, to James's annoyance, the earl was but a front for Sandys.

Sandys's fruitless attempts to negotiate with the crown a monopoly on England's tobacco trade—and to pay himself and Deputy Ferrar very well for managing it—smashed the last pretence of harmony. There were other tedious and unprofitable disputes, all tending to divide the company against itself, and cripple it.

On March 8, 1621, the affronted king suspended the lotteries granted to his friend Smythe nine years before. The company's budget for the twelve months ahead was £17,800, of which Sandys counted on the lottery for £8,000. At a stroke, the company lost nearly half its annual income and any chance of securing for the staggered administration any of the rest from subscriptions, debts, and loans. By May, Virginia Company shares were trading at forties to fifties, and another depression was setting in.

All over settled Virginia, colonists were going about their business the morning of March 22, 1622, when the Indians fell on them. About 350 English along the James and York Rivers died.

For protection, the survivors gathered in enclaves, a decision that curtailed the production of foodstuffs and led to more mortality, compounded by disease and the burden of new arrivals. More died that winter than had at the hands of the Indians in the spring.

Among other Sandys enterprises, the ironworks quietly folded—a predictable outcome even without the attack. Sandys's biographer Theodore Rabb wrote:

> Similar fates befell the attempts to encourage salt works, ship-building, glassworks, sawmills, silk production (patronized by the king himself), wine and naval stores. Either the artisans died, or the climate was unfavorable, or the necessary financing was unavailable. All were well intentioned undertakings which could have benefited the colony. But the Virginians could hardly be diverted from tobacco long enough to produce staple crops.

Lachrymose letters from the colonists to home begged for aid. The company quietly did what it could, which wasn't much, and hoped for the best. But that winter Samuel Butler, one of Rich's associates, visited the colony from Bermuda and returned to England to write a devastating indictment of Virginia's condition. His *Unmasked Face of Virginia* began a series of investigations that, in the main, supported allegations of mismanagement, negligence, pestilence, and starvation.

The Virginia Company attempted to rebut the charges by producing other letters painting pictures of a successful and contented colony. In the words of historian Wesley Frank Craven, "It was impossible for officers who were forced to admit that more than half the population had died, to prove that their people had led a happy and prosperous life." But they tried, and in the process transgressed orders from the king to eschew further factionalism, for which Sandys, Ferrar, and Ferrar's brother spent a few days under house arrest.

James instructed his attorney general to recall the company's charter, a litigious undertaking of about

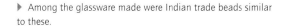

▲ The company hoped to mend its failing fortunes from glassworks.

▶ Among the glassware made were Indian trade beads similar to these.

eighteen months. A commission administered the company's affairs in the interim. The now-bankrupt Treasurer and Company of Adventurers and Planters of the City of London for the first colony of Virginia met for the last time June 7, 1624. Charles I declared Virginia a royal colony May 13, 1625, and the Privy Council gradually assumed administrative control.

What was lost and what was gained? On one side of the ledger there was this: Through the company, by good estimate, the Virginia enterprise had by 1624 enjoyed the benefit of £200,000 in investments. The general joint stock yielded £36,862 2s 9d of the sum; the rest came from the lottery, subsidiary joint stocks, and adventurers' developing their dividend lands. It was not even close to enough.

When the tottering business finally collapsed, the £200,000 was wasted, and the company was £2,000 in the red.

The cost in lives is tougher to calculate. Sandys said the company sent 6,070 people to Virginia—2,500 during Smythe's twelve years at a cost of more than £85,000, and 3,570 during Sandys's five years for about £30,000. Approximately 2,500 people remained. A tiny but forgotten fraction of the losses can be attributed to returns to England, but the bulk of them are deaths.

That Sandys offered such a comparison in his defense demonstrates how desperate matters were. His figures put the 1607–23 settler losses at 3,570, or 59 percent. He reported there were 1,000 colonists when he became treasurer, which meant 1,500 were lost during

Smythe's years—60 percent, or an average 125 a year, approximately. Sandys lost 2,070, or 45 percent of the souls for which he was responsible, a rough average of 414 annually, more than three times what Smythe had.

One of the investigating commissions, however, credited Sandys with sending 4,270—700 more than he reckoned—which would boost his figures to 2,770 lost, or 65 percent, for an annual average of about 554. The 1607–24 loss would become 63 percent.

A colonist sent a census to England in February 1624 that looks to be more accurate than all the figures compiled in London. It reported that though 300 colonists had arrived that summer, there were 1,275 English left. Using worst-case figures, the company wasted close to 5,795 English lives, a total loss of 82 percent of its human stock.

Putting it another way, as one of the investigations did, the exertions of the company under Sandys—the importation of as many as 3,295 people—had increased Virginia's English population by 275. The Sandys loss rate would be 83 percent.

No matter how the numbers are cast, they add up to this: Virginia was a death trap. Butler had written of the colony: "In steed of a Plantacon itt will shortly gett ye name of a slaughter house and soe iustly become both odious to our selvs & contemptible to all the world."

The other side of the ledger shows that for all its incompetence, shortsightedness, and greed, the Virginia Company of London adapted to North America the structures of English civilization.

On those foundations were built the republican form of government guaranteed by the Constitution in 1789. Though that Constitution mentions nowhere capitalism or free enterprise, the nation was built on the economic system that was part and parcel of the baggage that arrived with the Virginia Company. The Christianity the company established at Jamestown became America's mainstream religion and moral compass, albeit in many flavors.

In sum, the company brought to America the English culture with all its advantages, faults, parochialism, and pollyannishness—the sort of worldview expressed in a line of one of the company's propaganda poems: "We hope to plant a nation where none before hath stood."

That sort of sentiment and philosophy turned out to be, despite the company's failure, the best of the things it raised in Virginia's soil. Silent Cal Coolidge, the chief-business-of-the-American-people-is-business president, said centuries later:

> It is only those who do not understand our people, who believe our national life is entirely absorbed by material motives. We make no concealment of the fact that we want wealth, but there are many other things we want much more. We want peace and honor, and that charity which is so strong an element of all civilization. The chief ideal of the American people is idealism.

Captain John Smith

"an Ambityous unworthy and vayneglorious fellowe"

Halfway through the voyage, somewhere in the Canaries, the Jamestown fleet's leaders clapped Captain John Smith into custody and accused him of concealing an intended mutiny. At the next stop, across the Atlantic in the Caribbean, they offered to hang him and got as far as hammering together the gallows. Before his fellow settlers threw him out of Virginia thirty-two months later, they would again propose to stretch Smith's neck, to banish him, and even to murder him.

That is not the Captain John Smith story familiar to the history buff. Even some academic historians prefer to remember the positive elements of the now-popular captain's career. With some justification.

In his fifty-one years, Smith was a compiler and writer of exuberant travelers' tales, an explorer, a mapmaker, a geographer, an ethnographer, a soldier, a governor, a trader, a sailor, an admiral, and the editor of a seaman's handbook.

Enormously energetic, his adventures and travels touch Europe, Africa, and America, and match the boldest exploits of fearless knight-errantry. In this hemisphere alone, he was an early explorer not only of the Chesapeake but of New England's coast and, at home in England, an enthusiast in the cause of America's colonization.

By his admirers, Smith is credited with almost single-handedly preserving the first English Virginians from the ravages of their own sloth as well as from the hostility of their native neighbors. Except for his pen, chapters of America's earliest history would to us be lost, for much of the story of Jamestown comes from the captain. As an assembler of other men's accounts and a writer of his own, Smith is responsible for five swashbuckling, early seventeenth-century descriptions of the colony and its struggles, one richly

Captain John Smith in bronze guards Jamestown Island's south shore.
Behind the monument is the tower of the settlement's 1639 church.

CAPTAIN
JOHN SMITH
GOVERNOR OF
VIRGINIA
1608

illustrated. He produced seven other volumes and helped bring to the press a still stunning Virginia map.

Examining Smith's productions, it is difficult to conclude he is due less than a full measure of credit in the founding of the nation. Like many writers of the day, he was not an author to stint on praise of himself, the praise for which his fame is enshrined, once in awhile in bronze. Yet every story has more than one side, and Smith was a many-sided man.

It was June, two months after landfall in Virginia and more than four months after his arrest at sea, that the settlement's government got around to excusing Smith from custody. He took the liberty to join, some say engineer, a coup against President Edward Maria Wingfield in September.

By January, near his twenty-eighth birthday, Smith was condemned again to the noose, and only the last-minute arrival of a supply vessel this time saved his neck. That was just after Pocahontas, about thirteen, is said to have delivered him from a squad of Indian executioners.

Smith ousted another president in July and got himself elevated to that office in September. His enemies, eventually a majority of the settlers, suspected him of aiming to make himself a tyrant king. Smith denied the allegation; yet, by the end of his Jamestown sojourn, he did indeed reign alone, terrorizing Indians, bullying Englishmen, and flogging whoever happened to cross him. He once went so far as to command the assassination of a squad of turncoat colonists—by poison according to one account, by shooting and stabbing according to his own.

Before he had done, the aboriginals sorely wanted to brain him, some of his countrymen compounded to bar him from the settlement, and, penultimately, others conspired to shoot him in his sleep. In the end, the English resolved on sending Smith home to answer for, among other things, inciting Indians to attack them.

Dispatched on the same voyage were eight or nine witnesses against him and a letter that said in part: "This man is sent home to answer some misdemeanors whereof I persuade [myself] he can scarcely clear himself from great imputation of blame."

George Percy, who succeeded him as chief executive, wrote that this man Smith was "an Ambityous unworthy and vayneglorious fellowe."

Like the yeoman-class Smith, gentleman George Percy was an original Jamestown settler and a participant in its inaugural disasters. A witness to Smith's transactions, Percy is another primary source of the Old Dominion's oldest episodes. After Smith's self-aggrandizing books began to gain circulation, Percy took exception for the record. He wrote "that many untruths concerning These proceedings have been formerly published wherein The Author hath not Spared to Appropriate many deserts to himself which he never Performed and stuffed his Relations with so many falsities and malicious detractions."

Typically quoted by historians on the point of Smith's veracity is Thomas Fuller, author of a biographical dictionary called *The Worthies of England*. Publishing in 1661, only thirty years after Smith's death and while the memory of the captain was fresh, Fuller said that such were Smith's "perils, preservations, dangers, deliverances, they seem to me almost beyond belief, to some beyond truth. Yet we have two witnesses to attest them, the prose and the pictures, both in his own book; and it soundeth much to the diminution of his deeds, that he alone is the herald to publish and proclaim them."

In fact, Smith was not the only one to publish and proclaim them. In 1631, the year Smith died, the London press issued a satirical poem, *The Legend of Captain Iones*, by the Welsh clergyman David Lloyd. A bawdy, ridiculing parody of Captain Smith's autobiography, the poem's popularity sustained a half-dozen editions during the next forty years.

To quote a snatch of the epic:

. . . Tis known
Iones fancies no additions but
his own;
Nor need we stir our brains for
glorious stuff.
To paint his praise, himself both
done enough

In the twentieth century, historian Alden T. Vaughan wrote that the poem shows "Fuller's doubts about Smith must have been widely shared in the seventeenth century and . . . many of his contemporaries may have seen Smith more as a braggart, even buffoon, than as hero." More charitable, historian Samuel Eliot Morison concluded that Smith was "a liar if you will; but a thoroughly cheerful and generally harmless liar."

The Complete Works of Captain John Smith fill three volumes. Published for the Institute of Early American History and Culture, they were edited by the late Philip L. Barbour, the foremost modern Smith scholar. The best place to follow Smith's adventures is in those pages, but some of the more remarkable episodes are worth spotlighting here.

Smith reported he was imprisoned on the voyage to Virginia about February 21, 1607, just after the fleet stopped for water, wood, and food, because he was "suspected for a supposed Mutiny, though never so much matter." Barbour believed there may have been a dispute there over how to go about the gathering.

The fleet stopped again for supply at the Caribbean island of Nevis on March 28, 1607. Smith wrote in his 1630 *The True Travels, Adventures, and Observations of Captaine John Smith:* "Such factions here we had, as commonly attend such voyages, that a pair of gallows was made, but Captain Smith, for whom they were intended, could not be persuaded to use them."

A version of these events he published in 1612 is more illuminating. He had been

> restrained as a prisoner upon the scandalous suggestions of some of the chief [people] (envying his repute) who fained he intended to usurp the government, murder the council and make himself king, that his confederates were dispersed in all the three ships, and that diverse of his confederates that revealed it, would affirm it, for this he was committed as a prisoner: 13 weeks he remained thus suspected.

Once in Virginia, the colony's chief people wanted to ship him home for punishment straightaway, but Smith says he defended himself so fearlessly that he was allowed to remain. His account speaks for itself:

> He much scorned their charity, and publicly defied the uttermost of their cruelty. He wisely prevented their policies, though he could not suppress their envies, yet so well he demeaned himself in this business, as all the company did see his inno-

cency, and his adversaries' malice, and those suborned to accuse him, accused his accusers of subornation; many untruths were alleged against him; but being so apparently disproved begat a general hatred in the hearts of the company against such unjust commanders; many were the mischiefs that daily sprung from their ignorant (yet ambitious) spirits; but the good doctrine and exhortation of our preacher Master Hunt reconciled them, and caused Captain Smith to be admitted of the Council,

which helped the president run the colony, on June 10.

Smith, at least as he recounts it, often was unjustly accused of something or other. One of the earliest accusers was President Wingfield, Jamestown's president until September 10. That day settler Gabriel Archer presented Wingfield with a list of grievances and informed him that he was ousted and would stand trial. Captain John Martin backed Archer up, but Wingfield believed Smith was the first and only person to collect the charges against him. "Master Smith's quarrel" with him, Wingfield said, was "because his name was used in the intended and confessed mutiny."

Now John Ratcliffe became president. But Smith became powerful, signing on as Ratcliffe's chief agent, the man to take order of the work and, more importantly, the recruitment of food among the Indians. From that moment, Smith's grip on Jamestown closed. In a settlement invariably on the verge of starvation, control of the food supply could be control of everything.

If this was an unhappy development for the colonists, the Indians would regret it, too. On his very first call on a tribe for supplies, Smith attacked. He says the Kecoughtans, who lived near modern Hampton, scorned him and derided his offers to barter. So "seeing by trade and courtesy there was nothing to be had, he made bold to try such conclusions as necessity enforced, though contrary to his Commission: Let fly his muskets, ran his boat on shore, whereat they all fled into the woods." The Kecoughtans counterattacked, the English picked off a couple, the Indians sued for peace, and Smith sailed off with a boatload of corn.

Though not all of his trading encounters led to bloodshed, the first one made plain the possibilities of refusing to bargain. Promises of violence were frequent, and, though the orders from England were not to annoy

Smith said that in the summer of 1608 his party passed around the granite-spired, white-frothed falls of the Potomac River.

the natives, Smith ignored them as he judged circumstances to require.

It was a mission of trading and exploration along the Chickahominy River, just west of Jamestown, that gave rise to the Pocahontas legend. Smith made his way first in a barge and then in a canoe, scattering his company in his wake. Indian women lured two indiscreet soldiers ashore from the barge to their deaths in an ambush. Braves killed a third who guarded the canoe. Among the men killed were two called Robinson and Emery.

Smith walked inland into the arms of a Pamunkey hunting party. Marched roundabout to Powhatan, the "emperor" of the Tidewater tribes, Smith was promised his freedom in four days. As he told it in his *Generall Historie,* however, he was the next day summoned to Powhatan's house. Smith's account:

> At his entrance before the King, all the people gave a great shout.... [A] long consultation was held, but the conclusion was, two great stones were brought before Powhatan: then as many as could laid hands on him, dragged him to them, and

thereon laid his head, and being ready with their clubs, to beat out his brains, Pocahontas the King's dearest daughter, when no entreaty would prevail, got his head in her arms, and laid her own upon his to save him from death.

Powhatan decided he would instead regard Smith as a son, make him a tributary *werowance*—as headmen were called—and bestow on him a territory just downriver. Smith left for Jamestown two days later, the previously promised fourth day, skirting the site of what would be Williamsburg.

The last twenty-seven words of the passage quoted is the sum and substance of the Pocahontas story, repeated for 400 years and carved in stone in a frieze in the rotunda of the nation's Capitol. So far as the record shows, however, it is a story to which Smith forbore publicly even to allude until 1622—fifteen years after the fact—and not to disclose even in its scanty detail until 1624. In the interim he had published three other volumes of his Virginia experiences and one of other New World adventures.

▲ A creek loops and bends for the Chickahominy River in a wetlands that perhaps is little changed since the seventeenth century. An Indian hunting party pulled a captive Smith from a Chickahominy bog in December of 1607 and marched him away to Powhatan.

▶ If Indian princess Pocahontas saved Captain Smith from death at the hands of her father's headsmen, it must have been somewhere very near modern Purtan Bay on the York River at the long-vanished village of Werowocomoco, then Powhatan's headquarters.

By the time Smith shared the story with the printer, Pocahontas had been to England, where she died in 1617 after becoming famous. Powhatan, the other principal, was gone, too, and there was no one alive to contradict the captain.

Curiously, Smith's first book, *A True Relation,* published in 1608, less than a year after Smith's capture, describes in another context the same mode of execution he would eventually report he had escaped. Moreover, in the intervening years, a Spanish work with a strikingly similar Indian-princess-rescues-white-man-from-cruel-father's-execution tale appeared in London. And some historians see a Pocahontas parallel in the Miranda-Ferdinand episode from Shakespeare's *The Tempest.* That play, in turn, seems to have been inspired by the story of the wreck in Bermuda of a hurricane-tossed, Virginia-bound ship during Smith's Jamestown presidency.

Some nineteenth-century American scholars remarked on the delay in publication of the tale, noted discrepancies among Smith's various capture accounts, and questioned the authenticity of the Pocahontas rescue. Albert Bushnell Hart concluded Smith was one of the "great American historical liars," and essayist Henry Adams said, "It is perfectly clear that the statements of the *Generall Historie,* if proved to be untrue, are falsehoods of rare effrontery."

Proving them to be untrue is, of course, impossible. So, after so great a passage of time, is proving them authentic.

Barbour believes Smith misunderstood what had happened to him. It could be, he says, that Smith experienced an Indian naturalization or adoption rite in which he was symbolically killed, saved, and reborn with a status comparable to one of Powhatan's natural sons. Thus an obstreperously ungovernable Englishman would be transformed into a deferentially manageable sub-chief.

As uncertain as we are about the Pocahontas legend now, it was certain at the time that men in Smith's care had been lost on the expedition, and that President Ratcliffe and the council saw that as an opportunity to be rid of him. Smith's account goes:

> Some no better than they should be, had plotted with the President, the next day to have put him to death. . . . For the lives of Robinson and Emery, pretending the fault was his that led them to their ends, but he quickly took such order with such Lawyers, that he laid them by the heels till he sent some of them prisoners for England.

What happened, actually, was that Christopher Newport sailed up in the nick of time with new colonists and fresh supplies and arranged Smith's release. When Newport returned to England, Smith's friends-turned-foes Martin and Archer went with the ships, eventually to return and to get even.

The score-settling would wait until August of 1609; Smith would have twenty months of respite from what he described as their malice. By June, however, he was persuaded other comrades were conspiring to do him in. On a trading trip to the Potomac—a river he seems to have explored at least to the falls at modern Washington—he got into one of his scrapes with the Indians. After the dust settled, he said, "We were kindly used of those Savages of whom we understood, they were commanded to betray us, by the direction of Powhatan, and he so directed from the discontents at Jamestown, because our Captain did cause them to stay in their country against their wills."

In other words, Smith believed the Indians who ambushed him 100 miles from Jamestown had been put up to it by Powhatan to gratify and be rid of settlers who blamed Smith for being stuck in Virginia. If it is improbable, it may not have been impossible. It was what came into Smith's mind, and it was not the last time Smith would accuse subordinates of trying to undo him.

Eventually, the prophecies would fulfill themselves. In a hint of what was to come, colonists tried to keep him out of Jamestown, to leave him to his fate in the forest, when he returned from a November bartering expedition. Smith said they were jealous.

That summer he had authorized the ouster of his old friend President Ratcliffe and helped install his new friend Mathew Scrivener. Scrivener lasted a little more than a month; the council elected Smith president September 10, his term to run a year. By January, all other members of the council had died, several in supposed pursuit of yet another plot against the captain, and Smith was in sole and complete command.

King Powhatan comands C: Smith to be slayne, his daughter Pokahontas beggs his life his thankfullnes and how he subiected 39 of their kings. reade history.

printed by Iames Reeve

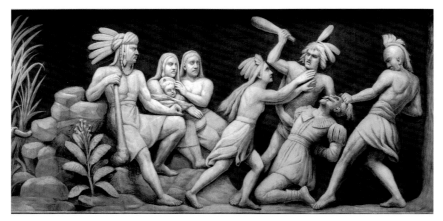

◀ ▶ Fact or fancy, the story of Pocahontas's rescue of the hapless Captain Smith is deeply engraved in American iconography. First illustrated in Smith's 1624 *Generall Historie* (above), the scene is portrayed in the Rotunda of the nation's Capitol. In the same chamber hangs John G. Chapman's huge and wildly romanticized painting of Pocahontas's 1613 baptism, with husband-to-be John Rolfe in attendance.

This was the winter of the no-work, no-eat order. Smith says he delivered it to the starving settlers in these words:

> Countrymen, the long experience of our late miseries, I hope is sufficient to persuade every one to a present correction of himself, and think not that either my pains, nor the [investors'] purses, will ever maintain you in idleness and sloth. I speak not this to you all, for diverse of you I know deserve both honor and reward, better than is yet here to be had: but the greater part must be more industrious, or starve, how ever you have been heretofore tolerated by the authorities of the Council, from that I have often commanded you. You see now that power rests wholly in myself: you must obey this now for a Law, that he that will not work shall not eat (except by sickness he be disabled) for the labors of thirty or forty honest and industri-
>
> ous men shall not be consumed to maintain an hundred and fifty idle loiterers. And though you presume the authority here is but a shadow, and that I dare not touch the lives of any but my own must answer it: the Letters patents shall each week be read to you, whose Contents will tell you the contrary. I would wish you therefore without contempt seek to observe these orders set down, for there are now no more Councilors to protect you, nor curb my endeavors. Therefore he that offends, let him assuredly expect his due punishment.

Among the individuals to whom Smith thought punishment was due were a group of renegade German colonists—Dutchmen, he called them—encamped with Powhatan. Smith had sent them off to amuse the emperor, and they had elected to stay. That was, after all, where the food was. With the help of confederates inside the fort, they were also stealing weapons and tools and proposed to lead an attack on Jamestown. Smith understandably called them traitors and ordered them assassinated. The idea was to poison them, or have them shot or stabbed, depending on who you believe. No matter, the runagates seem not to have come within Smith's reach; others did.

Every few months, it seems, a group of colonists would discuss hijacking Jamestown's pinnace and sailing for the English fishing fleets at Newfoundland. Smith credited himself with stopping each of these projects. "But if I find any more runners for Newfoundland with the Pinnace, let him assuredly look to arrive at the Gallows." He also made this an occasion to reinforce his strictures on work, declaring, "He that gathers not every day as much as I do, the next day shall be set beyond the river, and banished from the Fort as a drone, till he amend his conditions or starve."

Lesser infractions he punished at the pillory or with shackles.

Examples of Smith's hard usage of the Indians range from the petty to the perverse. Some he browbeat; others he imprisoned, psychologically tormented, kept in chains, or forced to labor. Once he personally administered twenty lashes with a rope, and the occasional village was sacked or burned. Smith said such measures were required to keep the Indians at bay and amenable to furnishing supplies. Historian J. Frederick Fausz has termed it terrorism.

Word of what was happening reached England at the end of October with a vessel fresh back from Virginia. The troubles of the Jamestown crew were publicly blamed on the "misgovernment of the Commanders . . . dissention and ambition among themselves, and upon the Idleness and bestial sloth, of the common sort, who were active in nothing but adhering to factions and parts, even to their own ruin."

Before this intelligence reached home, however, the colony's owners had redesigned Jamestown's administration, obtained a new charter, and dispatched a fleet of new settlers, the largest to date. Caught in a hurricane, the fleet arrived in pieces; but word of the new order of things got through. Smith was reproved and a replacement sent, though the captain was to be allowed a post as an Indian fighter.

By rights, Smith's presidency was terminated, and even Smith must have known it. But the papers to prove it were missing with the shipwrecked vessel on which they had been dispatched and, standing on ceremony, Smith declined to surrender power until his term expired September 10. Nor would he establish a new council with which to share power in the meantime. The newcomers settled for electing gentleman Francis West as a sort of president-in-waiting, and Smith moved to patch things up with his disappointed subjects. He also shored up his power by ingratiating himself with the fleet's sailors.

According to Percy:

Captain Smith fearing the worst and that the seamen and that faction might grow too strong and be a means to depose him of his government so Joggled with them by way of feastings Expense of much powder and other unnecessary Triumphs That much was Spent to no other purpose but to Insinuate with his Reconciled enemies and for his own vainglory for the which we all after suffered. And that which was intolerable did give leave unto the Seamen to carry away what victuals and other necessaries they would.

The settlers had arrived too late in the year to plant food for themselves, and Smith, though he had known since July they were coming, was in no position to provide for them all, either out of the colony's stores, nature's bounty, or the Indian trade. Rations were short, growing shorter, and all agreed on the need to disperse. The example of the Indians and experience had taught Smith to spread colonists out with winter's approach, so that they need not all depend on the resources of a single area.

West loaded a ship with munitions, food, and supplies, took 120 men to the falls of the James, the site of modern Richmond, and set them to building a fort near the river's edge. On a hill nearby was an Indian village commanded by a *werowance* the English called Little Powhatan.

West's settlers somehow got it into their heads that the river was the way to the South Sea, as the Pacific was called, and probably to the long-dreamed-of gold fields Virginia was thought to contain. They apparently decided a fort hard by the stream would command the route to riches and make them wealthy gatekeepers. The Indians objected and killed men who strayed from the compound.

At month's end Smith, who figured the Pacific lay beyond the Potomac, took five soldiers up the James to check on matters, met West coming down, and arrived at the falls to declare the ground of West's Fort too flood prone. He was probably right, but he was little credited.

Henry Spelman, a perhaps-confused young man who had only just arrived, was in Smith's party and years later wrote an account of what he thought happened next:

> I was carried by Capt[ain] Smith our President to the Falls, to the little Powhatan where unknown to me he sold me to him for a town called Powhatan and leaving me with him the little Powhatan, He made known to Capt[ain] West how he had bought a town for them to dwell in desiring that captain West would come and settle himself there but captain West having bestowed cost to begin a town in another place misliked it: and unkindness thereupon arising between them Capt[ain] Smith at that time replied little but afterwards conspired with the Powhatan to kill Capt[ain] West, which Plot took but small effect, for in the meantime Capt[ain] Smith was Apprehended and sent aboard for England.

Smith gave this explanation: He bought Little Powhatan's village all right, but Spelman was merely being apprenticed as an interpreter and was not part of the bargain. West's men spurned the deal, refused to budge, and denied Smith's authority. With his five men, Smith overawed all 120 and collared "all the Chieftains of those mutinies."

West's men, however, rallied, and drove Smith off. Falling back, Smith came to their ship, compounded with his latest friends the sailors, and took command of the vessel. Deprived of their ship and its stores, West's hungry men raided the Indian gardens on the hill, stole corn, beat and took Indians prisoner, and broke their houses. The Indians came to Smith to complain.

Percy said that "Capt[ain] Smith Perceiving both his authority and Person neglected incensed and Animated the Savages against Capt[ain] West and his company Reporting unto them that our men had no more powder left them then would serve for one volley of shot."

By Smith's account the Indians told him that, for love of him, they had endured the newcomers' hostile treatment but

they desired pardon if hereafter they defended themselves; since he would not correct them, as they long expected he would. So much they opportuned him to punish their misdemeanors, as they offered (if he would lead them) to fight for him against them. But having spent nine days in seeking to reclaim them; showing them how much they did abuse themselves with those great gilded hopes of the South Sea Mines, commodities, or victories, they so madly conceived, he set sail for Jamestown.

According to the captain, he had gone not half a league before his ship ran aground, and he could hear the attack in the distance. He was within easy reach of West's Fort when its men decided to submit themselves to Smith's mercy. They seemed to think he had some sort of sway over the Indian enemy.

Smith arrested six or seven of West's men, put the rest in the hill village, named the place Nonsuch, and made good the losses on either side, including the munitions and food he had captured and taken away himself. As Smith prepared to depart, however, Captain West reappeared, took command, and moved his men back to West's Fort by the river. Smith, by his account, threw up his hands and left for Jamestown by river.

Asleep in the boat, Smith said, he was terrifically burned when a spark fell from a match and touched off a gunpowder bag he wore at his waist. He jumped into the river to douse the flames and was recovered half drowned.

In those days a match was a pyrotechnic cord used to discharge a firelock musket or pistol. The practice was to light it and keep it burning when there was prospect of the need of force. Smith offered no explanation of why anyone attending him would be on the point of firing a weapon.

The pain of the burn, Smith said, was excruciating. More misery awaited him in Jamestown at the hands of Archer, Ratcliffe, and Martin. Smith said:

> Their guilty consciences, fearing a just reward for their deserts, seeing the President unable to stand, and near bereft of his senses by reason of his torment, they had plotted to have murdered him in his bed. But his heart did fail him that should have given fire to that merciless Pistol. So not finding that course to be the best, they joined together to usurp the government, thereby to escape their punishment.

THE PORTRAICTUER OF CAPTAYNE JOHN SMITH / ADMIRALL OF NEW ENGLAND.

Æra 37
Aº 1616

These are the Lines that shew thy Face; but those
That shew thy Grace and Glory, brighter bee:
Thy Faire-Discoueries and Fowle-Overthrowes
Of Salvages, much Civilliz'd by thee
Best shew thy Spirit; and to it Glory Wyn:
So, thou art Brasse without, but Golde within.

An engraving of stern-faced Smith illustrates his *Generall Historie*.

Smith says he decided to go home for treatment of his burn. But he never surrendered his now-expired commission, only let it be stolen before he had "taken order to be free from the danger of their malice."

Whatever Smith had decided for himself, his opponents had plans for him too. Percy, who also suffered from a burn and was heading home for treatment, was summoned from his ship to be made president in Smith's place. West would be returning to England.

Ratcliffe, Archer, and Martin delayed Smith's departure three weeks while they prepared charges and recruited wit-

nesses. What the point was isn't clear; until 1612 the Virginia Company of London had no authority to correct in England persons accused of crimes in Virginia. No copy of the charges seems to have survived nor any record of a trial.

Nevertheless, Smith looked to his defense by publishing in his *Proceedings of the English Colony in Virginia* of 1612 the testimony of two supporters, Richard Pots and William Phettiplace. From their relation, an outline of the indictment emerges:

> Now all those men Smith had either whipped, punished, or any way disgraced, had free power and liberty to say or swear any thing, and from a whole armful of their examinations this was concluded.
>
> The mutineers at the Falls, complained he caused the Savages assault them, for that he would not revenge their loss. . . . and this they proved by the oath of one he had oft whipped for perjury and pilfering. The dutch-men that he had appointed to be stabbed for their treacheries, swore he sent to poison them with ratsbane. The prudent Council, that he would not submit himself to their stolen authority. . . . Others complained he would not let them rest in the fort (to starve) but forced them to the oyster banks, to live or starve, as he lived himself. . . . Some prophetical spirit calculated he had the Savages in such subjection, he would have made himself a king, by marrying Pocahontas, Powhatan's daughter. . . . Some that knew not anything to say, the Council instructed, and advised what to swear. So diligent they were in this business, that what any could remember, he had ever done, or said in mirth, or passion, by some circumstantial oath, it was applied to their fittest use, yet not past 8 or 9 could say much and that nothing but circumstances, which all men did know was most false and untrue. Many got their passes by promising in England to say much against him. I have presumed to say this much in his behalf for that I never heard such foul slanders, so certainly believed, and urged for truths by many a hundred, that do still not spare to spread them, say them and swear them, that I think do scarce know him, though they meet him, nor have they either cause or reason, but their wills, or zeal to rumor or opinion.

And so Smith left Virginia, never to return; a man scorned, and a prisoner, just as he arrived.

Captain John Smith's Christmas

DENNIS MONTGOMERY

The ever-scribbling Captain John Smith wrote the first report of a Christmas celebration in English America. In a sentence often reprinted he detailed a Yuletide feast of shell food and meat and poultry and other jolly goodies devoured in the snug huts of a hospitable band of Indians beside the Chesapeake Bay.

His account occasionally is mistaken for the relation of the continent's original English Christmas, but Smith's anecdote is no more than the first description of one in the First Colony. There is a difference between the first time a thing happened and the first time that thing was written about. In any case, the captain detailed neither the first December 25 he passed in the brand-new Old Dominion, nor the first that Anglo-Saxons abided on these shores, nor the first that Europeans spent in the Western Hemisphere. Nor was it on what we call Christmas.

Nevertheless, Smith's sentence is worth reprinting again. It is part of a narrative that begins at Jamestown on December 29, 1608—by the Old Style calendar the seventeenth-century English used. As they often were in winter, the settlement's inmates were famished, and, not for the first time, Smith was off on the hunt of provender. With a barge, a boat, and forty-six men, he set down the James River. The plan was to round Old Point Comfort, where Virginia's Lower Peninsula pokes into the bay, make their way up the York, and land at the north-bank Indian village Werowocomoco to barter with Powhatan, headman of a loose association of Tidewater tribes, for a boatload of corn. Powhatan asked to be paid with construction of an English-style house, a grindstone, fifty metal swords, firearms, a cock, a hen, and, for good measure, copper and beads.

Smith's "dry smoaky" Christmas. Don Hulick as Smith, left, Anthony Fortune,
Christopher Jones, Lindsey Fortune, Monique Jones, and Carson Hudson.

The captain and his company, who would have sailed downstream with the outgoing tide, made about twenty-two miles the first day. They spent the night at Warraskoyack, an aboriginal enclave up Pagan Creek on the James's south side near modern Smithfield. It sounds as if in the morning a winter nor'easter—the direction Smith was going—was starting to blow. But, with twelve of his bunch, he left for Kecoughtan, a village of naturals about six miles across Hampton Roads, at the confluence of the James and today's Hampton River. Modern Hampton. Now the ingeminate sentence:

The next night being lodged at Kecoughtan; six or seaven dayes the extreame winde, rayne, frost and snow caused us to keep Christmas among the Salvages, where we were never more merry, nor fed on more plentie of good Oysters, Fish, Flesh, Wild-foule, and good bread; nor never had better fires in England, then in the dry smoaky houses of Kecoughtan.

The description originally appeared in Smith's travel tale *The Proceedings of the English Colonie in Virginia since the first beginning from England in the yeare of our Lord 1606, till this present 1612, with all their accidents that befell them in their Journies and Discoveries.* That 110-page tome was the third of more than a dozen of Smith's literary endeavors that fell from the press. Twelve years later, he recycled the passage in his eighth, the six-part, 248-page *The Generall Historie of Virginia, New-England, and the Summer Isles with the names of the Adventurers, Planters and Government from their first beginning in 1584 to this present 1624.*

Smith's Christmas narrative runs sixty-one words, but if you've been paying attention, you've noticed there is more to tell. The Werowocomoco expedition began four days after the anniversary of the Nativity. Smith spent December 25 at Jamestown. How is it, then, the captain said he kept Christmas at Kecoughtan? He didn't land there until December 31.

It is tempting to think that he meant to say he was celebrating New Year's Eve, but, by the Old Style calendar, New Year's Eve was March 24. The thing is that in Smith's day, by custom, Christmas began December 25 and lasted through Twelfth Night, or January 6.

To digress a little more, the New Style calendar, which we employ, as at the time did continental Europe,

ran ten days in advance of Smith's. So, by our reckoning, his party with the Kecoughtans began January 10, 1609.

That explained, your attention is recalled to the title of *The Proceedings,* which was given entire for a reason. It says the English embarked for Virginia in 1606. They must, then, have shared at least one Christmas—1607's—before Smith's food foray in the winter of 1608.

In fact, they had shared two, the first outbound aboard ship, the second in Virginia. The settlers took to their vessels December 19, 1606, Old Style, at Blackwall, near London; fell down the Thames with the midnight tide; and, waiting for favorable winds, anchored January 1—still 1606 because, remember, their New Year began March 25—in the Downs. Which is to say that, as colonists, the Jamestowners spent their first Christmas in England. At all events, Smith published no account of the offshore festivities, and neither, it seems, did anyone else.

In April 1607, the 104 guinea-pig pioneers dispatched for America reached the James. Thirty-eight lasted the eight months it took to gain their first Christmas on Jamestown Island. The other sixty-six were well and safely in their graves, felled by Indians, disease, sloth, starvation, cold, and melancholy.

Smith said that their minister, the Reverend Mr. Robert Hunt, who didn't die for a month or so more, was conscientious in his performance of the Church of England's rituals, so it is doubtful Hunt neglected services on Christ's birthday.

By the way, this was thirteen years before the settlement of Plymouth, so the Pilgrims are not even in first-Christmas running. They didn't like celebrating the holiday anyway.

Hunt probably offered his hungry parishioners communion at Jamestown's makeshift church, a structure Smith said was "a homely thing like a barne, set upon cratchets, covered with rafts, sedge, and earth." The captain wrote no account of that Yule's celebrations either; but he was absent, off foraging then, too, on a ramble that appears to have put him in a tight spot.

About December 10, 1607, Smith took a handful of men up the James and into the tributary Chickahominy scrounging for victuals. Within two days, the captain was snared, probably near today's Bottoms Bridge, by a hunting party that Powhatan's kinsman Opechancanough commanded. They began a trek north that, by best guess, put the Indians and their captive captain on the Rappahannock, the river next above the York, on Christmas Day.

In his description of these reverses, Smith mentions Christmas not at all, which, under the circumstances, is not hard to understand. After four or five days of wandering about, Indian village to Indian village, he and his captors fetched up on Werowocomoco, where Opechancanough introduced Smith to Powhatan. There, on December 31, it seems, occurred the episode in which Pocahontas, one of Powhatan's daughters, dissuaded her father's headsmen from dashing out Smith's brains. The next day Powhatan sent Smith back to Jamestown.

The year Smith escaped being brained was not, however, the year of the first English Christmas in North America. Not by twenty-three. Look again at the title of Smith's *Generall Historie of Virginia, New-England, and the Summer Isles.* It says the English colonies had "their first beginning in 1584."

Englishmen and Englishwomen first passed a New World Yuletide during the sixteenth-century attempt to settle Roanoke Island. Sir Walter Ralegh, the sponsor, dispatched exploratory voyages in 1584, and 108 settlers in 1585. Ralegh, by royal patent, was

> to discover, search, finde out, and view such remote, heathen and barbarous lands, countreis, and territories, not actually possessed of any Christian prince, nor inhabited by Christian people, as to him, his heires and assignes, and to every or any of them shall seeme good

and to govern all the territory within 200 leagues of the settlement. Roanoke Island is within the Outer Banks of today's North Carolina. Ralegh had christened all his holdings Virginia, in honor of his benefactress, the "Virgin Queen" Elizabeth I.

The Roanoke Islanders endured hardship, adventure, and privation for more than a year before catching a ride home with the passing Sir Francis Drake, headed for England fresh from a raid on the Spanish at Cartageña. During their stay, a party of Roanoke explorers ventured to the neighborhood of modern Norfolk, seem to have spent the winter, and may have become the first English to enjoy Christmas in modern Virginia

The Reverend Robert Hunt, portrayed by John Turner, administering communion to Willie Balderson as one of the first Jamestown settlers.

proper. But not a line about that December 25, in either place, seems to have survived.

No matter. The first Europeans to pass a Yuletide anywhere in Virginia were Spanish—a band of Jesuit missionaries encamped somewhere north of the James, perhaps in the region where Queen's Creek flows into the York, above modern Yorktown, in September 1570.

Safe to say the Catholic fathers celebrated mass that Christmas, but Indians killed them in February, and no description of their December 25 observance has come to light. By 1570, however, Spaniards and the Christian religion were unremarkable in the New World, and, anyway, the primary annual Christian celebration was of the Resurrection, which the Queen's Creek fathers lived not to see.

The first Spaniards treated to a New World Christmas were the crewmen of Columbus's fleet, the *Niña*, the *Pinta,* and his *Santa María.* About the Yuletide of 1492 the admiral, as Columbus was styled, wrote in the journal of the voyage that Christmas was the day his flagship sank.

The *Niña* and the *Santa María*—the *Pinta* had abandoned them—were cruising the Caribbean off Santo Domingo. According to the journal, at vespers December 6, by the New Style calendar, they put into a port that the admiral named Puerto San Nicolas "in honor of St. Nicholas whose day it was."

The eighteenth, off Haiti, Columbus ordered "the ship and caravel to be adorned with arms and dressed with flags, in honor of the feast of Santa Maria de la O, or commemoration of the Annunciation which was that day, and many rounds were fired from the lombards." Lombards are artillery.

A chieftain of the island came to the *Santa María* attended by counselors and found Columbus dining under the poop—the aftermost and highest deck of the ship, which formed the roof of the cabin in the stern. Columbus shared his meal and with his guest exchanged gifts. The admiral got a belt with pieces of gold worked thin. To the chieftain he gave the drapery from his bed, amber beads from his neck, a pair of colored shoes, and a bottle of orange-flower water.

On December 23, the admiral, still coasting off Haiti, sent ships' boats to investigate another reach of the island. When the boatmen returned, "They held it for certain that, if the Christmas festival was kept in that port, all of the people of the island would come, which they calculated to be larger than England."

Drifting in a dead calm on Christmas Eve from Santo Tomé toward Punta Santa—which seems to be Puerto San Nicolas—the *Santa María*'s tiller was entrusted, against standing orders, to an unqualified common sailor. About midnight, the dolt put the flagship on a sandbar east of Cap Haitien on the island's north coast.

Columbus and the master of the vessel, Juan de la Cosa of Santoña, clambered on deck and put a boat over the side, de la Cosa in command, with the idea of oaring the ship off. But de la Cosa, who owned the

Santa María, fled instead for the safety of the *Niña*—where the coward was driven off. In the darkness, Columbus ordered the *Santa María* dismasted to lighten and refloat her, but it was no use. "Her side fell over across the sea, but it was nearly calm. Then the timbers opened and the ship was lost."

The admiral sent two men ashore to ask the leader of the island's nearest village, Guacanagarí, for assistance with salvage. Much was rescued, and Columbus took heart at that much good fortune. Be that as it may, there was too little room aboard the *Niña* to accommodate the *Santa María*'s complement, and Columbus was forced to maroon thirty-nine sailors. With a year's provisions and a ship's boat, he left among them a caulker, a carpenter, a gunner, and a cooper with orders to build a fortress—the first Spanish outpost in America, and guardian of the claim of Ferdinand and Isabella to Columbus's discovery.

Yet the Spanish look to have been about five centuries too tardy to assert clear title to having been the first Europeans to pass Christmas in the New World.

About the year 1000, someone whose name is lost to time wrote on vellum *The Saga of Eric the Red.* A Norseman and a Thor worshiper, Mr. Red is credited with sailing from Iceland to Greenland and establishing a European colony in the Western Hemisphere years before.

For the purposes of a story about the first New World Christmas, a pagan's adventures matter not much. But, if the narrative is to be credited, by the time Eric's tale was written, the Vikings had introduced Christianity, and by implication Christmas, to North America, where they had also translated the custom of making merry at the Yule.

Before 1001, according to the tale, the Christian voyager Thorbiorn set sail from Iceland with a party of thirty, among them the Christian woman Guidrid. They arrived in Greenland, about fifteen of them surviving the trip. Eric and his wife, Thiodhild, a woman the newcomers seem later to have converted, welcomed them. Eric and Thiodhild begat Leif the Lucky—the Christian also known as Leif Eriksson.

Eric's narrative is quirky, but the grownup Leif, after a voyage to Norway, Ireland, and Scotland, returned and "proclaimed Christianity throughout the land, and the Catholic faith." A church was built, a structure named for Thiodhild, "and there she and those persons who accepted Christianity, and there were many, were wont to offer their prayers."

Thor's ways, however, were not neglected. The saga reports the twelve-day celebration of the Yule in honor of Odin at the following winter's solstice—Christmas time: "Preparations were made for the Yule feast, and it was so sumptuous, that it seemed to the people they had scarcely ever seen so grand an entertainment before."

Just when, the saga doesn't say, but about 160 of those people sailed south to Newfoundland a year or so later, where they met Indians with animal-skin-hulled canoes. The next year a party sailed farther south, perhaps to Nova Scotia. There they ran into more natives—whom they called Skrellings, which in Viking meant "savages"—spent the winter, and captured and baptized two Indian boys. Being good Christians, they presumably remembered Christmas.

The account may not be entirely reliable. It matter-of-factly records the surprise of a Uniped, a member of a race of one-legged men, who hopped away into the wilderness. Nevertheless, the saga, in its account of a Yule bash, comes close to detailing a Christmas observance. Which brings us back to Captain Smith.

If you are still paying attention, you've noticed that Smith's Kecoughtan banquet, like Eric the Red's winter feast in Greenland, lasted twelve days. The first relations of the first New World Christmases take on a sort of symmetry.

"no fayre Lady"

The Several Faces of Pocahontas

She was called Pokahontas. In a word, if not so beautiful as Venus, she was more simple than her doves, and her voice was not less sweet than the son of a seraph. . . . She hung wildly on the neck of the reprieved victim, weeping with a violence that choaked her utterance. The flame of love was now lighted up in the bosom of the Indian maid.

Here was the classic tale of Pocahontas as told by American novelist John Davis in 1804. On reading Davis's book *The First Settlers of Virginia,* Professor Louis Hue Girardin wrote from the College of William and Mary declaring that "we all here rejoice at the appearance of our interesting Indian Princess. You are a magician. Your wand possesses the power of animating even my heart." Thomas Jefferson, in Washington, declared that he had "subscribed with pleasure to his Indian Tale." However, the editor of the New York *Evening Post* dismissed the presidential endorsement as a forgery, while "a young Virginian gentleman studying at Edinburgh" began his review by asserting that "we never met with any thing more abominably stupid than this romantic legend about the Princess Pokahontas" and ended by damning the unfortunate author's style as being "made up of pedantry, vulgarity, affectation and conceit."

Today, thanks first to the exuberant writings of John Smith, the Pocahontas legend endures and continues to generate spirited if slightly more restrained debate. Whether or not, as novelist Davis put it, Pocahontas led Smith by moonlight to the falls of the river where "her passion discovered itself by a thousand wild charms" remains anyone's guess;

but her marriage to the scholarly John Rolfe and her subsequent importance as an instrument of both the Emperor Powhatan's and the colonists' policy are in no doubt.

In their zeal to control the Indian population, the bright ideas of the colonists and their Virginia Company masters in London had ranged from crowning Powhatan king of whatever he thought he already owned to the already married Sir Thomas Dale offering to marry another of the emperor's daughters. But no public relations ploy was more cynical than the proposal to ship Pocahontas and her well-meaning husband to London to demonstrate what could be made of a docile, Christianized "salvage."

To make sure that Pocahontas was recognized as real royalty, she arrived with a retinue of about a dozen Indians headed by Tomocomo, her brother-in-law—at least in English law—along with his wife and her half-sister Mat-

achanna, three female servants, and four Powhatan men. Some in this group of "divers men and women of thatt countrye" would stay to be educated in England.

On or about June 3 the *Treasurer* docked at Plymouth, where the distinguished passengers were greeted by Devonshire's vice admiral, Sir Lewis Stukely, who may have been surprised by the behavior of Pocahontas's guidance counselor. Tomocomo had been instructed by Powhatan to remember everything and everybody he saw, specifically to count the people, as he dutifully began to do by cutting notches on a long stick. However, probably even before he left the Plymouth quay, in John Smith's words, "he was quickly wearie of that taske." With the civic reception over and the national census stick tossed aside, the Rolfes and their retinue set out on the 173-mile journey to London. . . .

◀ ▶ The legend of John Smith's escape from execution through the intercession of Pocahontas became a favorite subject for nineteenth-century illustrators and for the souvenir vendors of enameled tin plates on the "War Path" promenade at the Jamestown Exposition of 1907.

It may have been someone's idea of a joke to book the Rolfes into the Belle Sauvage Inn on Ludgate Hill. But lest it be supposed that the name was changed to capitalize on the inn's American guests, records show that both the building and the name dated back to at least 1453. A hundred and sixty-three years later the inn was no four-star hotel and indeed had slipped down the hostelry ladder to the level of a tavern, as Ben Jonson recalled in his 1625 play *The Staple of News.* In it lawyer Picklock is talking to Pennyboy, a beggar, who says: "Let your meat rather follow you to a tavern."

Penny. A tavern's as unfit too for a princess.

Pick. No, I have known a princess, and a great one, come forth of a tavern.

Pick. Not go in, sir, though.

Penny. She must go in, if she came forth: the blessed Pocahontas, as the historian calls her, and great king's daughter of Virginia, hath been in womb of a tavern.

The historian was John Smith, who in 1624 had referred to "the blessed Pocahontas" in the dedicatory introduction to his *Generall Historie,* but the play's "princess" was a young woman from Cornwall, where, like many Indians, the people were commonly swarthy-skinned and black-haired.

Once in London, the Rolfes quickly became the city's latest curiosity. Just as they would be today, opinions were sharply divided on the wisdom of such a marriage, not so much on racial grounds as on religious. The Virginia Company's own enthusiasm for the idea of bringing over this example of a fair princess plucked from the devil's talons had wilted more than somewhat when the king made it clear that he considered John Rolfe's behavior little short of treason, prompting the council to debate the possibility that it might indeed be so. Whether these deliberations occurred before or after the couple's arrival is not clear, but James's opinion evidently softened to the point where he allowed Lord and Lady De La Warr to escort Pocahontas and Tomocomo (no mention of Rolfe) to Twelfth Night revels, which both he and his queen, Anne of Denmark, attended to watch a masque written by Ben Jonson. There may, however, have been a degree of irony in the invitation,

for Twelfth Night was traditionally the time to do honor to the swarthy biblical wise men of Bethlehem, "who are supposed to have been of royal dignity." Mock kings and queens, each chosen by finding a bean or a pea in a slice of cake, ruled the revels. Consequently, Jonson's *Masque of Christmas,* which he wrote for that occasion, included an usher "bearing a great cake with a been and a Pease." In the midst of such turnabout hilarity an Indian princess dressed like an English lady attended by Tomocomo in Indian attire would have provided London's smart set with added amusement.

Some authorities doubt that Pocahontas and Tomocomo were ever formally received by the king and queen, yet from John Smith's *Generall Historie* it seems clear enough that shortly after the Rolfes' arrival, and before Smith left for Plymouth to plan a New England voyage, Smith met Tomocomo in London, where the following conversation resulted:

Hee told me Powhatan did bid him to finde me [Smith] out, to shew him our God, the King, Queene, and Prince, I so much had told them of. Concerning God, I told him the best I could, the King I heard he had seene, and the rest hee should see when he would; he denied ever to have seene the King, till by circumstances he was satisfied he had: Then he replyed very sadly, You gave Powhatan a white Dog, which Powhatan fed as himselfe, but your King gave me nothing, and I am better than your white Dog.

The logic of his argument may be weak, but it is evident that Tomocomo did see the king, possibly at a levee along with so many other splendidly dressed people that he did not know who among them was the English Powhatan.

Whether or not Pocahontas was received by the king or queen would be of little pertinence to the James Towne story were it not that it relates to an object which allegedly survives as the sole relic of that meeting. I saw it first in 1968 in a singularly unlikely place, namely, in an office at the Sloane Street branch of Barclays Bank in London. I had been asked to go there on behalf of the Smithsonian Institution to examine a silver-mounted stoneware mug allegedly given by Queen Anne to Pocahontas, whose owner had a mind to sell it to the nation.

The jug was genuine enough. Made at Siegburg in the Rhineland in about 1580, it boasted a very ordinary silver mount on which were crudely engraved the initials T M R. Assuming that the middle letter stood for Pocahontas's Indian name Matoaka, the combination was supposed to represent the initials of Mr. and Mrs. Rolfe, a reasonable supposition, provided one forgot that John did not begin with a *T*. . . .

To help promote Pocahontas's acceptance in London's cruel society, John Smith had written to Queen Anne recalling all that Powhatan's daughter, "this tender Virgin," had done to help the colonists at large and himself in particular. Now that she had arrived from Virginia, "the first Christian ever of that Nation, the first Virginian ever spake English, or had a childe in marriage by an Englishman," Smith begged that she be well received. Seeking financial generosity (for which James was not renowned), Smith noted, too, that John Rolfe's financial status was such that he could not afford to dress his wife appropriately to be received at court, as was true. Although the Virginia Company did give the family four pounds a week, as historian Philip L. Barbour points out, the Levant Company hosting a single minor diplomatic visitor to London allowed him that much per diem solely for food, plus twenty pounds a month for lodging. In short, the Virginia Company was being extraordinarily stingy, reflecting its persisting ambivalence toward its colorful guests.

When Smith wrote his appeal to the queen, he claimed that he was "preparing to set saile for New-England" and so could not be of as much service to Pocahontas as he would have wished. That was true, as far as it went, but since Smith's grand design to reunite the Plymouth adventurers with the London Company in a new James Towne–like venture in Maine came to naught, it is surprising that he recorded details of only one meeting with Pocahontas in the seven months of her visit. It took place at the village of Brentford, possibly at Syon House, one of the homes of George Percy's illustrious brother Henry, Earl of Northumberland. He, however, would not have been there to receive the guests. First an enthusiastic supporter of Scotland's James VI when he came south to accept the English crown, Northumberland soon had difficulty concealing his con-

Polished by the touch of countless Jamestown visitors, the bronze hands of Pocahontas appeal for compassion toward all Native Americans. The statue by William Ordway Partridge was commissioned for the 1907 Jamestown Exposition at Norfolk.

clusion that a very few Scotsmen were more than enough. When the king learned that the earl's kinsman Thomas Percy, a ringleader in the Gunpowder Plot, had dined at Syon House the day before the scheduled explosion, Northumberland's loyalty was doubted, a suspicion that led to his prolonged imprisonment in the Tower of London—where Pocahontas reportedly was

Matoaks als Rebecka daughter to the mighty Prince
Powhatan Emperour of Attanoughskomouck als virginia
converted and baptized in the Christian faith, and
wife to the worfll Mr Joh: Rolff.

Si: Paß: sculp: Compton Holland excud:

Matoaks als Rebecka daughter to the mighty Prince
Powhatan Emperour of Attanoughkomouck als virginia
converted and baptized in the Christian faith, and
wife to the worfll Mr Joh: Rolff.

Pub. Aug. 10. 1793. by W. Richardson. Castle St. Leicester Square.

taken to visit him. That she should have been received at Syon House by his wife Dorothy is entirely possible for, like her husband, the Countess of Northumberland was an outspoken supporter of another longtime but recently released Tower prisoner, Sir Walter Ralegh.

Tradition has it that it was Ralegh who escorted Pocahontas to the Tower to meet his friend Northumberland, whose scientific interests had earned him the sobriquet of the "Wizard Earl." He was also an all-purpose tinkerer, and during the meeting with Pocahontas he noticed that one of her shell earrings was in need of attention. A pair of silver-mounted mussel shell earrings displayed in the National Park Services visitor center at Jamestown reputedly exhibits the Wizard Earl's handiwork.

However much John Smith may have professed affection for Pocahontas, his description of their Brentford meeting, though intensely human and likely to be true, does not stamp it as a social success. Perhaps overwhelmed by the glittering company, or perhaps by the emotion of seeing him for the first time since her childhood, Pocahontas failed to project a particularly sparkling or engaging personality. Smith recalled that, "After a modest salutation, without any word, she turned about, obscured her face, as not seeming well contented; and in that humour her husband, with diverse others, we all left her two or three houres, repenting my selfe to have writ she could speake English." She later demonstrated that she could; but she evidently, and not surprisingly, felt herself a tropical fish in an empty tank.

Although through the months that she was in England Pocahontas was well treated and entertained by many distinguished people having Virginia interests, behind her back she was considered an oddity and was referred to by

Three portraits of Pocahontas: the original 1616 engraving by Simon van de Passe; the much used but rarely, if ever, credited re-engraved and Anglicized version of 1793; and the controversial "Zuccelli" portrait, whose features more closely resemble the 1793 copy than van de Passe's original. The inscription inexplicably identifies her husband as Thomas rather than John Rolfe.

the gossipy letter writer John Chamberlain not as Mrs. Rolfe or Pocahontas, or even as Matoaka, but repeatedly as "the Virginian woman." On February 22, 1617, just a month before she was due to return to Virginia, Chamberlain wrote to his friend Dudley Carleton:

> Here is a fine picture of no fayre Lady and yet with her tricking up and high stile and titles you might thincke her and her worshipfull husband to be sombody, yf you do not know that the poore companie of Virginia out of theyre povertie are faine to allow her fowre pound a weeke for her maintenance.

Chamberlain evidently had sent his friend an engraving by the Flemish artist Simon van de Passe, one apparently commissioned by the compiler and publisher Henry Holland and sold by his supposed brother Compton at his shop near the Royal Exchange, where

merchants associated with the Virginia Company were likely to see it. The engraving shows a fierce-eyed, high-cheekboned, dark-countenanced woman with a strikingly regal yet witchlike look. A surrounding oval identifies her as Matoaka alias Rebecca (the name given her at her baptism), daughter of Powhatan, emperor of Virginia. As was common among engravings of this period, a lengthy inscription below the portrait repeats the information and adds that "Matoaks" was "wife to the Worshipful Mr. John Rolfe." Were it not for the fact that van de Passe added that his subject was aged twenty-one, we might be forgiven for guessing at forty.

The portrait is striking but by no means flattering, and one Pocahontas biographer has dismissed it as "mere caricature," a cheap copy of a portrait painted at the time of Pocahontas's presentation at court. There is no doubting, however, that the engraving came first and the

A Siegburg stoneware mug of about 1590, though of poor quality, is said to have been presented to Pocahontas by Queen Anne. Scratched on the silver rim mount are the letters T M R, the "M" allegedly the initial for Pocahontas's alternate name Matoaka, the "R" for Rolfe, and the "T" that better suits Thomas than John.

portrait a possibly belated second. The painting is stated in the *Dictionary of National Biography* to be the work of an Italian artist and to have come down in the Rolfe-related family of the Reverend Whitwell Elwin of Booton Rectory, Norfolk. In 1882 or 1883 the painting's then-owner Hastings Elwin wrote that his grandfather had been given it by a Mrs. Zuccelli and that he thought that Mr. Zuccelli might have been the artist. Perhaps because Elwin admitted to being unsure of the spelling, artist Zuccelli (if, indeed, he was an artist) has not been traced. All that can be said, therefore, is that the painting has no known history prior to the mid-eighteenth century.

Now in the National Portrait Gallery in Washington, D. C., the famous picture shows that the artist tried to Anglicize and soften the features, eliminating the chin cleft, weakening the cheekbones and the shadows under the eyes, and giving the flesh a warming injection of pink. In the engraving Pocahontas wears a tall hat with a broad band and a handsome side feather, but in the painting the feather is gone, and the plain hat begins to merge into the muddy background. The painter's changes to the hat, which seem to include a slight short-ening of the crown as well as omission of the feather, might be construed as part of the gentling process in the belief that van de Passe's hat was too theatrical. In fact, it wasn't (though it may well have been made for a man), for it is closely paralleled in Daniel Mytens's portrait of Spain's then-ambassador to England, the Count de Gondomar. The treatment of other clothing details in the "Zuccelli" portrait suggests that the artist did not fully understand how early-seventeenth-century garments were put together, thus supporting the likelihood that the engraving was copied some while after Pocahontas's death. But then again we cannot be sure that the "Zuccelli" portrait is not itself an imprecise copy of a now-lost original.

That the portrait was not painted from life is amply demonstrated by the fact that the long inscription under the engraving has been more or less slavishly transferred to the painting, something rarely, if ever, incorporated in that way into family portraits. The inscription reads like this:

Matoaks als [alias] Rebecka daughter to the mighty Prince Powhatan Emperour of Attanoughkomouck als virginia converted and baptized in the Christian faith, and Wife to the worll Mr Tho: Rolff.

Thomas Rolfe? Like the stoneware mug which came down through the same family, John Rolfe has been given the name and initial of his son. The "mistake" has to be deliberate, but why? There is no evidence that John changed his name for, after returning to Virginia, he continued to sign himself in that way. On the other hand, as we shall shortly see, the John-Thomas confusion is not the result of retrospective memorializing or fakery, for it began on March 21, 1617. One thing is certain: The painting was not commissioned by John Rolfe. But if not, then by whom?

The London historian William Kent has recorded that the landlord of the Belle Sauvage so profited from the fame or notoriety of his exotic lodgers that he put up a new sign bearing a portrait of Pocahontas. According to Kent, the association lasted at least until 1672, when the inn issued the second of two monetary tokens depicting "an Indian woman holding a bow and arrow." Is it possible, therefore, that the crude signlike quality of the "Zuccelli" portrait is no accident, and that it was the work of the Belle Sauvage sign painter, either as a gift to

the Rolfes or perhaps to hang in the taproom in the way that today's publicans hang signed portraits of celebrity visitors in their bars?

If that theory is to hold water, one needs to be able to produce the two tokens, the first of which (according to Kent) was issued in 1648. However, the standard catalog of English seventeenth-century tokens lists none for the Belle Sauvage, and the British Museum's Department of Coins and Medals states that it has no examples in its collection, nor has it heard of their existence. With the tokens sidelined, one has to wonder whether Kent's inn-sign story is any more reliable.

Out of all this uncertainty, only the Simon van de Passe engraving survives as an undeniably contemporary portrayal of the Virginian princess. Although the engraving seems to have been later bound with a book of English royal portraits printed by Henry Holland and published in 1618, it appears to have been first rushed out as a single sheet to exploit a short-lived market—the haste suggested by the absence of the corner embellishment common to these cartouche-style portraits. This, then, is the rationale for claiming that it was the Simon van de Passe portrait that John Chamberlain sent to his friend. It remains an open question whether the van de Passe rendering was taken from life or was copied from another now-lost painting or drawing.

In 1966 the Huntington Library's 1624 copy of John Smith's *Generall Historie* was reprinted in what was claimed to be a facsimile edition, and in it, on facing pages, were not one but two portraits of Pocahontas, the van de Passe version on the left and another healthier and more European version on the right. Assuming that "facsimile" meant an exact copy, I developed a thesis that Smith, believing that the van de Passe engraving failed to do justice to Pocahontas's memory, had the gentler version drawn for inclusion in his history's first edition. Although there are several ways to distinguish between the two versions when they are not seen side by side, the easiest is to note that the hat's feather breaks the oval in the first version but not in the second. The latter is by far the better known, for it was used to illustrate Edward Arbor's edition of Smith's *Travels and Works* (1910), which remained the standard text for more than seventy years. What Arber did not reveal, any more than did the 1966 facsimile edition,

St. George's Church, Gravesend, rebuilt in 1732 after fire destroyed the building in whose chancel Pocahontas was buried on March 21, 1617.

was the fact that a crucial line had been omitted from the bottom of the engraving. It reads, "Pub^d. Aug^r 10. 1793. by W. Richardson Castle St. Leicester Square." Thus John Smith had nothing to do with the short-feather engraving, and my thesis promptly collapsed. Only the van de Passe engraving had given Londoners their lasting impression of their exotic visitor, thin visaged, regal, yet still rather frighteningly "savage" beneath her European attire, and, as Chamberlain had slyly put it, "no fayre Lady."

One cannot help feeling sorry for John Rolfe. He came from a respectable Norfolk family of rural gentry who for generations had lived at Heacham Hall near King's Lynn. The area was a seedbed of Puritanism, and

that clearly had influenced the young man. It is clear, too, that he was a loner, more interested in growing tobacco than in involving himself in Virginia politics. As a letter to Sir Thomas Dale revealed, Rolfe was concerned lest God and his peers take a dim view of his marrying "an unbelieving creature," and he knew that once in London he was even more likely to encounter "the vulgar sort, who square all mens actions by the base rule of their own filthiness" and who he feared would tax and taunt him for what he saw as his godly labor. Lodged in an inn later renowned for its bedbugs and then frequented by fencers and theater people, where plays were performed in the yard, the quiet John Rolfe as the sole white gentleman in the midst of an Indian circus must have prayed for the day when he could return to Virginia and to isolated respectability.

Although Pocahontas was no better able to grapple with the climate and common sicknesses to which the English were hardened than were they to those of Virginia, she seems to have enjoyed her seven months in England. On January 18, 1617, Chamberlain, after describing the royal masque and Pocahontas's presence, wrote that "she is on her return (though sore against her will) yf the wind wold come about to send them away." This suggests that the Rolfes were by then aboard ship waiting for a favorable wind. Although winter was a vile time of year to sail out into the English Channel, it seems unlikely that the departure would have been delayed by all of nine weeks. Nevertheless, we know from both Smith and Chamberlain that Samuel Argall, as admiral of a three-ship fleet, was not ready to sail until about March 20—the day that Pocahontas died.

The ship *George* was then anchored at the mouth of the Thames off Gravesend. A small town of less distinction, it was nevertheless a major arrival and departure point for foreign visitors. Because it was closer to London than Dover and within rowing distance of the city, Queen Elizabeth had ordered that its lord mayor, aldermen, and officials of the civic companies were to go to Gravesend to receive all "eminent strangers and ambassadors . . . and attend them to London in their barges." It is likely, therefore, that the Rolfes went down the Thames to Gravesend by open barge. Anyone who has taken a tour boat from Westminster (if only as far as Greenwich) on a gray and windy March day can attest to the fact that you disembark with skin as blue as a bluefooted booby's feet. The probability that the already sickly Pocahontas caught a chill en route to Gravesend has more credence than the often favored view that her death was caused by exposure to the sea air while she waited aboard the *George* or while she lodged in a Gravesend cottage.

There is, however, another possibility, and it takes us back to the Simon van de Passe engraving and forward to 1620, when one of the Indian women left behind to be educated reportedly became "very weake of a concumpcon." Pulmonary diseases, which were common in seventeenth-century London, were exacerbated in the winter, when the city lay under a pall of yellow, choking fog, and the houses reeked of smoke from countless aging and often poorly built chimneys. As later bills of mortality show, hundreds died of tuberculosis and the other lung diseases collectively described as consumption. John Chamberlain's letter of January 18 had indicated that Pocahontas was leaving and waited only for a fair wind. It is conceivable, therefore, that the Virginia Company wanted her out of town before her deteriorating health generated critical gossip and that she did, in fact, go down to Gravesend several weeks before Argall's ships were to sail. That her drawn features were the product of a wasting disease and did not mirror her previous healthy appearance cannot be proved, yet it is hard to believe that any artist would have drawn the twenty-one-year-old "poor innocent Pocahontas," as Smith described her, in so unflattering a portrait had there been no reason to do so.

The funeral of Pocahontas took place in St. George's Church at Gravesend on March 21, 1617, the entry in the register reading "Rebecca Wrothe, wyff of Thomas Wroth gent. a Virginia lady borne, here was buried in ye Chauncell." The church burned down in 1732, and if a carved stone was laid in the floor (as seems likely, she being placed in so prominent a place in the church), it has long since disappeared. The parish registers survived, however, keeping alive the mystery of why, as on the mug and on the painted portrait, John Rolfe was there cited as T or Thomas.

As she lay close to death, Pocahontas had told her husband that, though all must die, it was enough that her child should live. But would he? The infant Thomas Rolfe had also been sick and remained frail and ill-prepared for the rigors of an Atlantic voyage. The Indian women who had been Pocahontas's servants and were now the child's nurses were also sick and themselves in need of nursing. Consequently, when the *George* reached Plymouth, John Rolfe sadly and reluctantly turned the boy over to Sir Lewis Stukely, the vice admiral who had greeted Pocahontas and all the others at quayside only ten months earlier. Rolfe never saw his son again.

Romancing Pocahontas

DENNIS MONTGOMERY

The artists never saw it the same way. In the first three centuries that engravers, painters, and sculptors imagined the tableau of Pocahontas saving Captain John Smith from her emperor-father Powhatan's headsmen, they presented the twelve- or thirteen-year-old Indian princess in fringed skirts, aprons and togas made of deerskin, tobacco leaves, and brightly colored, geometrically figured cloth. They dressed Smith in a doublet, armor, a cloth jacket, and starched collar-ruffs, high boots and low shoes. They braided Pocahontas's hair, put it up, put it down, and fastened it in a laurel wreath. They portrayed the event sometimes indoors and sometimes out.

In time, artists' conceptions of the Pocahontas-Smith drama came less to be encumbered by the idea of realism than informed by a view that forestalled more than rose-colored consideration of the episode. Or, perhaps, of its meaning.

They imagined the scene through the lens of their times and civilization, and, as centuries passed, came to see it less and less in terms of the early, almost journalistic representations of the moment, and more and more as reflections of their own, increasingly distant cultural ideas of what they believed was Smith's rescue. It was something like looking through the big end of a spyglass.

Which is what makes their images so informative. Their depictions reflect not so much what happened that December 31 in 1607 as they do the evolution and embellishment of the notions of swashbuckler Smith saved by a self-sacrificing Noble Savage as the moment grew in time more remote and romantic. The images on these pages reveal more about the artists and their publics than they do about the twenty-seven-year-old Englishman and the adolescent Indian.

King Powhatan comands C: Smith to be flame, his daughter Pokahontas beggs his life his thanfullneſs and how he ſubiected 39 of their kings. reade history.

printed by Iames Reeve

▲ From Smith's *Generall Historie of Virginia, New-England, and the Summer Isles,* first published in 1624, this may be the earliest, and perhaps most journalistic, representation of the rescue scene. What was long believed to be an attempted execution may have been an initiation.

▶ Sculpted in 1825 by Italian Antonio Catellano, this frieze of a reminiscently Roman rescue scene graces the rotunda of the nation's Capitol.

Today's historians suppose Smith, captured nineteen days before by a Pamunkey hunting party, was sentenced not to execution but to initiation—to be symbolically killed as an English commander and reborn as a tributary subchief who would deliver the remnant of the Anglo-Saxon tribe at Jamestown into the emperor's obedience.

In any case, every vision of the scene begins with the captive captain's description of being hauled into Powhatan's headquarters beside the River York:

> At his entrance before the King, all the people gave a great shout. The Queene of Appamatuck was appointed to bring him water to wash his hands, and another brought him a bunch of feathers, instead of a Towell to dry them: having feasted him after their best barbarous manner they could, a long consultation was held, but the conclusion was, two great stones were brought before Powhatan: then as many as could layd hands on him, dragged him to them, and thereon laid his head, and being ready with their clubs, to beate out his braines, Pocahontas the Kings dearest daughter, when no intreaty could prevaile, got his head in her armes, and laid her owne upon his to save him from death: whereat the Emperour was contented he should live to make him hatchets, and her bells, beads, and copper.

Think on Smith's words, look at the images, and ask whether our times encourage us to envision it through the proper end of the cultural telescope.

◀ An 1870 oil by Frenchman Victor Nehlig costumes the seaboard Powhatan Indians in the clothing of the Plains tribes.

▶ New England Chromo Lithography published its rendition of the rescue about 1870 in Boston.

▼ The firm of H. Schile of New York offered its version, with horses, in 1874.

"we are starved"

IVOR NOËL HUME

Next only to the arrival of the English in 1607 and their departure in 1781, the months of the winter of 1609–10, known as the Starving Time, rank atop the memorable events of Virginia's history. Hundreds of settlers died for want of food. Some were reduced to cannibalism. But who were the hungry and why did they starve? Neither question has been adequately answered, and more often than not historians have been content to say that it happened—but should not have.

Since the first English fleet dropped anchor in the river they named for King James, off the island where they raised Jamestown, there had been a steady flow of arriving colonists to hew a living out of the relatively benign Virginia environment. Crops grew easily and readily ripened, fish were plentiful, game abounded in the forests, and, if one was careful, wild plants, fruits, and nuts were edible. To transported Londoners this would have been as close to Eden as they could have imagined. So what went wrong?

The 1607 arrivals numbered 104 or 105 men and boys, half of whom were dead by year's end. Captain Christopher Newport who had commanded the original fleet returned with two ships of supplies early in 1608, but soon after he docked the fortified Jamestown caught fire. The conflagration destroyed most of the equipment and possessions already there. Rather than forwarding the settlement's progress, Newport's help focused on picking up the pieces from the charred ruins of the first year's meager accomplishments.

Nevertheless, his orders from the Virginia Company of London, the joint-stock enterprise that owned the colony, were to return with saleable commodities that would begin to repay the investors. Thus, the settlers spent a disproportionate amount of their time and

◀ The Starving Time Jamestowners, one of them portrayed here by Jared Larson, ran out of their beds "Cryeinge owtt we are starved."

▼ The wooden cross honors the Starving Time dead, scores of whom may be buried on the fenced ridge behind it.

energy sawing trees and splitting boards, not for their own home improvements but for building construction in England.

Although then-President George Percy identified the winter of 1609–10 as "this starveinge Tyme," it differed little from the periods of starvation that had beset the colony from the beginning. The settlers reported to the Virginia Company that as early as 1607

> they fell into extreame want, not having anything left to sustain them save a little ill conditioned Barley, which ground to meal & pottage made thereof, one smale ladle full was allowed each person for a meale, without bread or aught else whatsover.

The report, submitted by the "Ancient Planters nowe remaining alive in Virginia," said that had it not been for help from the Indians the colonists "had all utterlie by famine perished." By "ancient," they meant "among the earliest," and by "planters," "colonists."

Like twenty-first-century shortages, there was a surfeit of finger-pointing. The colonists were quick to blame the government, specifically the "misgovernment of Sir Thomas Smith," the Virginia Company's chief executive back in England, who

> aimed at nothing more than a perticular gaine to be raised out of the labours of such as both voluntarilie adventured themselves and were otherwise sent over at the common charge.

The survivors were saying that the company's primary interest was in getting the labor to Virginia and expecting it to fend for itself once it arrived while making money for the stockholders. In the light of the glowing reports of earlier English voyages to the New World that was a reasonable assumption—at least to company executives seated in the comfort of their London offices. It might have been reasonable too, if the apprentice settlers had known what they had to do and had the leadership to get it done. They didn't.

The locally governing seven-man Jamestown council—named before leaving England but not identified until it reached Virginia—spent more time jockeying for position than organizing the work force. Its president, Edward Maria Wingfield, was ineffective and malleable in the hands of more aggressive members of his fractious council. Consequently, when the first of two supply ships arrived at Jamestown in January 1608, the famished survivors of the original 104 or 105 were living in cabins—soldiers' tents—and holes in the ground. Ten were fit to work, the remainder being "at point of death, all utterly destitute of houses." The blame for this "misgovernment" rested as much on the shoulders of the ancient planters as it did on Sir Thomas Smith and the company.

The supply ships, the *John and Francis* and the *Phoenix*, brought 120 more settlers, reportedly worse provided for than their predecessors, adding to the burden of feeding the colony. Another supply ship, the *Mary Margaret*, arrived at the end of September, adding sixty more unseasoned helpers—"mostly gentlemen" and few or no tradesmen—all of whose supplies were exhausted within two months. By that time, however, the feuding councilors had been sidelined by their least-liked member, Captain John Smith.

Smith, for a time, provided the unified leadership the colony had lacked. But not even he could coax crops to grow overnight, and at the year's end the ancient planters said that although they had cleared four acres for agriculture there was "hunger & sickness not permitting any great matters to be donne."

Salvation—if there was to be any—lay in the hands of the Indians, whom the colonists called savages. Trading copper and beads for corn and even swords for turkeys kept England's precarious foothold alive through the winter of 1608–09. Had the Indians not been beguiled by the Europeans' tools and trinkets, the colony would have collapsed and the course of American history changed. Instead, the Indians traded their corn for a future of persecution and privation—a deal personified by the at-first nubile and later tragic figure of Pocahontas.

Although Smith said he did everything he could to whip the colony into shape, survivors of the old guard were plotting against him—and rats were in the storehouse. Not until it was too late did Smith discover that

> in searching our casked corne, wee found it helfe rottern, the rest so consumed with the many thousand rats (increased first from the ships) that we knewe not how to keepe that little wee had.... This did drive us all to our wits end.

◀ Swiftly running through the provisions shipped from England, the colonists did not plant enough to feed themselves and were reduced to "one smale ladle" of gruel a day. Interpreter Lindsay Gray accepts his pittance from interpreter Carol Farmer.

▼ In *The New World*, Native Americans—Q'orianka Kilcher here as Pocahontas—traded food to starving Englishmen in 1608–09.

A frying pan proved a sorry tool for catching fish. Interpreter Lindsay Gray flails at fish "lying so thicke" but comes up empty-handed.

Smith's solution was to divide the colonists into three groups, one to go downriver to modern Hampton at the mouth of the James to live on oysters, another to go upriver to establish a fort by the falls at modern Richmond, and the rest to remain at Jamestown. The Hampton group did more arguing than fishing while contentions at the falls fort resulted in many being killed by the Indians or deserting to join them.

If we are to believe Smith, had his best endeavors not been frustrated by "envious authority," the Starving Time to come would have been averted. Even so, Smith's planning seems to have its shortcoming—like going fishing without a net.

In June, 1608, Smith had headed an expedition to explore the estuaries of the Chesapeake Bay. Sailing in an open barge were the colony's doctor, seven gentlemen, and as many soldiers, one of whom was identified as "Jonas Profit a fishmonger." The fish, Smith said, were "lying so thicke with their heads above the water, as for want of nets . . . we attempted to catch them with a frying pan: but we found it a bad instrument to catch fish with."

Netless fishing was but one of the many almost farcical failures that beset the colony before and after John Smith's presidency—which unexpectedly ended with a bang. On his way back from the fort at the falls a bag of gunpowder ignited and burned him so severely that he was expected to die. When he did not, and after an aborted assassination attempt, the Jamestown councilors shipped him home to England—in the interests of his recovery and future well-being.

The ailing George Percy, one of the remaining original councilors, succeeded Smith as president. He had inherited a virtually empty storehouse. But thanks to Smith's efforts, crops had been growing and, with the numbers of mouths to feed decreased as disease and the Indians took their toll, the situation was not as dire as it might have been. Besides, Percy knew that help was on its way.

On Friday, June 2, 1609, a fleet "of seven good ships and two pinnaces, weighed anchor from Plymouth Sound," bound for Jamestown. The flagship *Sea Venture* led the way with Admiral Sir George Somers in command and with a new charter and a governor, Sir

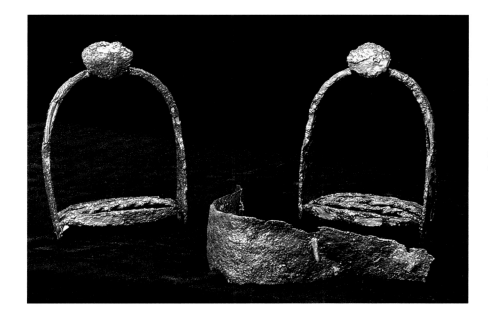

Stirrups and bridle recovered from Jamestown, useless after the English ate their horses and were reduced to eating rats, snakes, and mice and to grubbing for roots. When those resources were exhausted, colonists turned to eating the dead.

Thomas Gates, to replace the Percy administration as well as Captain Newport and other senior officers aboard. Astern sailed the heavier transports loaded with supplies and 500 soldiers and settlers, among them an unrecorded number of women and children. All went well until July 23 when "the clouds began to thicken around . . . and a dreadful storm commenced from the north east." The hurricane raged for three days, wrecking the *Sea Venture* on a Bermuda reef and scattering and battering the rest of the fleet. After reassembling and assessing the damage, the fleet limped into the James on August 11 having suffered "a great loss of men by calenture," a tropical fever "and most of them all much weatherbeaten."

To the embattled Percy, the rescue fleet was no help. The new governor had apparently been lost at sea, but three argumentative colleagues, Ratcliffe, Archer, and Martin, who had gone home the year before were now back with their own axes to grind. Unable to house the near 500 new arrivals, Percy billeted them in the colony's seven-acre field of planted corn which they "in three days at the most, wholly devoured."

Faced with spreading disease and the likelihood of insurgency, Percy decided to once again split the colony into three parts. He reduced Jamestown to a small garrison, ordered the inexperienced twenty-two-year-old Cap-

tain Francis West upriver to the falls, and Ratcliffe to build forts at the mouth of the James to augment another on the south side held by the difficult John Martin.

Martin soon quit and returned to Jamestown, leaving his men to fend for themselves. Mutiny followed and so did the Indians. The mutineers fled and were killed as were the remaining soldiers. Percy next sent Ratcliffe with a fifty-man force to the emperor Powhatan to trade for maize and corn. The negotiations did not go well. Sixteen men made it back—empty-handed—Ratcliffe having been flayed and burnt alive by Indian women "and so for want of circumspection miserably perished."

Percy sent West with thirty-six men in a small ship called the *Swallow* to trade with the Indians of the Potomac, which they did. Returning to Ratcliffe's fort at the mouth of the James, West was assured that Jamestown was in dire need of the corn, apparently heard that there was cannibalism, and urged to proceed upriver with all possible speed. The *Swallow's* crew had a better idea. It headed to sea and ate the corn on the voyage home to England.

The hard winter of the Starving Time reduced a population of about 500 to barely sixty, "the reste beinge either sterved throwe famin or cut of by the Salvages," Gabriel Archer among them. Everything from the horses

The Jamestown fort at the edge of the James River, where, as George Percy wrote, "There were never Englishmen left in a forreigne Countrey in such miserie." After the Starving Time of 1609–10, perhaps sixty of 500 English had survived famine, disease, and Indians.

brought by the Gates fleet to rats, snakes, mice, and roots dug from the forest were consumed, and emaciated survivors took to eating the dead.

On May 22, 1610, two small ships appeared in the James. Aboard were the crew and passengers of the wrecked *Sea Venture,* all well nourished from nine months of relatively easy living on the islands of the Bermudas. The survivors the new governor, Gates, saw as he entered the fort at Jamestown were, wrote Percy,

> lamentable to behowlde them for many throwe extreme hunger have Runne outt of their naked bedds being so Leane that they Looked Lyke Anotamies Cryeinge owtt we are starved.

The settlement, Gates wrote, looked more like "the ruins of some auntient" fortification "then that any people living might now inhabit it."

Having no immediate remedy and no knowledge of any relief coming from London, Gates resolved to abandon Jamestown and take the survivors home. On June 7, they boarded his small ships and left their dilapidated fort and ruined houses to be picked over by the Indians. Powhatan had won. England's Virginia colony was no more.

But for Jamestown, as Winston Churchill wrote in the context of a later disaster, that was only the end of the beginning.

"things which seame incredible"

Cannibalism in Early Jamestown

MARK NICHOLLS

The English settlers who arrived in Chesapeake Bay aboard the *Susan Constant* during the spring of 1607 landed in a new world, mentally as well as physically. Expectations were high. Vast tracts of unexplored country beckoned with minerals, with rich land, and with the prospect of an easy trade route to the Indies. High hopes, however, were the while accompanied by profound fears. The Algonquian tribes of Virginia's Native Americans—the Powhatans—seemed friendly enough, to begin with, but there was already a "back catalogue" of incomprehension and mistrust in the relations between Indian and European, fuelled by a belief that this state of affairs must necessarily endure. Englishmen sailing to North America anticipated savagery and barbarism in the peoples that they encountered; they found it hard to accept the humanity even of those who welcomed them and gave them succor. They expected none of their civilized norms, such as they were. These expectations, of course, proved self-fulfilling.

The human consumption of human flesh is as old as mankind—evidence survives from prehistoric and more recent societies across the world—but there was, in 1607, novelty in the word "cannibal," and novelty added to the frisson for the thousands of readers of travelers' tales, sitting in comfort back home. Contemporary writers, who knew their market, applied the term broadly, vaguely, and quite often for effect. Although Columbus refers to *Canibales,* predatory tribes living on the islands of the West Indies, the word unequivocally takes on its modern meaning in the mid-sixteenth century. "Cannibal" derives from a Spanish version of a Carib term meaning "strong men." In the earliest records it is applied to intractable peoples encountered throughout the New World, those who resist the overtures of European traders and settlers. Antagonism of this kind was

▲ Driven by desperate famine, a colonist in the Starving Time killed and ate his pregnant wife. Willy Balderson portrays the madman, Trish Balderson the unfortunate wife.

◀ Likely part of purification or martial rites, cannibalism was practiced by some Indian tribes, here in Theodore de Bry's 1592 scene.

naturally unwelcome to those Europeans, and it had to be dealt with, militarily but also in the mind. One way to denigrate the truculent was to focus on their least palatable habits, and, given the stigma attached on the eastern side of the Atlantic to the eating of human flesh, any suggestion that Native Americans devoured their fellow men, women, and children helped convey the notion that they were altogether less than human: fearsome enemies, expensive to defeat, but also fair game for bloody acts of reprisal.

The writings of George Percy, youngest son of the eighth Earl of Northumberland and a prominent member of the original band of Jamestown settlers, offer an insight into the mind-set of those early colonists. Like every other man in Jamestown, Percy had come across tales of cannibalism in the Americas. On the outward voyage, he repeated what he had heard about the natives of Dominica in the West Indies, that they would "eate their enemies when they kill them, or any stranger if they take them," would "lap up mans spittle, whilst one spits in their mouthes in a barbarious fashion like Dogges."

"These people," Percy wrote, "and the rest of the Ilands in the West Indies, and Brasill, are called by the names of Canibals, that will eate mans flesh."

Cannibalism was practiced in some contemporary Native American societies, particularly among tribes of the north and the west. Jesuits living with the Iroquois recorded it, like torture, among the victors over those defeated in battle, and there is evidence that these customs endured into the eighteenth century. But the Iroquois, Mohawk, and other peoples surrounded their cannibalism with strict and complex taboos; never simply gastronomic, it was usually confined to strengthening or purification rituals, or to the systematic humiliation of foes. Recorded instances are often tied up and confused with tales of human sacrifice, which may from time to time be seen as a sublimation of cannibalistic rites. There is no real evidence that such customs were found on the Virginian littoral, but a bad press is hard to shake off. Confronted with the Jamestown settlers and their suspicions, Indians of the Powhatan confederacy could not win.

When they captured Captain John Smith, they fed him, by his account, very generously. In this there were perhaps courtesy and a demonstration that the tribe was

Boiled boot leather, being cooked up here by interpreters Calvin Jenkins, left, and Patrick Strawderman, was eaten when better sources of food had vanished.

strong enough to eat well, but Smith, writing years later and aware his readership would welcome a good yarn, said he saw through the charade. Surely he had been fattened for slaughter. Vague tales of Virginian cannibals—always among the remoter tribes, just beyond the western horizon—persisted to the 1680s, when the minister John Clayton recorded tales of revenge cannibalism on defeated enemies.

Ironically, it is the English who demonstrably resorted to cannibalism in the early days of the Jamestown colony. When grisly reports reached England, carried by runaways on board the *Swallow* in the summer of 1610, they caused a stir. To allege cannibalism among one's erstwhile comrades was suspect in men guilty of deserting a beleaguered colony, but their tales won credence in London. If exaggerated, they were fundamentally accurate. When death and disease swept through Jamestown, reducing its population perhaps by 80 percent in the catastrophic Starving Time of 1609–10, some individuals had turned to cannibalism out of hunger. As Percy and other survivors told it, sporadic cannibalism was a manifestation of a partial breakdown in civilized society, in the face of inescapable disaster:

Sir George Percy in a nineteenth-century portrait by Herbert Luther Smith, who copied an earlier work.

A worlde of miseries ensewed as the Sequell will expresse unto yow, in so mutche thatt some to satisfye their hunger have robbed the store for the which I Caused them to be executed. Then haveinge fedd upon our horses and other beastes as longe as they Lasted, we weare gladd to make shifte with vermin as doggs Catts, Ratts and myce all was fishe thatt Came to Nett to satisfye Crewell hunger, as to eate Bootes shoes or any other leather some Colde come by. And those beinge Spente and devoured some weare inforced to searche the woodes and to feede upon Serpentts and snakes and to digge the earthe for wylde and unknowne Rootes, where many of our men weare Cutt of and slayne by the Salvages. And now famin beginneinge to Looke gastely and pale in every face, thatt notheinge was Spared to mainteyne Lyfe and to doe those things which seame incredible, as to digge upp deade corpes outt of graves and to eate them. And some have Licked upp the Bloode which hathe fallen from their weake fellowes.

Percy, aware of the causes and trying to put events at Jamestown in context, turned to his books, mitigating these actions by pointing to precedents in colonies and settlements planted by England's European rivals. Even there some standards had been maintained. Whenever cannibalism occurs in the history of exploration in the New World, he suggests, it comes about in extreme circumstances, as an unwilling, necessary act:

> If we Trewly Consider the diversety of miseries, mutenies, and famishmentts which have attended upon discoveries and plantacyons in theis our moderne Tymes, we shall nott fynde our plantacyon in Virginia to have Suffered aloane. . . . The Spanyards plantacyon in the River of Plate and the streightes of Magelane Suffered also in so mutche thatt haveinge eaten upp all their horses to susteine themselves withal, Mutenies did aryse and growe amongste them, for the which the generall Diego Mendosa cawsed some of them to be executed, Extremety of hunger inforceinge others secrettly in the night to Cutt downe Their deade fellowes from of the gallowes and to bury them in their hungry Bowelles.

There are earlier narratives that made the same point, including a few relating to the Newfoundland voyages. But Percy is saying something else here. Life in Jamestown, for all the conscious mimicry of English tradition, is fundamentally different from life back home. On the very edge of the known world, such security as there is in England does not apply. More than once in the course of their long ordeal the settlers must have given up hope, the ghosts of their dead comrades clustering about them in the emptying fort. These traumatized settlers clung to the distinctions that set them apart from their Algonquian neighbors while adopting fleeting new conventions and customs that were subsumed into a more stable, more English construct later in the century.

Here, graphically demonstrated, is an "emergency society." Abnormal stresses lead to actions intolerable under a more established and comfortable way of life. Look, for example, at how laws are modified, or set aside, to suit a new, extreme life. English common law had come to discount evidence gained by torture, but in Jamestown the infliction of pain in pursuit of incriminating testimony is routine. Percy tells us how, in his capacity

Colonists searched the wife eater's home for pieces of her body, and he was seized, hanged by his thumbs until he confessed, and burned alive. From left, bottom, interpreters Lindsay Gray, Dennis Farmer, Calvin Jenkins, Willie Balderson, and Dennis Strawderman.

Yielding to the pangs of cruel hunger, colonists, portrayed by Calvin Jenkins and Carol Farmer, dug up corpses for food.

as interim president of the colony, he dealt with a man accused of killing, salting, and eating his pregnant wife.

When related by the *Swallow* refugees, the story had been indignantly rejected as a falsehood by the Virginia Company of London, the joint-stock enterprise led by Sir Thomas Smith that was responsible for the colony and its supply. But by the time that Percy wrote, about 1625, he no longer saw a reason to be coy. He conceded that he passed a sentence of death on the wretch—if for murder rather than cannibalism—having extracted an admission under torture, hanging his prisoner "by the Thumbes with weightes att his feete a quarter of an howere before he wolde Confesse the same." Though Percy did not say so, the man was burned alive, a punishment that follows no conventional penalty for murder under English law.

That punishment paled in comparison to the ad-hoc torments inflicted by Sir Thomas Dale. Deputy gov-ernor in 1611, Dale showed no patience with those "idell" colonists who preferred sloth or desertion to hard work. That impatience was apparent when he set out upriver to found a settlement, eventually named Hen-rico after the king's eldest son, Prince Henry. Deep in Powhatan territory, Dale took a tough line with recap-tured deserters. Percy records the consequences:

> Some he apointed to be hanged some burned some to be broken upon wheles others to be Staked and some to be shott to deathe, all theis extreme and crewell tortures he used and inflicted upon them To terrefy the reste for attempteinge the Lyke. And some which Robbed the store he cawsed them to be bownd faste unto Trees and so sterved them to deathe.

This is what the English did to their own. They were no more respectful of norms and guidelines in their relations with the Indians. The routine execution of spies may be familiar, but Percy also recounts the slaughter, in cold blood, of an Indian "queen" and her children, taken prisoner in a military operation. It is the fault of his followers, he writes, as the children are thrown into the water and shot while swimming, and the woman is led off and "putt to the sworde" in the woods. Reprisals against enemy captives were not unknown and had loomed large in the Elizabethan Englishman's experiences in Ireland, but the bloodlust shown by both sides in the early Indian wars, the absence of charity toward women and children, illustrates a mutual contempt and fear unusual in the wars between major European nations. Those at the mental frontier between "civilized moderation" and "unfettered savagery" engaged in a struggle for survival, finding that respect and self-esteem may vanish and that relentless siege and mounting hunger begin, step by step, to overwhelm nicer feelings. Percy is correct, up to a point. Incidents of the Jamestown kind of cannibalism must be seen in this context.

Can we, however, accept Percy's argument that cannibalism such as Jamestown's is never universally countenanced, that it is regarded as a repulsive action of last resort? Curiosities in the accounts make us wonder whether the full tale is being told. Reports, composed almost exclusively by the gentlemen among the settlers, say that the "lower orders" were the first to indulge in such acts; social norms were thus preserved in the written record. But who *were* the individuals who dug up and consumed corpses? They are never named. It is curious in so small a society that any man, wellborn or poor,

could have enjoyed the privacy necessary to slaughter his wife and eat her over time, piece by piece. Did he get away with this because so many people were dying—and morale was so low—that one face more or less was not worthy of remark? Or was there connivance of some kind? Observe how the bodies of men, including at least one Indian, are buried before being surreptitiously dug up and consumed. Note, too, how carefully human flesh is prepared: "boiled and stewed with roots and herbs," "powdered," "carbonadoed." This suggests concerted action, perhaps widely beneficial, and perhaps verging on ritual. Is the implication of method and planning a later elaboration, or does it accurately reflect a starving man's obsession with food?

We touch on deeper fears: that human meat might prove addictive. One of the colonists, it is said, acquired the taste. He could not be restrained from cannibalism and had to be executed. True story, or a trope on where such bestial behavior can lead? From the Aztecs to the Fijians, history suggests that whole societies can develop a lust for human flesh, and that consumption ritualized keeps the craving within bounds. In this obsession, hunger, and pain, it is a relief to encounter a touch of bleak humor, directed not against Indians who had come up with a novel way of tormenting starving people, but rather against the influential men in England who had so signally failed to relieve the settlers' want:

> Soe miserable was our estate that the happyest day that ever some of them hoped to see, was when the Indyans had killed a mare they wishing whilst she was boylinge that Sir Thomas Smith was uppon her backe in the kettle.

"such a dish as powdered wife I never heard of"

DENNIS MONTGOMERY

Accounts of Jamestown anthropophagy have never, shall we say, been palatable. As horrific in the seventeenth century as they are in the twenty-first, reports of man-eating were, nevertheless, as readily accepted and credited then as they are quickly doubted and discounted now.

Perhaps it's because today they come as something of a surprise.

The earliest relations of Virginia made no bones about it: In the winter of 1609–10, the Starving Time, the English were reduced to consuming, as colony President George Percy put it, what they "could come by." And not for the last time.

Modern writers, however, are more circumspect; so tactful, in the main, that modern readers and students have seldom heard of such a thing, and commonly disbelieve it when they do. At that, some ask what purpose is served by recalling these ancient unpleasantnesses when there are to be recounted more inspiring, and less embarrassing, passages in the Jamestown saga.

That would leave the saga incomplete, like telling the story of the Oregon Trail and not mentioning the Donner Party. Without it, the understanding of how narrow were Jamestown's circumstances and what it took to create America's first permanent English settlement would be less than fully formed.

News of Jamestown cannibalism arrived in England with a runagate crew of settlers and circulated widely. It reached the ears of the Spanish ambassador, who wrote June 14, 1610, to his king:

When hunger-mad colonists turned to eating human flesh during Jamestown's Starving Time, some were said to "lay wait and threatened to kill and eat" those who seemed better nourished. From left, interpreter Patrick Strawderman is stalked by interpreters Dennis Farmer and Lindsay Gray.

Sire—From Virginia there has come to Lyme, a harbor of this Kingdom, a ship of those that remained there lately, and those who arrived in it, report that the Indians hold the English surrounded in the strong place which they had erected there, having killed the larger part of them, and the others were left so entirely without provisions that they thought it impossible to escape, because the survivors eat the dead, and when one of the natives died fighting, they dug him up again, two days afterward, to be eaten.

Among other tales, the Jamestown deserters, who had stolen off in a small vessel named the *Swallow,* retailed a story of a man who devoured his wife. In the years to come, nearly every time the story appeared in print, more details were disclosed.

The Virginia Company of London, the joint-stock enterprise that ran the colony, got it to the press first, that December. In *A Declaration of the Estate of the Colony in Virginia, with a confutation of such Scandalous Reports as have tended to the disgrace of so worthy an enterprise*, a promotional tract that downplayed the starving and the cannibalism, the company said:

James and Margaret Reed of the Donner Party, which, trapped in winter, resorted to cannibalism in the nineteenth century.

There was one of the company who mortally hated his wife and therefore secretly killed her, then cut her in pieces and hid her in divers parts of his house. When the woman was missing, the man suspected, his house searched, and parts of her mangled body were discovered. To excuse himself he said that his wife died, that he hid her to satisfy his hunger, and that he fed daily upon her. Upon this, his house was again searched, where they found a good quantity of meal, oatmeal, beans, and peas. He thereupon was arraigned, confessed the murder, and was burned for his horrible villainy.

This version of the tale came by way of Sir Thomas Gates, the colony's new governor. The company staggered to its death in 1624, the year a group of Virginia survivors wrote *A Brief Declaration of the Plantation of Virginia during the first Twelve Years . . . down to this present time.* It said famine had compelled them to consume

those Hogs, Dogs & horses that were then in the Colony, together with rats, mice, snakes, or what vermin or carrion soever we could light on, as also Toad-stools, Jewes ears, or what else we found growing upon the ground that would fill either mouth or belly; and were driven through unsufferable hunger unnaturally to eat those things which nature most abhorred, the flesh and excrements of man, as well of our own nation as of an Indian, digged by some out of his grave after he had lain buried three days & wholly devoured him; others, envying the better state of body of any whom hunger had not yet so much wasted as their own, lay wait and threatened to kill and eat them; one among the rest slew his wife as she slept in his bosom, cut her in pieces, powdered her & fed upon her till he had clean devoured all parts saving her head & was for so barbarous a fact and cruelty justly executed. Some adventuring to seek relief in the woods, died as they sought it, & were eaten by others who found them dead.

By "powdered," they meant salted.

Virginia's General Assembly that year inscribed in its minutes:

One man out of the misery he endured, killing his wife powdered her up to eat her, for which he was burned. Many besides fed on the Corpses of dead men, and one who had

gotten unsatiable, out of custom to that food could not be restrained, until such time as he was executed for it.

Captain John Smith left Virginia before the colonist ate the wife but collected a report of the affair to flesh out his *Generall Historie of Virginia, New-England, and the Summer Isles,* which fell from the press in 1624.

Nay, so great was our famine, that a Salvage we slew, and buried, the poorer sort took him up again and eat him, and so did divers one another boiled and stewed with roots and herbs: And one amongst the rest did kill his wife, powdered her, and had eaten part of her before it was known, for which he was executed, as he well deserved; now whether she was better roasted, boiled or carbonado'd, I know not, but of such a dish as powdered wife I never heard of.

By "carbonado'd," Smith meant barbequed.

Percy the same year penned *A Trewe Relacyon,* though not all of it reached print until the 1930s. Among other things, Percy said:

This was most Lamentable That one of our Colony murdered his wife Ripped the childe out of her womb and threw it into the River and after chopped the Mother in pieces and salted her for his food. The same not being discovered before he had eaten Part thereof.

It was not the last Virginia-related case of cannibalism in extremis. Bermuda, claimed for England by settlers shipwrecked on the way to Jamestown, knew one in 1615. Smith reported that seven men, among them Andrew Hilliard, fishing from a boat, were blown by a tempest to sea. Six died, five of them to be buried in the ocean. Hilliard could not push overboard the last,

for so weak he was grown he could not turn him over as the rest, whereupon he stripped him, ripping his belly with his knife, throwing his bowels into the water, he spread his body abroad tilted open with a stick, and so lets it lie as a cistern to receive some lucky rain-water, and this God sent him presently after, so that in one small shower he recovered about four spoonfuls of rain water to his unspeakable refreshment; he

The dedication of Percy's *Trewe Relacyon,* which recounted the desperate acts and official retributions of the Starving Time.

also preserved near half a pint of blood in a shoe, which he did sparingly drink of to moist his mouth: two several days he fed on his flesh, to the quantity of a pound.

Currents carried Hilliard to land, and, Smith said, he was still alive in 1622. There was, however, at least one more instance of Virginia-related cannibalism, this one in January 1649.

Sixteen men and three women fleeing to Jamestown from Cromwell's Protectorate were marooned by the crew of the *Virginia Merchant* on an island off the East-

ern Shore. Provisions aboard had run so short that the meat of rats trapped in the bilges was prized. The passengers were not. The castaways, among them Colonel Henry Norwood, kept starvation at bay for six days on rations of oysters and birds until supplies failed and famine returned.

Norwood, chosen leader, counseled cannibalism:

Of the three weak women before mentioned, one had the envied happiness to die about this time; and it was my advice to the survivors, who were following her apace, to endeavor their own preservation by converting her dead carcass into food, as they did to good effect. The same counsel was embraced by those of our sex: the living fed upon the dead; four of our company having the happiness to end their miserable lives on Sunday night the ____ day of January.

Indians rescued the survivors five days later, and the English made their way to settlements in February.

There are, then, at least a half-dozen written seventeenth-century reports of Starving Time cannibalism, each of which corroborates another in one or more details. Two documents have the multiple endorsements of resident Virginians—the colony's legislature and Starving Time survivors. The company's account of the man who ate his wife is backed not only by the authority of Jamestown's president at the time, but his successor's, not to mention the men of the *Swallow.*

How widespread was the Starving Time cannibalism? For sure, if the records are to be believed, a Native American and an Englishwoman were killed and consumed. But, we are told, "Many besides fed on the Corpses of dead men" and that "Some adventuring to seek relief in the woods, died as they sought it, & were eaten by others who found them dead." "Many" is an indefinite word, but, by the usage of dictionaries then and now, designates a large number. More than that, no one can say.

We can, however, be certain that accounts of Jamestown anthropophagy are as horrific now as they were then, just as unpleasant, and just as dreadful.

The Mystery of Sir George Somers and His Bermuda Triangle

IVOR NOËL HUME

Nothing intrigues a historian more than history with a hole in it. In this case, it is a ninety-eight-day hole in 1610 when Sir George Somers and his thirty-ton ship *Patience* vanished in a triangle cornered by Jamestown, Sagadahoc in Maine, and Bermuda. That is more northerly than the Bermuda Triangle of legend, but Somers's disappearance is as baffling as any anywhere.

The story of Sir George steering the doomed *Sea Venture* onto Bermuda's reefs July 25, 1609, saving its crew, its Jamestown-bound passengers, and dog, is graven in the annals of maritime lore. Not so well remembered is what happened afterward.

Somers, born in 1554, began a career at sea thirty-nine years later. An expansionist inspired by the writings of Richard Hakluyt and Thomas Hariot, Somers made his first American voyage in 1595. It was essentially a buccaneering exploit led by Sir Amias Preston to the Spanish Caribbean that resulted in the sack of St. Iago de Leon. There Somers reportedly displayed much heroism.

In the last years of the sixteenth century, Spanish treasure fleets generally passed out of the Caribbean through the strait between Cuba and Florida en route to Spain. The English tried to intercept them when they reached the Azores, but more often than not, the timing was off, and the English captain sailed home empty-handed—to the chagrin of the London merchants and courtiers who bankrolled the expeditions. One such enterprise was launched in 1597 by Sir Walter Ralegh, supported by Lord Thomas Howard, the sixth Lord Mountjoy, and the not-yet-knighted Somers. It was no more successful, and in a storm off the Azores, Somers's ship was separated from the rest of the fleet and given up for lost. But in 1600, he was flotilla hunting on the same sea-lanes as captain of the *Vanguard* and faring no better.

A life portrait of Admiral Sir George Somers by Paul van Somer.

Bad luck or bad timing did nothing to sully Somers's reputation as a seaman in the mold of the great Elizabethans, and in the following year, he commanded the *Swiftsure* as part of an English squadron attacking a Spanish fleet at Kinsale in Ireland. In September 1602, he captained the *Warspight* in one more fruitless Azores voyage. After that, he became a country gentleman living on his estate at Lyme Regis in Dorset. Writing in 1661, biographer Thomas Fuller called him "a lamb on land, so patient that few could anger him: and (as if entering a ship he had assumed a new nature) a lion at sea, so passionate that few could please him."

Somers was knighted in 1603 in recognition of his exploits and soon was elected the Member of Parliament for his hometown. Three years later he became mayor. At the then-advanced age of fifty-one, Somers seemed ready to rest on his seafaring laurels. But the writings of publicist Hakluyt and accounts of others' voyages of New World exploration led to his becoming a founding shareholder in the Virginia Company of London, the joint-stock enterprise set up for Jamestown.

When the company was chartered in April 1606, the king headed his list of "our loving and weldisposed subjects" with Sir Thomas Gates and Somers. When a second charter was granted in May 1609, dividing the business between a company based in London and another in Bristol and the West Country, Gates and Somers still headed the London branch. In the same month, the Virginia Council named Gates "governor of Virginia and Sir George Summers, Knight and Admirall of Virginia." It was clear Somers was in command while at sea and Gates in control when they landed.

That made sense. Somers was a sailor and Gates a soldier knighted for valor during the 1596 assault on Cadiz that disrupted a Spanish plan to invade England. Gates subsequently accompanied Sir Henry Wootten to Vienna when the latter was appointed ambassador. Two years later, while the English were allied with the States General of Southern Holland, Gates was garrison commander at Oudewater. In short, he was a man of courage and leadership.

Together, in 1609, Gates and Somers commanded a blue ribbon fleet of eight vessels bound for Virginia. They sailed from Plymouth on June 2 and headed west on the well-traveled course via the Azores, it being speedier and less likely to run afoul of Spaniards than would the old route through the Caribbean. Aboard the flagship *Sea Venture* were Somers as admiral and old Virginia hand Christopher Newport as captain, along with Gates and a bevy of gentry that included future-governor George Yeardley. The company had risked all its best eggs in one wooden basket.

On July 21, the onset of a hurricane scattered the fleet, and it was only through Somers's bravery and seamanship that the *Sea Venture* escaped sinking in deep water. She wound up on a Bermuda reef, where she

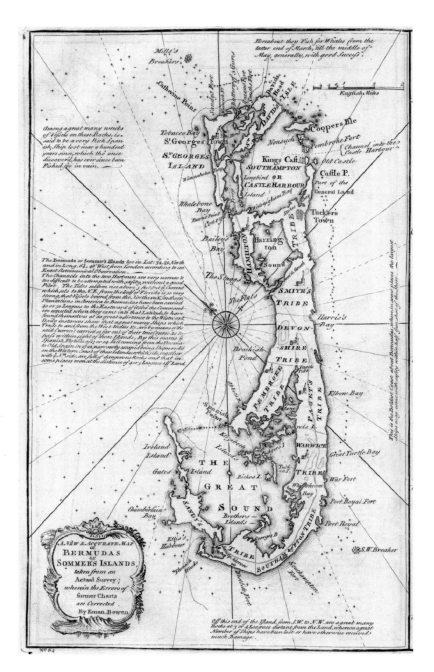

▲ Somers, portrayed by Charles Stayton on Jamestown Settlement's *Discovery*, built the *Patience* from the wreckage of the *Sea Venture*.

◀ Sommers Islands, Bermuda, on an eighteenth-century map.

▶ A nineteenth-century engraving of the wreck of the *Sea Venture*, stranding Admirals Somers and Gates in the Bermudas.

wedged partially submerged between two coral outcrops. Passengers, crew, and the ship's dog got safely ashore and later salvaged almost everything but the ribs of the ship.

Spaniards, who lost several galleons on its reefs, called Bermuda the Isle of Devils, but it teamed with wild life, fruit, birds, and hogs. In its waters, fish of every description were to be caught. The castaways were in hog heaven and not overly anxious to put to sea again.

Gates exercised his powers as governor and set up his base on the smaller of Bermuda's two islands while Somers and his crew encamped on the main island to the west. The inference seems to be that Gates relied on the gentry and Somers took charge of the seamen. In all, there were 150 souls to be saved, and between them Gates and Somers agreed that two ships should be built out of the wreck of the *Sea Venture*'s remains. There

being four carpenters, Gates gave Somers two to build the smaller of the escape ships. Although the two leaders seemed to have kept in regular touch with each other, it is clear that they operated independently. It is equally clear that Somers was more interested in Bermuda than Gates, whose sole aim was to leave it. Gates called the ship his carpenters were building the *Deliverance;* Somers named his the *Patience.*

Gates saw himself as the thoughtful administrator. Somers was more comfortable doing what had to be done. Soon after arrival, he had taken one of the longboats and sailed around the islands drawing a detailed map. He established a garden, experimented with vegetable cultivation, and was the first to hunt the island's hogs.

It took a year to construct the ships, during which time petty feuds among crew and passengers erupted in

Jamestown almost self-destructed before Lord De La Warr's arrival in 1610.
A nineteenth-century engraving by Mosely Isaac Danforth.

mutiny. Ringleaders in Gates's group said that once off the ship and in a place other than Virginia he was no longer their governor and without power over them. The trouble spread to Somers's men, whose desire to remain on the islands was equally strong and no less fervent. Twice Gates seized ringleaders and threatened to hang them, but twice he relented. A third dissident he ordered turned off, but when the man said he was a gentleman and entitled to be shot, Gates complied.

Among the gentry, William Strachey, who was part of the Gates faction, and Silvester Jourdain, who seems to have been with Somers, recorded much that happened. Jourdain wrote almost nothing about the mutiny but had his report printed in 1611; Strachey, who said too much, had to wait until he was dead to be published. Jourdain was enamored of Somers and told how, when building the *Patience,* "He laboured morning unto night as duelie, as any workman doth labour for wages."

When the little ship was completed, she was twenty-nine feet in the keel, eight feet deep, and drew six feet of water, and as Jourdain noted, she was constructed from local cedars "with little or no yron worke at all."

After nine months on the islands, when *Patience* and *Deliverance* were ready to sail, the number of passengers and crew remained unchanged, deaths and births having offset each other. Three of the mutineers, however, had fled into the woods and had not been found. At least two of them were sailors in Somers's command, and although he made an effort to find them, it is possible he saw them as a skeleton garrison to hold Bermuda for England. Be that assumption right or wrong, Sir George Somers had a more than passing interest in the future of the Bermudas.

After an eleven-day voyage, the ships arrived safely off the Virginia coast May 21. But at Jamestown, Gates and Somers were appalled to find the colony in extremis. Of 800 settlers there in the previous year, about sixty were left, and those on the point of starvation. The relatively well-fed *Sea Venture* survivors had brought only enough food for the voyage. There was little they could do to help the colonists or themselves. So, in concert with the leadership at Jamestown, Gates and Somers agreed to quit the settlement and sail north to Newfoundland's fishing grounds, where they hoped to find ships willing to carry everyone home to England. To the colonists' bitter disappointment, a new relief fleet and a new governor, Thomas West, Lord De La Warr, arrived in time to prevent the exodus.

Although the fleet carried supplies, it brought more than 600 additional mouths to feed. Lord De La Warr readily accepted Somers's offer to return to Bermuda for a shipload of hogs. With him went Captain Samuel Argall aboard the *Discovery,* the smallest of Jamestown's original three ships. Somers chose his Bermuda-built pinnace the *Patience.* Both captains took sealed orders from De La Warr, a detail that seemed hardly necessary, and sailed June 19. Before leaving, Somers wrote that he expected to be back "before the Indians doe gather their harvest"—which would have been mid-August at the latest.

After clearing the Chesapeake Bay, contrary winds prevented the ships from sailing southeast as intended; they went north toward the Newfoundland fishing banks. As so often happens in that region, a fog came up to halt progress. Argall wrote that "the weather was so thick, that we could not see a Cables length from our ship." When at last the fog lifted, Somers's *Patience* was nowhere to be seen. On August 3, Argall ordered his sailing master to open the orders but neglected to tell us what they were. He remained off the New England coast fishing until the twenty-first, then gave up, and returned to Jamestown, arriving off Cape Charles at noon on the thirty-first. Sailing down from Cape Cod took Argall a week. So where during all this time was Somers?

John Smith in his history of Bermuda wrote:

> Sir George Somers all this time was supposed lost, but thus it hapned, missing the Bermondas, he fell also as did Argall with Sagadahock, where being refreshed, would not content himself with that repulse, but returned againe in the search; and there safely arived. But overtoiling himselfe in a surfeit died.

There is no documentation to confirm Smith's account, but we know Argall waited near Sagadahoc from July 26 to August 3 before opening his orders. Although the fog had been dense and the winds variable, there was no obvious reason for the *Patience* to be so long delayed. If Somers had been in trouble, he could

Charles Stayton, second from right, as Somers with crew members played by interpreters Ron Carnegie, Jared Larson, Dennis Strawderman, and WIllie Balderson (left to right).

have been back at Jamestown by the end of August.

In another passage Smith said:

> But such was his diligence with his extraordinary care, paines and industry to dispatch his businesse, and the strength of his body not answering the ever memorable courage of his minde, having lived so long in such honourable services the most part of his well beloved and vertuous life ... finding his time but short, after he had taken the best course he could to settle his estate, like a valiant Captaine he exhorted them with all diligence to be constant to those Plantations, and with all expedition to return to Virginia.

Somers died November 9, but the *Patience* did not return to Virginia. His nephew and heir, Matthew, was on board and ordered his uncle's body embalmed and returned to England. Smith later reported that in 1619, Bermuda Governor Nathaniel Butler,

> founding accidentally a little crosse erected in a by place, amongst a many of bushes, understanding there was buried the heart and intrailes of Sir George Summers, hee resolved to have a better memory for so worthy as Souldier, then that.

Butler had a "great Marble stone" brought from England.

Nobody wrote anything about the missing months. Matthew Somers arrived in England, where his uncle was buried with honors at Whitchurch in Dorsetshire. But why did the nephew not do as bidden? According to Smith, Matthew Somers's accounts of what had happened were "beleeved as but travellers tales"—until the Virginia Company decided Bermuda might merit closer scrutiny. When in 1612 it did, Matthew Somers's name was conspicuously absent from the listing of beneficiaries.

Although it is unlikely that proof will be found, it is possible to build a case that Somers's affection for Bermuda grew when he saw the deplorable conditions at Jamestown. His relationship with Gates was likely to have been strained, and when De La Warr arrived to impose a new government, Somers saw a future uncertain.

During the voyage that eventually took him to Bermuda, and after a month of fruitless sailing, Somers could have concluded that he was by then too late to provide help for the floundering colony. He elected to remain in Bermuda, completing the survey he had begun during his previous stay on the islands. Later records show that during those missing months he was in cordial touch with the three mutineers who had remained when the *Deliverance* and *Patience* departed and who, having built themselves a house and garden, intended to stay. There can be little doubt that the prospect of founding a colony of his own was close to Somers's heart. Was that the reason he wanted it to be buried there—if, indeed, he did—or was the removal of such body parts a prerequisite for embalming?

Of one thing we can be reasonably sure. The crew of the *Patience* had no desire to return to Jamestown—and nephew Matthew Somers had his inheritance to look forward to in England.

Watching the little ship sail away, the three mutineers may have laughed as they waved goodbye and settled back to the good life of ease, free of masters or mistresses. Centuries later, essayist Washington Irving would dub them "The Three Kings of Bermuda," but no one ever asked what they knew about Admiral Somers and those missing months in 1610.

The Reverend Robert Hunt

Jamestown's First Minister

LEWIS WRIGHT

By the Old Style calendar used in those days, it was April 26, 1607, when three ships of the Virginia Company of London, the *Susan Constant,* the *Godspeed,* and the *Discovery,* entered the Chesapeake Bay and anchored off the sandy southern cape at its mouth. Three days later, before the fleet pushed upstream, a party of soldiers, sailors, and settlers erected a wooden cross on the promontory—which they named Cape Henry—and one of their number, the Reverend Mr. Robert Hunt, offered prayers of thanksgiving for their safe passage. Hunt had joined the voyage to establish the first permanent parish of the Church of England outside the British Isles.

The ships, the Jamestown fleet, had sailed down the River Thames from Blackwall in London on December 19, 1606, and had traveled about 5,000 miles. The captains thought the crossing would require two months, but it took more than four. The ships had floundered south of the English coast for six weeks waiting for good winds to begin the journey.

Aboard the vessels were 144 or 145 men. All but about forty were to remain in the New World as colonists. Their officers opened a box in which the company had sealed a list of the men appointed to govern Virginia. One of them, George Percy, recorded the details, including the election of Edward Maria Wingfield as their first president.

It is almost certain that their minister, the only official of the colony whose rank and role in Virginia were known from the outset of the trip, was the Robert Hunt born in Hampshire about 1569. That Robert Hunt graduated from Magdalen Hall, Oxford, with a bachelor's degree in 1592, and was awarded the customary master's degree three years later. Magdalen Hall was not the same as Magdalen College. It had been founded more

HERE AT CAPE HENRY FIRST LANDED IN
AMERICA, UPON 26 APRIL 1607, THOSE
ENGLISH COLONISTS WHO, UPON 13 MAY 1607,
ESTABLISHED AT JAMESTOWN, VIRGINIA, THE
FIRST PERMANENT ENGLISH SETTLEMENT
IN AMERICA.
ERECTED BY

Erected in 1935, the memorial is a reminder of the service Hunt led when the Jamestown settlers reached Virginia and the oak cross they raised.

than a century earlier as the grammar school of the college and became a respected senior institution that would eventually merge with Hertford College. Records of Hunt's two ecclesiastical appointments in England specify that he had bachelor's and master's diplomas. At the time, most English clergy did not have academic degrees. His place of birth and the dates and places of his baptism and ordination have not been discovered. But Hunt was a common name in the Romsey area of Hampshire.

His first parish appointment was as vicar of St. Mary's at Reculver in Kent, a few miles from Canterbury, where he served from 1594 to 1602. He married Elizabeth Edwards of Canterbury in 1597. According to the marriage register, he was twenty-eight and his bride sixteen. In 1602, for reasons unknown and by mutual agreement, he exchanged parishes with the Reverend Barnaby Knell and became vicar of All Saints Church at Heathfield in Sussex.

In 1606 he arranged for his curate, the Reverend Mr. Tristham Sickelmore, to take charge of the parish indefinitely and prepared to leave for North America. Since he did not resign the post, Hunt probably hoped to return. His will, written in November 1606, left bequests to his son and daughter, Thomas and Elizabeth, and to two servants. His wife was to inherit the balance of the estate unless "during my life or if after my death before the proving of my will she staie and abide in the same house or other place whatsoever with John Taylor the oldest sonne of John Taylor of Heathfield." Domestic problems apparently played a role in his decision to accompany the group to America.

The Reverend Mr. Richard Hakluyt, one of the founders of the Virginia Company, had been named rector of the colony. In his mid-fifties, he was an esteemed clergyman, a well-known maritime historian, and for five years had been chaplain to the English embassy in Paris. He decided against going with the expedition, however, and approved Hunt as the chaplain. Wingfield, another founder of the Virginia Company, who knew him and may have been a distant relative, had also endorsed Hunt.

Hunt fell ill just after the expedition got under way, but recovered. In the course of the rest of the voyage, he earned a reputation for skill as a mediator and peacemaker in shipboard disputes.

Sailing up the first large tidal river they discovered inside the Chesapeake, a stream they soon renamed the James in honor of their king, the English selected an island for James Fort, later known as Jamestown. There, vessels could be moored to trees at the edge of the river. That eased the unloading that began May 14 and gave the settlement the protection of the ships' guns.

The local Indian tribe, the previous occupant of the island, was the Paspahegh. Rather than risk offending them, Wingfield forbade the erection of defenses any more elaborate than brushworks. But after a May 26 attack, the colonists set about cutting timber and constructing a triangular-shaped palisaded enclosure.

The council and Hunt instituted two daily religious services from the *Book of Common Prayer* of the Church of England. Captain John Smith wrote, "We had daily Common Prayer morning and evening, every Sunday two sermons, and every three months the Holy Communion."

At that time, less than a century after the English Reformation, the Church of England was strongly influenced by continental Protestant reforms. It required priests to celebrate the Eucharist, or communion, at least three times a year—Christmas, Easter, and Whitsunday. Most clergymen celebrated it more often. The usual Sunday morning service in parish churches lasted hours and consisted of the prayer book offices of morning prayer, the litany, and the antecommunion—the eucharistic rite up to the canon or prayer of consecration—accompanied by a long sermon.

Hunt conducted the first Jamestown services beneath a canvas canopy. Smith wrote, "We did hang an awning (which is an old saile) to three or four trees to shadow us from the Sunne . . . our seats unhewed trees . . . our Pulpit a bar of wood nailed to two neighboring trees."

The first church within the fort was built of wattle and daub. Captain Christopher Newport, commander of the three ships, volunteered his sailors for the construction. Smith said: "We built a homely thing like a barne, set upon cratchets, covered with rafts, sedge, and earth."

Historians have long reported that the first Anglican Eucharist in the present-day United States was celebrated

June 21, 1607. It is more likely that the first was the required Whitsunday celebration, which was May 24. There is, however, documentation of the June 21 celebration—a special service celebrating the resolution of factions in the colony and the departure of two of the ships the next day for England.

During the months that Wingfield served as council president, nearby Native Americans seem to have been unsettled on several Sunday mornings. On these occasions, the service was put off until later in the day and was shortened by omitting the sermon. Wingfield wrote: "The preacher did aske me if it were my pleasure to have a sermon. I made answere . . . that if it pleased him we would spare him till some other tyme."

Make no mistake, however; Wingfield was attentive to the church's rituals. When only two gallons of sack, a wine of many uses, remained, he put them aside for communions. Nevertheless, the factious colonists ousted him from the presidency that winter, partly on the suspicion that he was a secret Roman Catholic.

There was occasion for Hunt to officiate at more than communions, Sunday services, and daily prayers. There was a staggering number of funerals. By September, half of the colonists had died. Medical historian Wyndham B. Blanton, as well as others, blames the high mortality mostly on starvation and dietary deficiency diseases instead of infection. Burial after nightfall became customary to keep the Indians from learning the exact size of the colony. About forty English survived when relief finally arrived.

On January 2, 1607, the ship *John and Francis,* captained by Christopher Newport, entered the bay. By today's reckoning, the date was January 12, 1608, but the English still followed the Old Style, or Julian, calendar, not adopting the New Style, or Gregorian, calendar we use until 1752.

On January 4, by Jamestown's calendar, the ship reached the settlement. It brought 102 new colonists and fresh provisions. But three days later a fire destroyed most of Jamestown and nearly all the colonists' possessions not still aboard the ship. Colonist Thomas Studley, who ran the colony's store, wrote, "Good Master Hunt, our Preacher lost all his Library, and all he had but the cloathes on his backe: yet none neuer heard him repine at his losse."

A representation of the minister himself.

The Robert Hunt Shrine on Jamestown Island depicts the minister with his flock worshipping beneath a canvas canopy.

Hunt died in early 1608 between mid-January and early April. His gravesite is lost. Captain Smith wrote: "Master Robert Hunt, our courageous Divine; during his life our factions were oft qualified, our wants and greatest extremities comforted, that they seemed easie in comparison of what we endured after his memorable death." Without a priest, the colonists continued daily services in the church consisting of prayers and the reading of a psalm.

The *John and Francis* sailed April 10 and carried news of Hunt's death to England. His widow, Elizabeth, qualified as executrix. His will was probated in the Pre-rogative Court at Canterbury on July 14. Probate in Canterbury was required because he owned properties in two archdeaconries. The widow Elizabeth married Noah Baker, a yeoman, and not the forbidden John Taylor, at All Saints Church at Lewes in Sussex on August 10, 1608. Speedy remarriage was not unusual, and there were several children of this match.

The Reverend Richard Buck was appointed to replace Hunt at Jamestown. On his way to North America in the summer of 1609, Buck was shipwrecked in Bermuda and did not arrive until the spring of 1610.

Hunt was seldom remembered until the tercentennial celebration of Virginia's founding renewed interest in all things Jamestown. But he was not entirely forgotten, either. In the 1890s, a series of stained glass windows of geometric design by the Tiffany Company were installed in Old St. Luke's Church near Smithfield, Virginia. A window near the gospel side of the altar was dedicated to Hunt.

The class of 1907 at Virginia Theological Seminary, Alexandria, gave a stained glass window depicting Christ at the Last Supper and dedicated it to Hunt. At the Jamestown celebration in 1907, a large cast bronze plaque depicting Hunt celebrating the Eucharist under the canopy of a sail suspended from trees was installed in the surviving brick tower of the mid-seventeenth-century church. Designed by George T. Brewster, it was cast by the Gorham Company, a leading maker of church furnishings and ornaments.

In 1922, the plaque was incorporated as the reredos of the outdoor altar at the Robert Hunt Shrine, a few yards upstream from the brick tower. Financed by donations from Episcopal dioceses in Virginia and West Virginia, the shrine was often used for religious services in the twentieth century.

Among the men who ministered there in 1907 was another priest who succeeded to Hunt's post—the Reverend Doctor W. A. R. Goodwin, the founder of Colonial Williamsburg.

The ceremonial mace of the College of William and Mary, used in academic processions since 1923, is engraved with the names of individuals who played prominent roles in the history of Virginia and America. Among these are the names of Hunt and Hakluyt. At Cape Henry, Virginia Beach, a stone cross was erected in 1935 commemorating the landing of the colonists and their placement of a wooden cross on the beach.

In the early 1960s, as Emmanuel Church in Harrisonburg, Virginia, was being completed, a series of figural stained glass windows in a contemporary style were installed in the nave. They record individuals and events significant in the history of the English church. Made by Willet Glass Company of Philadelphia, one of the windows on the south aisle depicts Hunt celebrating the Eucharist.

Hunt is also commemorated in Washington Cathedral. Nestled in a niche above an arch in the crypt, near the outside entrance to the Bethlehem Chapel, is a statue representing Hunt. Sculpted by Marian Brackenridge, it was installed in 1976.

All Saints Church in Heathfield, Sussex, England, dates from the thirteenth century, though it was renovated in the nineteenth. In 1957, a stained glass window depicting Hunt administering communion to the colonists was installed. It was the work of Laurence Lee, who also designed windows for the new Coventry Cathedral, constructed adjacent to the ruins of the old cathedral after the end of World War II. A poor box in the church, carved from a single oak tree, may have been in use at the time of Hunt's tenure.

The Saxon-era church dedicated to St. Mary at Reculver, Kent, which had been built within the ruins of a Roman fort, was demolished in the early 1800s. Its two towers were left as navigational markers and they exist today.

Until recently historians thought the James River had, through bank erosion, washed away the site of James Fort. Archaeological study directed by William Kelso, however, shows that much of the site survives. A large brass book clasp thought to be from a Bible, along with a type of book boss often used on liturgical texts at the time the colony was established, have been retrieved within the past few years from a fort trash pit. They could be remnants of Robert Hunt's library.

John Clarke's Tale

Cold War Skullduggery . . . 1600s style

ANDREW GARDNER

Worthy of the pen of John Le Carré, "John Clarke's Tale" is a Cold War spy saga . . . with a small difference. This cold war spanned the earliest years of the seventeenth century, when two European nations faced off in a struggle for the New World's riches. All the classic spy-thriller ingredients are here: powerful adversaries, Spain and England; ideologies that divided the world, not communism and capitalism, but Catholicism and Protestantism. Adding to the flavor of a simmering international soup are heretics, grubby politics, and the lust for lucre.

At stake was control of riches—gold and silver—that would give the winning nation means to wage more war and to carve out an even bigger empire. In such circumstances, skullduggery was a prized personal attribute.

It's said that John Clarke was a simple English seafarer in the wrong place at the wrong time, caught up in an international heavyweight-slugging contest. But was he really just a pawn on the chessboard of early 1600s intrigue? Perhaps he wasn't quite as simple as he made out. Whatever the truth, John Clarke's tale is reminiscent of the standoffs between the United States and the old Soviet Union in the 1950s, '60s, and '70s. As Mark Twain said, "History does not repeat itself, but sometimes it rhymes."

On July 29, 1588, John Clarke was thirteen years old and living in Rotherhithe, a suburb of London. It would be a day to remember. That morning coastal beacons flashed a fiery warning from Cornwall to Dover. The feared Spanish Armada was coming up the English Channel. With 130 galleons, 8,000 sailors, and 18,000 soldiers, Philip II of Spain aimed to trample Queen Elizabeth's heretical Protestant realm into submission, and to reestablish the Roman Catholic faith across the shires of England.

A modern view of Old Point Comfort and Fort Monroe.

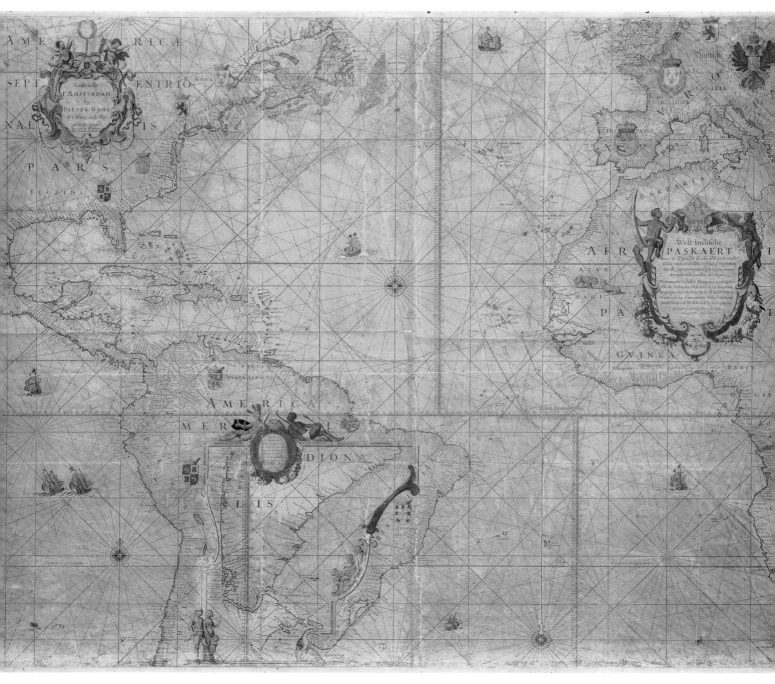

A Dutch map shows the American prizes Spain and England hoped to hook.

But the Spanish king was thwarted. His fleet—which had cost ten million ducats, or about $375 million in today's prices, to build and equip—was wiped out by the superior tactics of the English navy, commanded by Lord Howard and Sir Francis Drake, and by horrendous weather. Fifty-one Spanish ships and 20,000 Spaniards never made it home. It was Spain's last attempt to bring England to heel. Within days, young John Clarke was listening to the great bells of old St. Paul's Cathedral clanging a celebration of England's victory. It was enough to make any boy run away to sea.

And, apparently, that was what Clarke did. Rotherhithe had always been a favorite place for old sea captains to retire to, and Clarke, perhaps inspired by their stories of daring and glory, soon packed his kit bag and followed in their sea-dog footsteps. Next time we catch sight of him is in 1609 in Malaga, Spain. He'd spent his days at sea and had become an experienced, well-traveled mariner, hailed as a pilot and well acquainted with coastlines and anchorages at home and abroad.

In early March 1611, Clarke sailed from London as pilot of a small squadron of merchant ships bound for Virginia. He had visited Virginia only once before, or so he said. One wonders how he got the job based on that rather slim experience. But there weren't many English mariners experienced on the coasts of America, so Clarke's voyage may not have been out of the ordinary.

There were three ships bound for the four-year-old colony. The cargo was 600 barrels of flour, fifty tons of gunpowder, and a consignment of arquebusses, seventeenth-century handguns. In addition 100 cows, 200 pigs, 100 goats, seventeen mares, and 300 soldiers—"men of war"—were crowded into the vessels. This was no up-market Caribbean cruise. Two and a half months later, after an uneventful Atlantic crossing, the expedition began off-loading the men of war at Fort Algernon on Point Comfort, just inside the Chesapeake Bay, and took the supplies upriver to Jamestown.

The English colonists were not the first to have settled these shores. Half a century before, a Spanish adventurer, Antonio Velasquez, had planted his country's flag here, and the French, too, had raised forts along the Atlantic coastline in an imperial contest aimed at securing the biggest slice of the North American pie.

But by 1600, the French had turned their colonial gaze toward Canada, and the new Spanish king, Philip III, had given up on the region. There were richer pickings further south in the Caribbean.

The arrival of the soldiers must have raised the spirits of the fledgling Virginia colony. Tensions had eased between the English and Spanish in the twenty years since the defeat of the Armada, but the peace was uneasy, and Jamestown was ever fearful of a Spanish attack. Which was not surprising. In her day, the English queen, Elizabeth, had consistently turned a blind eye to the English swashbucklers who harried the treasure-laden galleons along the Spanish Main. The Spanish took a dim view, but Elizabeth's successor, her cousin James, continued to cheer on the privateers. The potential prize was enormous. At the end of the 1500s the Spaniards were plundering gold and silver from Central and South America to the tune of $300 million yearly, and the enterprising buccaneers, as well as the English sovereign, were intent on getting a share.

And there was also the little matter of religion. The Spaniards and their Jesuit priests saw it as their Christian duty to export their Catholic religion to their new colonies. They viewed the Protestant English as heretics and might have been happy to burn them at the stake given half a chance.

As this witches' brew of international distrust, resentment, and intrigue simmered along America's Atlantic seaboard, the Spanish king resisted his generals' calls for a preemptive strike against the English colony. Above all he wanted to avoid a costly war. But when Don Pedro de Cuniga, the Spanish ambassador in London, sent word to Madrid of the Virginia Company's plan to send 2,000 more settlers to Jamestown, alarm bells rang. The Spanish secretary of state for war pointed out the threat the English settlers would pose to the treasure ships, but Philip was not swayed. He proposed a subtler course, just keeping an eye on the English in Virginia. It was suggested that two English Jesuit priests from the Catholic English seminary at Seville, loyal to Spain, might be dispatched to stake out Jamestown, spy on the fortifications, and report to Madrid.

Intelligence briefings came from the governor of Florida, Pedro de Ybarra, as well as knowledgeable

From the rudimentary fort at Old Point Comfort, John Clarke and two
English soldiers uneasily watch the approach of a Spanish ship. Carson
Hudson portrays pilot Clarke, pointing, and interpreter Willie Balderson,
left, and master shoemaker Al Saguto wield the muzzleloaders.

King Philip III of Spain was wary of openly confronting the British but sent spies to scout the Virginia colony.

▶ In Havana, Clarke faced prison interrogation.

sources in London. On June 14, 1610, as Jamestown recovered from a winter famine, a new Spanish ambassador in London, Don Alonso de Velasco, reported to his political masters that the colony was in trouble and said that "it would be easy to undo it completely by sending a few ships to finish off the survivors." But King Philip declined to take advantage of "this excellent opportunity" to rid the New World of the English interlopers.

Instead, under orders from the Spanish Council for War in the Indies, Captain Diego de Molina and his ensign, Marco Antonio de Perez, slipped out of Lisbon harbor April 13, 1611, aboard the caravel *La Nuestra*

Señora del Rosario bound for Havana on the first leg of a spy mission.

Their cover story was that they were going to recover the artillery of a wrecked ship. Their real job, however, was to reconnoiter Jamestown. If there was any diplomatic fallout, the Spanish would deny it and blame their renegade Florida governor for overstepping his authority. Also aboard the *Nuestra* was a *confidente,* an Englishman who was a Spanish spy. Some mystery still shrouds his identity, but he was known as James Limry or Limrick. Perhaps he, too, was a pilot. Perhaps an interpreter. No one knows. What is certain is that had

The captive Juan Clerg, as the Spanish named John Clarke, droops on board *La Nuestra Señora del Rosario*, anchored off Old Point Comfort.

he known what he was getting himself into, he would have opted to stay at home.

The story of what happened next is brought to life from documents in the Spanish archives in Seville and Simancas. Depending on whose account you read, it is possible to find very different stories of how events unfolded the day *La Nuestra Señora del Rosario* sailed into the Chesapeake and dropped anchor at Point Comfort. It's not hard to imagine the reaction among the English in Fort Algernon. The enemy was nigh.

According to the account Clarke later gave to his Spanish interrogators, Molina, posing as a sailor; ensign Marco Antonio de Perez; and Francisco Lembri, their English pilot-interpreter, came ashore from the ship's boat and were met in all civility by Clarke, Captain James Davis, and English troops. Later, Clarke says, they all sat down for a meal. The caravel, the boat, and the crews remained offshore.

After eating, Davis suggested the caravel be brought into a safe anchorage for the night, and Clarke was ordered to help pilot the *Nuestra* into position. But when Clarke was safely aboard the Spanish vessel, the crew thought he was trying to move the ship into better range of an English attack for seizure. They refused to budge, and Clarke became a Spanish prisoner.

In Clarke's book, it was the Spanish who had started it all. The *Nuestra's* captain said that it was the "dirty English" who had double-crossed them by taking Molina, Perez, and their interpreter prisoner and that Clarke was trying to lure the Spanish ship into danger.

What really happened that day may never be unraveled, but the upshot was that the captain of *La Nuestra Señora del Rosario* upped anchor and high-tailed it back to Havana, leaving behind the two Spaniards and the English turncoat as prisoners of the Virginians.

Now there was an international incident to sort out. First, from Spain's point of view, two of their citizens had been captured and accused of spying. Shock. Horror. The Spanish king went on the offensive. He was at pains to avoid admitting anything about the voyage. He didn't want an expensive war to result from this botched mission. He instructed his ambassador to appeal to King James "to procure the liberty" of the two Spaniards and to insist that the *Nuestra* had been on a search for a lost vessel, not spying.

But the Spanish were little farther forward. Molina contrived to smuggle out intelligence, reporting of the colony:

> Last year there were seven hundred people and not three hundred and fifty remain.... Some have deserted to Indians and been killed, others have gone out to sea, being sent to fish, some have died of hard work and short supplies.... The forts which they have are of boards and so weak that a kick would break them down, and once arrived at the ramparts those without would have the advantage over those within because its beams and loopholes are common to both parts—a fortification without skill and made by unskilled men. Nor are they efficient soldiers, although the rulers and captains make a great profession of this because of the time they have served in Flanders on the side of Holland, where some have companies and castles. The men are poorly drilled and not prepared for military action.

But all the Spanish really had to show for their troubles was John Clarke the pilot, locked up in a Havana dungeon. It was time to pick Señor Clarke's brains.

The prospect of being interrogated by Spanish inquisitors, albeit the military wing in Havana, cannot have inspired Clarke—or Juan Clerg as he is named in the transcript—with joy. From the record of his interview on July 23, 1611, it is obvious that he sang like a canary, telling his interrogators exactly what they wanted to hear. Who can blame him? His aim was to get home alive and in one piece.

But he did seem exceptionally well versed in the details for someone who had visited the coast of Virginia just once before. He drew charts of the bay showing the fathoms. He described the fortifications in detail, the placement and sizes of the guns, the number of men and boats—the whole shooting match. He explained how the colonists grew maize and gathered walnuts for food, and sometimes there was fish and sometimes there was not. But there was more. Much more.

He broke the news for which his captors had been waiting. A hundred leagues, or 300 miles, into the mountains there was gold in Virginia. He was lying. The gold was a figment of Clarke's imagination, but it was worth his life.

Hearing that his ambassador in London was arranging a transfer of prisoners, King Philip ordered that Clarke be shipped from Cuba, "brought henceforth to the prison of the Casa de la Contratacion in Madrid," and treated well. On February 18, 1613, Clarke was again interviewed. Little changed in his account, except that this time he said he was forty years old, and a Roman Catholic. Eighteen months before, in Havana, he had said he was thirty-five and a Protestant. Even here, John Clarke's tale is not all that it might appear. The records of the Virginia Company allege a Spanish effort to "turn" John Clarke into a double agent. They say that "he was carried to Spayne and there deteyned fower years thinkinge to have made him an instrument to betray the Plantacion."

Clarke was still in Madrid under house arrest in 1616, four years after his arrival. The Council of War saw to it that his keepers maintained him "in good custody and guard, giving him good entertainment and comforts," and paid the prison charges, as well as his food and lodging.

Finally the spy-swap deal was done, and the English doubtless got the best of it. For the release of John Clarke in Madrid, Captain Diego de Molina was the only prisoner handed over to the Spanish ambassador in London. Ensign Perez died in captivity, and it was reported that the traitorous English spy was hanged from a yardarm by Sir Thomas Dale, Virginia's governor.

With his freedom regained, Clarke was soon back at sea. In 1619, with a one-time pirate, Captain Thomas Jones, master of the *Falcon,* he crossed the Atlantic and delivered another cargo of cattle to Virginia. In 1620, Clarke was hired as master's mate and pilot of the *Mayflower.* It would be his most famous voyage, yet it could hardly have been as memorable as his adventure to Jamestown nine years before.

On February 13, 1622, the Virginia Company honored John Clarke for his service, voting "that he might be admitted a free Brother of the Companie and have some shares of land bestowed upon him." To exercise his holdings he set off to Virginia on April 10, 1623, in Captain Daniel Gookin's ship *Providence.*

John Clarke died soon after he landed.

Henricus

A New and Improved Jamestown

MARY MILEY THEOBALD

The Virginia Company of London's Sir Thomas Dale shipped up the James River in the summer of 1611 searching for a place to plant a new and improved version of Jamestown—the flagging, first permanent English settlement in America thirty miles downstream. It would be called the Citie of Henrico, or Henricus, in honor of Prince Henry, heir to the English throne and a great supporter of the Virginia colony. The town would have a shorter life than its namesake—a dozen years to the prince's eighteen—but its significance was greater than that suggests.

While Dale scouted for a suitable site, laborers in Jamestown were ordered to start cutting "pales, posts and railes to impaile his proposed new Towne." Instructions to Dale and to Governor Thomas Gates from the Virginia Company, which owned and financed the Virginia enterprise, made clear that Henricus would become the colony's new seat and so required a location that was healthier and easier to defend than Jamestown.

It was not the Indians who worried the English, but the Spanish. Virginia colonists were intruding into what Spain considered its own "Iberian lake," the Atlantic Ocean. The Spanish had claimed ownership of much of the Americas since 1494, when Pope Alexander VI bestowed it upon them. The world's only superpower, Spain could not be expected to ignore such an affront by the upstart English. Spanish ships had explored the Chesapeake Bay, which Spaniards called the Bay of Santa Maria, but their effort to settle Jesuits to Christianize the Powhatan Indians in the late sixteenth century had been disastrous for both sides. The Powhatans murdered the missionaries; the missionaries and their shipmates introduced Old World diseases. The experience with the Spanish prepared the Powhatans to deal more astutely with the English arrivals in 1607.

At Henricus Historical Park, Nathan Hall, left, and Lindsay Gray re-create life inside the settlement Sir Thomas Dale built in 1611 to replace the ailing and vulnerable Jamestown.

If the English doubted how the Spanish might react, they had only to recall Spain's brutal extermination of a small French settlement in Florida, Fort Caroline, in 1565 and its slaughter of a band of shipwrecked Huguenots a few days later. The war between England and Spain that began in 1585 and saw the defeat of the Spanish Armada had concluded in 1604, but the peace was uneasy. Spies and statesmen kept their monarchs scrupulously informed about the goings-on in Virginia. The Spanish ambassador to England repeatedly urged his king to wipe out the trespassers before they became entrenched. Don Diego de Molina, a Spanish prisoner at Jamestown, smuggled out a letter in 1613 imploring Philip III, king of Spain and Portugal, "to stop the progress of a hydra in its infancy" before it became a "gathering-place of all the pirates of Europe."

Virginia's answer to the Spanish threat was Henricus. Removing the colony's principal town farther upriver would make it harder for Spanish warships to attack. The Virginia Company instructed Dale to build Henricus some distance from deep water, beyond the range of enemy ordnance, "where he can never march with horse" or drag cannon through the forest. Whistling in the dark, the English put their faith in the fragility of long supply lines, trusting that, if attacked, they could hold out until Spanish soldiers became "wearied and starved."

Dale selected a peninsula that matched the company directive. "I have surveyed a convenient strong, healthie and sweete seate to plant a new Towne in," he wrote. London promoter Robert Johnson's 1612 pamphlet reported:

The Colonie is removed up the river fourscore miles further beyond James towne to a place of higher ground, strong and defencible by nature, a good aire, wholesome and cleere (unlike the marish seate at James towne) with fresh and plentie of water springs, much faire and open grounds freed from woods, and wood enough at hand.

Dale took a ship to the Henricus site, but most of the three hundred men in his command walked. The Indians harassed them along the way and after their arrival. But Dale was the real bane of the men's existence. He drove them mercilessly. Accused of horrendous cruelties and heartily despised, he built the town in record time. In ten days the settlers completed a vertical log palisade securing seven acres of land, then built corner watchtowers, a church, and storehouses. Only then, according to a history written by long-gone Captain John Smith, did Dale "thinke upon convenient houses for himself and men."

Descriptions of Henricus conflict. De Molina had ringing contempt for English construction, saying that 500 Spaniards could easily destroy the colony because "the forts which they have are of boards and so weak that a kick would break them down." He was prisoner in one near Old Point Comfort near the mouth of the bay, built by 1609. Captain Ralph Hamor, in a 1614 account repeated almost verbatim by later authors, wrote:

> There is in this towne, 3 streets of well framed howses, a handsom Church, and the foundation of a more stately one laid, of Brick, in length, an hundred foote, and fifty foot wide, beside Store houses, watch houses, and such like: there are also, as ornaments belonging to this Town, upon the verge of this River, five faire Block houses.

The minister at Henricus, Alexander Whitaker, wrote in a 1612 pamphlet promoting donations for the Christianization of Indians that the weather at Henricus was idyllic and assured readers in England that there were not more than three sick people in the settlement: "Many have died with us heretofore thorough their owne filthinesse and want of bodilie comforts for sicke men; but now very few are sicke among us."

A Virginia Company pamphlet describes cheerful workers building fine brick homes:

At Henricus, Jill Pesesky cards wool, demonstrating a step in the craft of spinning. The seventeenth-century settlement lasted a dozen years.

> Being thus invited here, they pitch, the spade men fell to digging, the brick men burnt their bricks, the company cut down wood, the Carpenters fell to squaring out, the Sawyers to sawing, the Souldier to fortifying, and every man to somewhat. And to answer the first objection for holesome lodging, here they have built competent and decent houses, the first storie all of bricks, that every man may have his lodging and dwelling place apart by himselfe.

Most historians believe the upbeat tracts were propaganda intended to persuade Englishmen to send more of their money and their sons to the colony. Archaeologist Nick Luccketti, who has excavated the area around Henricus, says, "The buildings they describe are far grander than the sort built in Virginia in the 1610s and 1620s."

Across the river, Dale began additional fortifications, creating a suburb of sorts. Here the colonists were reported to have erected palisades and five tiny fortified dwellings across a narrow peninsula. Inside the pale they constructed "a retreat, or guest house for sick people," called Mount Malady, the first English hospital in America. Areas inside the palisade were given optimistic names—Coxendale, and Hope in Faith, for example—

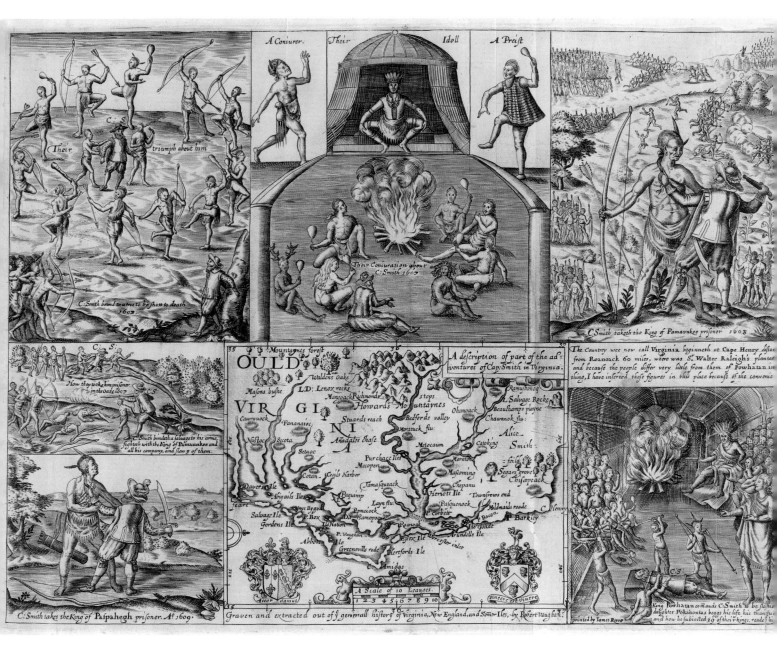

John Smith's *Generall Historie* depicts his encounters with Indians, including his imminent but aborted execution, lower right. Indian attacks ultimately spelled the end of Henricus.

At Arrahatak, a re-creation of an
Indian village at Henricus Historical
Park, Pete McKee shows his skill with
bow and arrow.

and nearby Whitaker built "a faire framed parsonage
house" called Rock Hall. It was to Rock Hall that young
Pocahontas came after the English kidnapped her, and
where she lived while Whitaker instructed her in the
Christian faith, baptized her, and married her to John
Rolfe in 1614.

Christianizing Virginia's Indians was a priority with
the Virginia Company and King James. They planned
to build a college at Henricus to teach Indian children
trades useful to the English and to train them as missionaries to their own people. One hundred English tenants were sent to work ten thousand acres of college land
to provide income for the school's support, and more
than £2,000 sterling was raised in churches throughout
England to get the institution off the ground.

But it was not to be. The Indians proved "very
loathe upon any tearmes to part with theire children,"
Governor George Yeardley said, and the Powhatan
uprising of 1622, in which about 350 English died, sent
colonists looking for revenge instead of converts. When
the College of William and Mary was established seven
decades later, it did include an Indian school, the Braf-
ferton, but it was built in Williamsburg, not Henricus.

The Citie of Henricus, like Jamestown, did not
thrive. The seat of government did not move upriver. In
1616, Henricus's population stood at about sixty. During
their 1622 uprising, the Powhatans burned part of the
town—or perhaps all of it—and killed an unknown
number of colonists. One year later, a visitor, Captain
Nathaniel Butler, reported that he

> found the Antient Plantations of Henrico and Charles Citty
> wholly quitted and lefte to the spoile of the Indians, who not
> onely burned the houses saide to be once the best of all oth-
> ers, but fell upon the Poultry, Hoggs, Cowes, Goates and
> Horses whereof they killed great numbers to the greate griefe
> as well as ruine of the Olde Inhabitants.

But local planters said Henricus lingered and that
seven large guns were still there in 1624.

Remnants of the town and a great ditch Dale had
dug along the palisade were visible more than a century
later. William Stith, rector of Henrico parish and one of
the governors of the College of William and Mary,
wrote in 1747 that "the ruins of this Town are still
plainly traced and distinguished, upon the Land of the

late Col. William Randolph, of Tuckahoe." As late as the Civil War, a historian wrote that Dale's breastworks "and vestiges of the town are indicated by scattered bricks showing the positions of the houses."

As it turned out, the Spanish never attacked. The Powhatans did. Why didn't the Spanish act? A small fleet could have wiped out the pathetic English colony easily during its early years, and advisors to Philip III recommended just that. The king agreed to the plan they proposed. But the "all devouring Spaniard" so feared by Jamestown's leaders never laid his ravenous hands upon Virginia.

Both kings wanted to maintain the fragile peace between their countries. Long years of war and piracy had depleted their treasuries. The Spanish military had to concentrate on suppressing a Dutch rebellion. The peace treaty with England guaranteed that the English would stop helping Dutch Protestants in their fight for independence and that they would stop privateers from preying on Spanish vessels. Besides, reasoned Philip, the Jamestown colony was unlikely to survive—reports from his spies about starvation, disease, and Indian troubles must have had him chuckling—and Virginia had no gold or silver. Why not sit back and enjoy watching James I get sucked into the Virginia money pit? If the price of English pacification was one miserable colony in Virginia, Philip was prepared to pay.

Like Wolstenholme Towne, seven miles below Jamestown, and other settlements destroyed by the Indians in 1622, Henricus would not be rebuilt. There was scant need for towns in the early plantation economy, so in a sense, Henricus was a victim of Virginia's economic success. As self-contained tobacco plantations prospered, the larger ones became miniature villages themselves with storehouses, docks, essential trades, and sometimes a church. The only reason for a town to exist was the business of government, and one was enough. Jamestown, and later Williamsburg, was the colonial capital, the place where the governor resided, the courts convened, and the legislature met.

The exact site of Henricus is lost. The area has been disrupted during the past three centuries, from the Civil War, when Union forces cut a canal to straighten out the river, to more recent gravel mining and the construction of a Dominion Virginia Power electric power station. Three serious archaeological attempts since the 1970s have turned up a few nails and some lead shot but no other evidence of the settlement.

The town, however, is represented by Henricus Historical Park, peopled by costumed interpreters in reconstructed buildings.

More than 800 acres surrounding the historical site form the Dutch Gap Conservation Area, home to blue herons, eagles, and other rare birds. The Audubon Society lists Henricus–Dutch Gap as one of the top sites for birding in Virginia.

Archaeologist Luccketti speculates that the town was slightly behind the reconstruction of the village, on what was once a broad, high clearing a short distance from the river. If so, it was destroyed by the gravel mine. Today the Dutch Gap Conservation Area and a Dominion Virginia Power plant coexist where once stood the Citie of Henricus.

No Wine Before It's Time

CHARLES M. HOLLOWAY

The Virginia Company colonists who sailed down the Thames for the Chesapeake in 1606 took along a taste for the grape . . . and for beer, and for aqua vitae, and for Madeira, and for porter, and for canary, and for sack, and for ale, and for drink in most of its forms and flavors, fermented or distilled, in general and in particular. In their time, a time when water was not to be trusted, Englishmen drank per capita forty gallons of alcohol a year. The libation business was in those days lucrative, and no small part of the trade was the wine crossing the Channel from the Continent bound for England's tables and taverns. It was part of the reason the Virginia Company's three-ship fleet was making its way to sea.

The merchants and gentlemen of the company who invested in the voyage intended from it to profit. Such things as gold mines and the Northwest Passage were uppermost in the company's calculations. But commodities figured in its schemes as well. Virginia was set up for a trading colony, and its managers expected from its servants such manufactures as glass, iron, naval stores, silk, and wine. Such New World imports looked to fetch tidy sums.

In the end, it was tobacco that made a market, but in the beginning wine looked more likely. The chronicle of Virginia viticulture thus begins at Jamestown, the scene of many failures and blasted hopes. Its history is sometimes desultory, and it is often discouraging, but four centuries later, the enterprise is at last paying off.

Captain John Smith, who made the four-month trip to the colony with the original 104 settlers, later wrote that at Jamestown there were vines "in great abundance in many parts that climbe the toppes of the highest trees." The company's records say Virginia

Jamestown Settlement interpreters Michael Lund, Homer Lanier, Steve Martin, and Joseph Freitus, costumed as seventeenth-century sailors, lower a cask of Virginia wine into the hold of the replica *Susan Constant* as if for shipment to England.

"yeeldeth naturally great store" of grapevines "and of sundry sorts, which by culture will be brought to excellent perfection." Smith said that "of hedge grapes, we made neere 20 gallons of wine, which was neare as good as your French Brittish," and that if they were "properly planted, dressed and ordered by skillful 'vinearoones' we might make a perfect grape and fruitfull Vintage in short time." By "vinearoones" he meant vignerons, people who cultivate grapevines.

For decades, however, thirsty Virginians would make do with the much distrusted water, try their hands at home brew and cider, and look for ships from home, like the *Mary and John,* captained by Samuel Argall. In 1609, Argall "came to truck with the Colony, and to fish for Sturgeon, on a ship well-furnished with wine and other good Provision." Along the James River shores he found ready customers, settlers often reduced to drinking from the wide, muddy tidal stream, and who sometimes paid for the gamble with their lives. In the first year, colonist George Percy wrote, "Our drinke Cold water taken out of the River, which was at a floud verie salt, at low tide full of slime and filth, which was the destruction of many of our men."

After the *Mary and John*'s departure, the company ordered Sir Thomas Gates, Virginia's new governor, to "use the labour of your owne men in makinge wines." In 1611, Gates's successor, Thomas Dale, established a three-acre vineyard of such native grapes as scuppernong, or muscadine, and Catawba to test their adaptability for the production of salable wine. The next chief executive, Lord De La Warr, brought Smith's vignerons. Frenchmen, some of them said the English treated them more like slaves than employees, and none got a wine business going. Their failure was blamed on climate, soil, lack of equipment, and browsing deer.

In 1619, at the meeting of the first representative assembly in English America, Speaker John Pory said, "Three things there bee which in a few yeares may bring this Colony to perfection: the English plough, vineyards and cattle." The burgesses, sitting in the Jamestown church, passed "Acte 12," which required colonists to plant vineyards and, to feed silkworms, set out six mulberry trees a year.

Among the first to comply was yeoman John Johnson, who patented eighty-five acres known as Jockey's Neck on a plateau four miles east of town. Much of it is now the heart of the Williamsburg Winery, established in 1985, where more than fifty acres are under cultivation. One of its popular vintages is Acte 12 Chardonnay.

But that's getting ahead of the story. What little wine came of early Virginia efforts was bitter and traveled badly, and to the lack of proper drink was attributed some of the cause of the colony's failure to approach anything resembling perfection.

In 1622, Governor Francis Wyatt wrote to London:

> When we dated our letters in June last, the Colony stood admirably to health, within ten days succeeded great sickness and mortality: This was scarcity and want of meanes: Understand it rightly, want of beere, poultry, mutton &c . . . To plant a Colony by water drinkers was an inexcusable errour in those, who layd the first foundacion, and have made it a received custome, which until it be laide downe againe, there is small hope of health.

Virginians found indeed other beverages to drink their health. As their colony expanded, a modest form of prosperity developed, accompanied by the encouragement of ordinaries, as taverns were sometimes called. In 1649, a writer reported that "six publike Brewhouses" served Virginia and that its 5,000 settlers had plenty of barley and excellent malt and brewed "their owne Beere, strong and good."

The Virginia Company of London hoped squadrons of Jamestown ships would be freighted with wine and profits. The plans did not bear fruit.

William Byrd of Westover plantation wrote that at Caroline Courthouse, "Colonel Armistead and Colonel Will Beverly have each of 'em erected an ordinary well supplied with wine and other polite liquors," and "besides these, there is a rum ordinary for persons of more vulgar taste." Not much later, planter Robert Beverley said, "Their richer sort generally brew their small beer with Malt, which they have from England. . . . the poorer sort brew their Beer with Molasses and Bran. Their strong drink is Madeira Wine."

Governor William Berkeley, for one, would not give up on the native grape. He experimented with wine growing and bottle making at his Green Springs estate just west of Jamestown. During a visit in 1663, Beverley's father saw tree plantings that formed a trellis to support extensive grapevines. Berkeley said his wine was "as good as any that came out of Italy."

Berkeley dispatched Captain Henry Batt to explore western Virginia, and Batt reported that he found "grapes of an incredible Plenty, and Variety, some of which are very sweet" and "grapes so prodigiously large they seem'd more like Bullace than Grapes." A bullace is a plum.

By the late seventeenth century, most Virginia homes stocked wine and spirits in variety and in quantities exceeded only by such self-produced potations as pear wine and hard apple cider. A 1686 inventory of William Fauntleroy's cellar in up-country Rappahannock County listed ninety gallons of rum, twenty-five gallons of lime juice, and twenty dozen bottles of wine.

Visitor Durand de Dauphine found that "merry-making," including the consumption of large quantities of beer, was extensive. In 1686, he stopped at Bedford, the plantation of William Fitzhugh, and said his host provided "the largest hospitality—he had a store of good wine and other things to drink." He noticed the local Indians drank no wine but imbibed beer, cider, and a punch made of beer, brandy, and nutmeg.

Religious and political unrest in France stimulated the emigration of a new wave of colonists, this time Huguenots—Protestants and Calvinists who fled to England in 1685. More than 800, among them vignerons, sailed to Virginia with a Breton nobleman, Olivier de la Muce, and settled above the falls of the James. In 1699, the Huguenots founded Monacan Town

and were soon producing wine and brandy, including what they called "a Noble, strong-bodied claret."

Williamsburg was chartered and became Virginia's capital the year of Monacan—sometimes Manakin—Town's founding. In a May Day speech to Governor Francis Nicholson and the General Assembly, a student from the six-year-old College of William and Mary said the city already had many of the essentials of a metropolis, including "a Church, an ordinary, several stores, two Mills, a smiths shop a Grammar School, and above all the Colledge."

The ordinary may have been John Bentley's. In 1697 he was licensed to operate a tavern in Captain Matthew Page's house. Five years later, a Swiss traveler reported that there were eight taverns in the capital. Among their keepers were entrepreneurs like Jean Marot.

Licensed in 1707, Marot's ordinary, the English Coffee House, became one of Williamsburg's larger and more popular establishments. Marot operated a couple of stills nearby, and his inventory in 1717 listed such refreshments as Madeira, Canary, red port, Rhenish, brandy, and beer. Later, Henry Wetherburn's tavern stocked libations like arrack, port, Madeira, claret, beers, and rum.

An idea of the variety of spirits available can be had from the records of an expedition to the west undertaken in 1715 by sixty-three gentlemen known to history as the Knights of the Golden Horseshoe. Among them was John Fontaine, who said the group carried "Virginia red wine and white, Irish usquebaugh, brandy, shrub, two sorts of rum, champagne, canary, cherry, punch, water, cider, etc."

Hugh Jones, a clergyman who taught mathematics and philosophy at the college from 1717 to 1721, said Madeira was the most popular wine, "for it relieved the heat of summer and warmed the chilled blood and the bitter colds of winter."

Robert "King" Carter, the wealthiest Virginian of his day, died in 1732, leaving many of his plantations to his son Charles. Educated in England, the young man wrote a tract on "a whole new system of Virginia Husbandry . . . wherein the business of Tobo farming, improving lands and making Wine, are largely treated of and earnestly recommended."

Charles Carter became a burgess from King George County, worked with the Royal Society of Arts, and

▲ Interpreter Dan Hard, delivering goods to Williamsburg's Raleigh Tavern, draws a mug of wine without falling off the wagon.

◀ Interpreters Clayton Williams, William Webb, and Bob Brown, left to right, lift a glass in a Raleigh Tavern toast.

Thomas Jefferson, a wine connoisseur, tried winemaking at Monticello. Above are bottles and corking equipment in his cellar, which stored imported as well as domestic vintages.

corresponded with Peter Wyche in London, chairman of the society's agriculture committee. They discussed the production of varieties of French, Spanish, and Portuguese wines in Virginia, though Wyche thought the colony's location, terrain, and soil made it a less than ideal place to bottle good wines. In 1762, Carter had 1,800 vines in his vineyard but, because of drought, doubted he would produce more than a hogshead of wine.

In 1768, Virginians exported to Britain a little more than thirteen tons of wine while importing 396,580 gallons of rum from overseas, and another 78,264 from other North American colonies.

Two years later, the General Assembly designated Frenchman Andrew Estave winemaker and viticulturist for Virginia. He was described as a long-time resident of France who "hath a perfect Knowledge of the Culture of Vines, and the most approved Method of making Wine." Estave had lived in the colony two years, studied the soil, and cultivated wild grapes. Now he took 100 acres, a house, and three slaves, promising to make

"good merchantable Wine in four years from the seating and planting of the Vineyard." Like all before him, he failed. Estave thought his stocks of European grapes—*vitus vinifera*—were too fragile for the climate.

Virginia's planters looked to London wine merchants for regular supplies—the opposite of what was intended in 1606. George Washington was ordering wines from Robert Cary & Co. in London in 1759. About the time of his wedding to Martha Custis, he asked Cary to "order from the best House in Madeira a Pipe of the best Old Wines." Two years later, thinking perhaps that he might attempt to grow his own, he ordered "a Butt of about one hundred and fifty gall'ns of your choicest Madeira. And if there is nothing improper, or inconsistent in the request a few setts or cuttings of the Madeira grape."

Thomas Jefferson's affinity for French culture and his curiosity led him to plant vineyards at Monticello, and in 1773 he turned over 2,000 acres of rolling land to a Tuscan, Filipo Mazzei, to "prove the value of native grapes." But Monticello winemaking failed, perhaps

Modern Virginia is a force in winemaking. The wine at left was made by Gabriele Rausse Winery of Charlottesville with Monticello-grown Sangiovese grapes. Above, vintner Steve Warner samples a barrel at the Williamsburg Winery.

MILFORD PUBLIC LIBRARY
330 FAMILY DRIVE
MILFORD, MI 48381

because of the advent of the Revolution, or because lice infested the roots and leaves.

Elected president in 1801, Jefferson spent $10,000, a fortune, for wines during his administration, and to hold them ordered a sixteen-foot-deep wine cellar constructed adjacent to the White House. The pit was shaped like a flower pot and built of absorbent clay bricks. A wooden superstructure protected the wine against the weather, and bottles were racked on a platform floor above a bed of ice, replenished monthly and packed in sawdust.

Under Jefferson's influence, and with the cooperation of wealthy planters, a Virginia winemaking industry began to flower in the early nineteenth century, but the disruptions of the Civil War wiped out the business along with the rest of the state's economy.

Later in the century, the concept of prohibition gained wide support in Virginia, stifling any revival of winemaking, and by World War I, the state had gone dry. In 1919, the federal Eighteenth Amendment made national the ban on the import, export, manufacture, sale, or transportation of intoxicating liquors.

Virginia's tidelands became fertile ground for contraband liquor because of its natural resources and access to open water and smugglers' boats. Sheriffs sought out stills with land, sea, and air patrols. Williamsburg's *Virginia Gazette* reported prohibition arrests for moonshining, sale of illegal alcohol, and drunk driving.

After the repeal of the Eighteenth Amendment in 1933, Williamsburg became the first city in the state to end Prohibition, and by 1934 state liquor stores opened. It was not until the mid-1970s that Virginia began to compete again in the national wine market, using French hybrids, *vinifera* varietals, and new fertilizing techniques that helped counteract disease and mildew. The Farm Winery Law of 1980 boosted the industry, and technical aid from the United States Department of Agriculture and state universities helped accelerate the growth and quality of its product.

At Monticello, Jefferson's northeast vineyard was replanted in 1985 and his southwest vineyard in 1993. Visitors to the historic home have the opportunity to buy bottles of gift-shop wine.

There were six Virginia wineries in 1976, and more than seventy by 2002. Virginia ranked tenth in the nation in volume, and its wines were winning national and international acclaim—almost four centuries after the sailing of the first Jamestown fleet.

Tobacco

Virginia's Mother Lode

ALLAN C. FISHER JR.

Leaves of gold pressed into hogsheads were planters' treasure chests. Tobacco notes served as a monetary basis for sprawling plantations worked by slaves.

What do you think when you read the name John Rolfe? Most people recall only one thing: his marriage to the Indian princess Pocahontas, arguably the most famous wedding in our history. It led to eight years of peace with the great chief Powhatan, father of Pocahontas. But Rolfe should be remembered with gratitude for something far more remarkable and significant. To him can be credited the economic salvation of the Virginia colony. Four times previously the English had tried and failed to establish a foothold in the New World, but in Virginia Rolfe assured them of success.

On July 20, 1613, a year before Rolfe and Pocahontas married, the good ship *Elizabeth* docked in England with something that proved more valuable than gold, something historians have claimed was "of momentous importance." Rolfe had grown and shipped several hundred pounds of an experimental crop, tobacco. Its superior quality drew huzzahs of excited praise from London merchants. Seldom had soil, climate, and commercial plant combined for a more salubrious result. London wanted more, much more, all that could be grown. Tobacco became Virginia's raison d'être. It rescued the colony from a threadbare, toehold existence and assured its future.

Tobacco's demands gave birth to the plantation system, from the great estates of Robert "King" Carter, William Byrd II, and many others to the smaller holdings of

Improved by 380 years of experience and experiments, a crop of Virginia leaf ripens in the Southside sun of late October near Danville.

yeoman farmers and former indentured servants. Two or three plantings of tobacco exhausted even virgin soil, so growers believed they had to keep clearing new ground. But geography was on their side. Land in abundance stretched out all about them, much of it along navigable rivers such as the James and York in Virginia and the St. Mary's in Maryland, easily accessible to deep-draft trading vessels sailing to isolated estates and farms. An early governor of Maryland commented, "Tobacco requires us to abhor communities or townships . . . a planter cannot carry on his affairs without considerable elbow room."

The lure of the golden leaf swelled an unending flood of immigration. From tidal Virginia new settlements spread into the Piedmont and Carolina. As one pundit put it, Virginia was a colony "founded upon smoak." To a major extent, the same could be said of Maryland and North Carolina, and tobacco became a valued cash crop and item of trade in Massachusetts, Connecticut, and Delaware.

And in Virginia, in particular, it became money, actual legal tender. You could pay debts with it, purchase supplies, pay your preacher, the militia, and your taxes, and, in the seventeenth century, even buy a wife. Leaf of gold indeed.

Tobacco and its various uses had swept the world in the sixteenth century after its introduction to Europe by the first explorers of America, who were given it by the natives. On October 12, 1492, Columbus noted in his journal that the natives of San Salvador (if that island indeed was his first landfall, presently a matter of dispute) offered him leaves which "gave off a distinct fragrance." But he had no idea of its uses until two men he sent on an explorative sortie in Cuba saw natives smoking tobacco. One of these two men, Rodriguez de Jeréz, became a confirmed smoker and probably introduced the custom to Europe. The smoke coming from his mouth and nostrils so terrified his neighbors in Ayamonte, Spain, that the Spanish Inquisition imprisoned him for seven years, which no doubt broke his habit.

When the Spanish and Portuguese slashed their way into the New World, they soon cashed in on tobacco. In the 1500s Portuguese traders spread its use from Central and South America to Japan and China, and the Spaniards began cultivating it in the West Indies, Venezuela, and Mexico for the world market. In the conquered lands several species were used widely by the Mayas and other peoples for smoking, chewing, snuff, therapy for ills, and offerings to the gods. All these uses were part of a way of life centuries before the arrival of the conquistadors.

When tobacco finally came to the attention of scientists, its genus was named *nicotiana* for Jean Nicot of Nîmes, a sixteenth-century French ambassador to Lisbon. He is said to have received from a Portuguese scientist seeds that he sent as a present to Catherine de Medici, queen of France. New World natives had some 600 names for the plant, among them a word that sounded like "tobago"—as Columbus called it—hence tobacco.

The genus has many species, all but two native to America. The Spaniards found their conquered people grew what became known as *nicotiana tabacum,* and today most kinds of commercial tobacco belong to that species. But they also cultivated *nicotiana rustica,* or weed tobacco, widely grown by Indians in North America, including the Powhatans. The English thought this Indian plant "poore and weake, and of a byting tast." But the Spaniards, wisely and expertly, soon learned to cultivate only *tabacum,* which became known as "sweet-scented," and it dominated the European market, particularly in England.

Sir Francis Drake and Sir John Hawkins obtained "a great store of tobacco," in plundering the Spanish Main, but not seed; it was illegal for the Spanish to sell it or give it away, and the successors of the conquistadors guarded this treasure more successfully than they did their gold. But in 1586, when Drake took home to England the survivors of the first attempt to settle Roanoke Island, he also had in his hold some tobacco

plants and seed of the Indian weed tobacco. Sir Walter Ralegh, an inveterate smoker, grew the seeds on his estate in Ireland. When King James I condemned him to death, it is said he went to the axman's block in 1618 smiling and smoking his favorite pipe of cork-oak.

Perhaps Ralegh did so as a final jab at King James, who to this day ranks as perhaps the greatest tobacco phobe of all time. In 1604 he published anonymously his *Counterblaste to Tobacco,* containing, among many vehement denunciations of the "precious stink," this memorable summation: "A custome Lothsome to the eye, hatefull to the braine, dangerous to the Lungs, and in the black, stinking fume thereof, neerest resembling the horrible Stigian smoke of the pit that is bottomlesse." This condemnation became known as the king's work and eventually was acknowledged as such. How ironic that in the colony and along the river named in James's honor, tobacco should enrich his royal coffers.

Through the years a cacophony of other voices and pens in Europe called tobacco "the devil's weed" . . . "stinking" . . . "pernicious" . . . "foul." But voices in praise of tobacco were just as numerous and loud. Many claimed it a divinely sent remedy for the ills of mankind; you name it, tobacco cured it or helped. It was used as a powder, poultice, unguent, cathartic, even a dentifrice. William Byrd II called it "that bewitching vegetable" and wore it on his clothing and hung it in his home to ward off disease. "Divine tobacco" . . . "the holy, healing herb" . . . "sublime" . . . "a sovereign remedy to all diseases" . . . tobacco users vied in their claims and their praise. And, like the Indians, they smoked it, chewed it, snuffed it.

At the time of Jamestown's founding in 1607 Spanish exporters held a virtual monopoly on the London tobacco market. Not many people wanted the harsh Indian tobacco, although it was grown in the Midlands. They preferred leaf from the West Indies, Venezuela, and Mexico, which came in compacted shapes, such as twisted rolls, called "pudding," "ball," and "cane." And the Spaniards prospered like successful bandits, a merchants' counterploy to the freebooting English Sea Dogs. They sometimes obtained the equivalent of $125 a pound for their choice tobacco, and ordinary varieties brought prices equal to $17.50 a pound. The rich paid, and so did others with a demanding habit. The expense was the chief reason English pipes had small bowls.

Rolfe, a pipe smoker, had rueful knowledge of the expensive London market, and he had the wit and the will for Virginia to cash in on it. No one knows how, but he obtained some of the treasured Spanish *nicotiana tabacum* seed, probably from Caracas or Trinidad, but perhaps, as some believe, from Varina, Spain, then site of an estate growing fine, mild tobacco. Rolfe named his plantation Varina Farms, and to this day it continues to be a working farm, though tobacco hasn't been planted there in 300 years. Whatever the source, concealing seeds in small bags and smuggling them out of Spanish territory should have been easy; there are more than 350,000 tobacco seeds in an ounce.

In 1614 the secretary of Virginia, Ralph Hamor, writing in praise of Rolfe, said he "first took the pains to make trial [of the new seeds, in 1612], partly for the love he hath long borne [tobacco] and partly to raise commodity to the [settlers]." Hamor himself had grown some of Rolfe's seed. After leaving Virginia for England, Hamor wrote, "No country under the Sunne, may, or doth afoored more pleasant, sweet, and strong Tobacco."

After his marriage Rolfe took Pocahontas to England in 1616 to show off his exotic bride and to promote Virginia. He sent King James a brochure extolling the new land, but of tobacco he wisely took an apologetic tone, calling it "the principall commoditie the colony for the present yieldeth."

Pocahontas soon died in England, and, when Rolfe returned to Virginia, he found his colleagues growing tobacco wherever they could, even in the streets. Thomas Dale, the deputy governor, feared the colony would revert to the Starving Time of 1609–10, so he ordered no man could raise tobacco unless he also "manured and maintained" two acres of corn. But the rich London market drew the colonists like the pot of gold at the end of the rainbow.

The Virginia Company, then controlling the colony, authorized its agents in 1618 to pay settlers three shillings per pound for the best quality leaf and eighteen pence for second quality in trade at the company store. These were rich prices, and in 1620 Virginia tobacco sold as high as eight shillings per pound on the London market, a remarkable return considering the high value of sterling at the time. That modest first shipment from Virginia in 1615 increased to 60,000 pounds in 1622 and six years later to 500,000 pounds. In the four years 1637–40 annual exports averaged 1,395,063 pounds. Each year until the Revolution, except in years of crop failure, exports increased.

But the exorbitant prices when Spain had a stranglehold on the market could not continue. In successive moves the crown stopped English farmers from growing tobacco and charged the Virginia and Bermuda Companies an import duty of a shilling a pound, a violation of the crown's agreement with the two companies but an amount half that charged the Spanish. Then, probably with ill-concealed pleasure, the crown narrowly limited the importation of Spanish tobacco and lowered the import duty on colonial leaf from twelve pence to nine pence per pound. That gave the colonials a guaranteed market, but at controlled prices, and they had only one market, London; later Bristol and Scotland were added. Until the outbreak of the Revolutionary War prices paid growers ranged from a maximum of about three pence a pound to a half penny or even less. Not often did the price exceed two pence.

Colonials chafed under the British monopoly, and some historians have said the resentment fueled anti-British sentiment at the time of the Revolutionary War. When the British were preoccupied with civil war or foreign wars, American tobacco moved to other markets, particularly in Holland, but the British Navigation Acts of 1651 and 1660, the latter strongly enforced, kept free trade to a relative trickle.

Overgrowing of tobacco, which frequently flooded the market, and the Navigation Acts contributed to a severe depression in tobacco areas for two decades after 1660. Twice Virginia led the colonies in attempts to raise prices by controlling production, only to be thwarted by Lord Baltimore. If planters were poor, said Baltimore, "it is not from the low price of Tobacco, but from their own sloth, ill husbandry, and profusely spending their crops on Brandewine and other liquors." Depressed prices and depressed minds also helped fuel Bacon's Rebellion of 1675–76 in Virginia, a bloody internecine battle against Governor Berkeley's authority;

and in the same general time period Culpeper's Rebellion in Carolina was a direct, if doomed, insistence upon free trade. In the next decade, groups known as the "Cutters and Pluckers" attempted to control prices by destroying fields of tobacco in Virginia's York, Middlesex, Gloucester, and New Kent Counties.

But the ups and downs of a one-crop economy did not keep Virginia, and later Maryland and Carolina, from growing and prospering. Tobacco enriched many owners of big plantations. "King" Carter amassed some 300,000 acres; William Byrd II increased his inheritance of 43,000 acres to 179,000. Members of the fecund Randolph clan, so dominant politically, nearly all had large, profitable holdings. In 1703 Colonel Robert Quary, reporting on Virginia conditions to the Board of Trade, wrote, "In every river there are from ten to thirty men who by trade and industry have gotten very competent estates." Such large plantations thrived on slave labor, introduced in 1619, but slaves were not imported in large numbers until later in the seventeenth century. For a crop with a weed ancestry, tobacco culture made many demands requiring labor. Its cultivation included such steps as planting, hilling, transplanting, weeding, topping, suckering, cutting, hanging, stripping, and prizing. The finest tobacco, "sweet-scented," came from the sandy, loamy soils along the James and York Rivers. One small plantation on the York near Yorktown, that of Edward Digges, a mid-seventeenth-century settler, grew the lightest, mildest Virginia leaf, and for many years it brought the highest prices. Maryland, Delaware, and Carolina mostly cultivated orinoco, and it too had an assured market. Indeed, through mutation, orinoco evolved into the preferred kind.

Planters consigned their hogsheads of tobacco to favored British merchants, and in return a merchant shipped his client whatever he ordered: tools, textiles, fine furniture, china, fashionable clothing, and all the many other things not made in the colonies. The nominal commission earned by a merchant was only 2.5 percent of gross sales, but that became 8 to 10 percent of the net proceeds, because the commission applied to government duties and other charges. Planters never knew how much they made on a crop until the following growing year, or even later, so they tended to fall into debt, often

From Theodore de Bry's *Grands Voyages,* 1590, this illustration of a North Carolina Secota village of 1585 shows Indian cultivation of tobacco at top center and lower left. It was the first depiction of tobacco farming in America.

deeply. By the reign of George II about two-thirds of Virginia's planters were so involved and trapped.

Through the years, fifteen male members of the powerful Randolph family amassed large debts with London merchants, mostly because of extravagance. Thomas Jefferson, himself heavily in debt to London and Glasgow firms, said of the consignment system, "These debts had become hereditary from father to son, for many generations, so that the planters were a species of property, annexed to certain mercantile firms in London." The system at times worked amicably, in some cases in the planters' favor, but often they thought themselves underpaid or even cheated. George Washington asserted that in four years out of five the tobacco he shipped on consignment brought lower prices than those quoted on the home market.

Of course, British factors complained that the planters were extravagant and poor managers, and nearly all tried to live like English country squires and some like lords of the realm. If they worked hard, they usually played even harder. But some of the British merchants were indeed dishonest, underpaying their growers, cheating their government on duties, even trading in smuggled tobacco. Planters had their own adept sharp practices, such as stuffing the middle of tobacco hogsheads with stems and sticks and other trash, a practice that became known as "nesting." The entire system was so loose and so poorly managed and governed that it invited dishonesty. It didn't improve until passage of the Inspection Act in 1732.

In the eighteenth century, tobacco cultivation moved above the fall line into the Piedmont, where it became the staple of agrarian livelihood for yeoman farmers. Ocean-going vessels could not reach this upland area, so canny Scottish merchants and some English factors sent representatives to set up stores for growers and to buy tobacco directly, making shipping to England and Scotland their responsibility. But they owned vessels in the tobacco trade, and such shipment could be painless, even profitable; the law required tobacco be hauled to market only in British built, owned, and manned vessels. On the eve of the Revolutionary War one large factor operated seven stores in Maryland and fourteen in Virginia and owned and operated a large fleet in the Virginia trade alone. In this period the percentage of tobacco sold by consignment declined steadily, though most of the big, long-established tidewater planters either clung to the practice by choice and habit or were enmeshed in it.

By the late 1650s pressure for tobacco land had become so compelling in Virginia's choice tidewater areas that colonists began moving south into the Chowan River and Albemarle Sound areas. Albemarle boasted an assembly that passed generous laws promoting immigration, and it marketed its tobacco in Virginia because Carolina harbors were shoal draft. But the first state labeled its offspring "Rogues' Harbour" and closed its market to Carolina tobacco. That provided a lucrative, if illegal, opportunity for New England traders. They had shoal-draft coasting vessels and, in defiance of the Navigation Acts, they moved into the Carolina trade. Not until 1731, when London's Privy Council threw out Virginia's exclusion laws against its neighbor, did the impasse resolve, though many Carolinians and Virginia buyers and shippers managed to circumvent the restrictions. In the meantime, angry Carolinians developed a better shipping outlet, Port of Brunswick on the Cape Fear River.

Today it's hard to imagine tobacco as actual money. It was far more bulky than currency or coinage; it could spoil or suddenly decrease in value; it had to be stored in protective enclosures such as warehouses; it varied in quality; it was not easily divisible. In short, ownership could be a chancy pain in the neck. Historians have said more laws were passed in colonial America to control tobacco's price, quality, and marketing than for anything else that concerned legislators. But the colonists had to use something as a standard of value for goods and services, since they had relatively few coins or much currency. Virginia tried several times to produce copper coins, but, lacking British support, failed.

Throughout colonial history the British never provided specifically for colonial coins. So colonists turned to Spanish "pieces of eight" and the Portuguese "joes," obtained mostly from the West Indies. But these silver and gold coins had to be valued in terms of the British pound. For example, a Spanish piece of eight, or milled dollar, for years was valued at four shillings six pence; after 1727 the official value in Virginia was fixed at six shillings. But there were never enough coins of any kind.

All of the thirteen colonies issued paper money during the eighteenth century, but Virginia, one of the last to do so, didn't print any until 1755 and only then to pay heavy debt incurred during the French and Indian War. As with coinage, there was never enough currency.

So tobacco had to suffice as money. When single women arrived at Jamestown in 1619, bachelors and widowers claimed them at 120 pounds each of the best leaf. Later the salaries of clergymen were fixed at 16,000 pounds of leaf per year. You could be married for 200 pounds, buried for 400. A tax of a penny a pound on certain exported tobacco helped found the College of William and Mary.

Such use of the tobacco tax aroused the ire of a royal minister, Sir Edward Seymour. Told the new college would prepare clergymen who would save souls, Seymour ranted, "Souls! Damn your souls! Make tobacco!"

Rarely did the British government stray from single-minded self-interest in its tobacco policy. After 1685 English import duties soared for the remainder of the colonial period, becoming four to six times the price ordinarily paid the planter. But when British merchants exported their tobacco purchases to Europe, they paid no duties. Instead, the government gave them drawbacks, or refunds, of the original duties paid when the tobacco came from America to Britain, duties planters had been charged for by their factors.

Many times Virginia's legislature tried conscientiously to assure the quality and value of tobacco for the British market and domestic uses. One of its first acts, in 1619, required inspection and burning of "mean" or inferior leaf. Laws limiting production were passed in 1619, 1621, and 1629. In 1633 the assembly ordered tobacco be brought to warehouses for inspection prior to sale. That failed, as did similar attempts, but in 1713 and 1730 laws were passed requiring effective inspection by licensed inspectors in bonded warehouses. They could issue to growers "tobacco notes" as receipts for their crops. While not true mediums of exchange, these notes and letters of credit given by British merchants to growers were often used as money, especially to pay certain taxes and legal fees.

In 1733 Robert Walpole, the crown's first minister, tried to introduce in England a law similar to Virginia's requiring bonded warehouses for receipt and sale of tobacco. Walpole knew merchants cheated their government by false weights, and he wanted to stop it and develop a tax that would ease the burden on landholders. But the merchants, even the honest ones, aroused such a hue and cry the move was defeated.

Williamsburg merchants established a kind of central market for tobacco. They took the latest advices from the

Colonial Williamsburg cooper Lew LeCompte readies tobacco for prizing into a hogshead.

British market, applied them to the local supply and demand situation, and came up with a basic price. When the price became accepted by a considerable number of sellers and buyers, it was said to be "broke," and it became known as the "Court price." Even outside Williamsburg, where the kind and quality of tobacco might be different, the court price proved influential.

But in many years the fluctuating price of tobacco proved a serious disadvantage in its use as money. Take, for example, the celebrated "Parson's Cause." Salaries of Virginia clergymen had been set at 16,000 pounds of tobacco annually, assessed on tithe payers, and in 1755 and 1758 the legislature declared the value of tobacco to be two cents per pound. But that amount soon fell below the going rate, and the Privy Council in London, on petition of the clergy, threw the law out. So one of the preachers, on behalf of all the others, brought suit against tithepayers for the difference they felt was owed them. They "won" in a jury trial in which Patrick Henry, the tithepayers' lawyer, declared the king a tyrant. The jurors, obviously sharing that belief, awarded the parson one penny in damages.

By the time of the Revolution, Virginians owed British mercantile houses some £2,000,000, as much as all the rest of the colonies combined. But the figure is somewhat misleading, for it includes seven years' interest and does not account for the harvest of 1776 that largely went to France. Nevertheless, Thomas Jefferson thought the indebtedness twenty to thirty times the value of all the money circulating in Virginia. So in October 1777, the Virginia assembly passed a law of sequestration for debts owed the British. This meant planters could deposit money in the state loan office to pay the merchants, now enemies. Some £275,000 was raised in that manner, and to Americans that was enough, since Corn-

wallis's troops in Virginia had destroyed 10,000 hogsheads of tobacco and many tobacco properties. Jefferson himself had suffered grievous loss of leaf stored at his plantation on Elk Island, yet he did not claim immunity from any part of his £10,000 indebtedness.

The Treaty of Paris in 1783 reaffirmed the claims of British creditors, and suits forcing collection ruined many old plantation dynasties. The controversy over debts continued for twenty years, until the American government finally paid £600,000 to the British in satisfaction of all claims.

Leaf of gold had helped win America's freedom. Though British warships seized an estimated 34,000,000 pounds of tobacco during the war, some 53,000,000 pounds evaded capture, reached foreign markets, and helped finance the rebellion. In 1777 Benjamin Franklin in Paris obtained 2,000,000 livres against a contract to deliver 5,000 hogsheads of Virginia leaf. George Washington, appealing to his countrymen for help, said, "If you can't send money, send tobacco." Many did.

After the war tobacco exports recovered quickly on the world market. In 1783 leaf from Virginia alone jumped to more than 86,000,000 pounds compared to an average of 12,000,000 during the war years 1776–82. But in 1803 the much condemned and extolled plant that had sustained Virginia in particular during more than a century and a half of colonial rule finally lost its status as the nation's principal export crop to King Cotton and, later, as Jefferson had predicted, to wheat. The use of tobacco as money faded under a new nation free to mint its own coins and print its own currency. But the United States, as during colonial days, continues to be the major source of the finest leaf and remains the world's largest exporter. Tobacco is still, quite literally, the leaf of gold.

Sailor, Soldier, Scoundrel

Captain John Martin, the Last of the First Jamestowners

MICHAEL LOMBARDI

He was a swashbuckler and a privateer, bold, energetic, entrepreneurial, greedy, and unscrupulous, the quintessential Elizabethan adventurer. He circumnavigated the globe with Sir Francis Drake. He was in on the rescue of Sir Walter Ralegh's first colony. He was a founder of Jamestown, an original officer of the colony, and briefly its president. He raised the fort that preserved the settlement from early annihilation.

He was accused of malingering. He suffered from gold fever—with which he infected others. He plotted and schemed for power. He tried to erect a feudal estate on a bend in the James River wilderness. He promoted the suppression of the Indians. And he was the last of the first English Virginians to die. But for all the theatricality of his checkered life, he lies in a forgotten grave, his name unremembered save by scholars and history buffs, a footnote in history.

History, like every endeavor, has its stars. When the tales of the first English-American settlements are told, the romantic and tragic Ralegh is bound to play a lead. The drama and adventure of Captain John Smith's life makes him big box office. Pocahontas is a matinee idol. Captain John Martin never makes a marquee. But Hollywood could hardly improve upon his story.

Martin was born about 1562 into a family that embodied an era in which talent, daring, and contacts could overcome humble birth. His father, Richard Martin, had moved to London as a young man and apprenticed himself to a goldsmith. By 1558, the elder Martin married Dorcas, the daughter of Sir John Eggleston, and he and his partner at the Sign of the Harp had become goldsmiths and bankers to Queen Elizabeth, financers

◀ John Martin, portrayed by Al Saguto, examines his patent for hundreds of acres along the James River. His claims were disputed.

▼ Martin sailed with Sir Francis Drake, here in an eighteenth-century Jacobus Houbraken portrait.

of her endeavors. Richard Martin became warden and master of the mint, a London alderman, and three times lord mayor.

John, his third son, studied law but gave it over to become a sailor, soldier, entrepreneur, and fortune hunter. His father's connections and financial support almost surely secured the sixteen-year-old a crewman's place when Drake boarded the *Golden Hind* in 1578 and began his voyage around the world.

When Drake was dispatched to the Americas in 1585 to attack Spanish settlements in the West Indies and Florida, Martin sailed along as captain of the *Benjamin*. He participated in the sack of St. Augustine and helped bring home the distressed settlers of the initial attempt— there would be three—at Roanoke Island colonization.

When the Virginia Company of London attempted a foothold further north, Martin was in the landing party. On April 29, 1607, the *Susan Constant, Godspeed,* and *Discovery,* commanded by Christopher Newport, sailed past the Virginia Capes into the mouth of the Chesapeake Bay. To port was the river they would name the James. Aboard the *Susan Constant,* the leaders of the expedition opened a sealed box containing instructions for the trading station they were to establish. Newport, Bartholomew Gosnold, John Ratcliffe, Edward Maria Wingfield, George Kendall, John Smith, and Martin were appointed to its governing council. Wingfield was elected president, a position granted two votes to a councilor's one.

Soon after they went ashore, near modern Hampton, the English skirmished with a band of Native Americans. Martin and four other councilors were hurt. Binding their wounds, they turned upriver and selected for settlement a marshy peninsula suited more for defense than habitation. Martin, named master of the ordnance, had the responsibility for fortification against Spanish warships and the Indians, whose attacks continued. By June 20, he had seen to construction of three-sided James Fort and, with others, had found time to collect a barrelful of what Martin said was gold.

Newport took the barrel to England when he returned for supplies. A London assay found a tiny amount of genuine ore, and a lot of fool's gold, as if the sample had been salted. Was Martin, the goldsmith's son, deceived, or was he trying to deceive? Sir Walter Cope, a Virginia Company official, wrote:

> In the ende all turned to vapore, & Martyne hath cosyned the pore Captaine, the Kinge & State and meant as I hear to have cosyned his own father, seeking to have made unto himm somm sullpyes, which otherwise he dowted never to procure.

Virginia surely needed supplies—arms, armor, medicine, clothes, food, and drink. Indian attacks, sickness, cold, and hunger killed the colonists, among them Martin's only son, John Martin Jr., who died August 18. Captain Martin blamed President Wingfield for the boy's death—"He hath starved my sonne, and denied him a spoonful of beere" —and joined Smith and Rat-

cliffe in a September coup that led to Wingfield's arrest for general incompetence, his trial, and his ouster. Ratcliffe took his place.

Thus began the disputes and revolts that plagued early Jamestown. Martin was often at their center, bending his legal training to the forms of charging and prosecuting enemies.

Wingfield and Kendall tried to commandeer the colony's pinnace, the small *Discovery,* fitted out for trade, to abscond for England. Kendall was eventually tried for mutiny and convicted, Martin pronouncing the sentence. Soon after, the Indians captured Smith and briefly kept him a captive. In Smith's absence, Ratcliffe used the president's two votes to elect Gabriel Archer to the council over Martin's objection. Now Martin and Smith combined to depose Archer and install Mathew Scrivener.

The colonists could have better bent their efforts to survival. When Newport returned to Jamestown on January 8, nearly 75 percent of them were dead. He brought more settlers and composed the councilmen's differences. The infighting subsided with Martin, Ratcliffe, Smith, and Scrivener in charge.

Soon, however, the lure of gold divided the colony's leaders. Martin must have believed that gold would be found. He led a faction that spent much of its time trying to prove him right. Smith dismissed their efforts as "golden inventions" and wrote: "The worst mischeife was our guilded refiners with their golden promises, made all men slaves in hopes of recompense; there was no talke, no hope, no worke, but dig gold, wash gold, load gold."

The supply ship *Phoenix* arrived April 20, and when the colony leaders debated how to freight her for return to England, the gold controversy came to a head. Martin wanted to load the ship with what Smith called "his phantasticall gold." Smith and Scrivener favored a cargo of cedar. When the *Phoenix* sailed June 2, 1608, it carried a load of Virginia cedar, and Martin, bound for home.

Martin was sick at the time but also "desirous to injoy the credit of his supposed Art of finding the golden mine." He reached England when it was apparent that the colony had to have a new charter and new leadership, and Martin was there, with others, to argue for it. The second charter transferred governance and control of the colony from the crown to the Virginia Company. Thomas West, Lord De La Warr—Delaware in modern orthography—was named governor, with Lieutenant Governor Sir Thomas Gates and new councilors to administer the colony until De La Warr could sail.

In June of 1609, Martin shipped as captain of the *Falcon* in a nine-vessel Jamestown fleet commanded by Admiral Sir George Somers. It carried the new charter and commissions, Gates, and 500 passengers, including seventy artisans and skilled laborers whom Martin had recruited. A hurricane struck and scattered the flotilla. Somers and Gates were shipwrecked in Bermuda with about 180 passengers, as well as the commissions for Virginia's new officials.

Martin brought his ship safely to Jamestown, where he discovered Smith had become president. While Martin began to rebuild the settlement's structures into more permanent buildings, political battles began anew.

Absent the shipwrecked commissions, Smith refused to accept any new councilors or yield his authority. At first Martin allied himself with Ratcliffe and Archer against Smith. But in August or September, when Smith's term ended, he and Smith had reached an understanding. Martin would join Smith on the council, take over the presidency, and resign in favor of Smith. Martin served for three hours before thinking better of it.

Archer and Ratcliffe took it upon themselves to name Captain Francis West, Lord De La Warr's brother, as chief executive. In October, Smith sent West to the Falls of the James with 100 men. West's party was ambushed and several were killed or wounded. West called for help and Smith led a relief party. Here the stories diverge.

West said Smith betrayed him to the Indians, saying his men had powder for one volley. Smith said West mistreated the Indians. Smith sailed back to Jamestown, a gunpowder bag on his belt. Somehow, the powder ignited and badly burned Smith. He saved himself by jumping into the river and nearly drowned. Smith's authority was weakened by his wounds. Martin changed sides again, joining Ratcliffe and Archer. Smith said they "plotted to have murdered him in his bed," but there was no assassination attempt. Instead, Martin and the others deposed Smith and sent him back to England to stand trial for unspecified "misdemeanors."

That winter the Indians laid a kind of guerilla siege to Jamestown, and the colonists, almost trapped in their fort, had little to eat. When Gates and Somers reached Jamestown on May 24 carrying the second charter and the survivors of the shipwreck, they found a town of sixty people in deep distress. The colonists voted to abandon the place and return to England, with a single exception. John Martin voted to stay.

The colonists glided down the James just as a new supply fleet, led by De La Warr, sailed into sight. It brought food, clothing, doctors, skilled laborers, and real authority for the colony's governance. Everything the colony needed to reopen Jamestown.

Lord De La Warr did not take Martin into his council, so for the next few years the captain contented himself with experiments in the cultivation of tobacco and silkworms, and schemes for the future. Martin had his eye on a peninsula twelve miles above Jamestown. That winter he sailed back to London to sell tobacco and pursue his hunger for land.

Martin had influential contacts in England. Sir Julius Caesar, his brother-in-law, was on the King's Privy Council, and his father was still an important financial figure. The Virginia Company granted ten shares of land in November 1616. A share was usually 100 acres, but Martin maintained his were valued at 500 each. He claimed 5,000, total, and named the parcel Martin's Brandon to honor his wife's maiden name. Martin was not finished. Marshalling his political clout, he persuaded members of the company, among them Sir Julius, to issue a patent that gave Martin rights unlike any before granted in English America.

He was to have trading and fishing rights along the James, the right to build and operate mines, shipyards, iron and corn mills, and the right to govern Martin's Brandon without interference from the colonial government "save only to defend it against it's foreign and domestical enemies." Martin was essentially a feudal lord.

The colony's resident government was unhappy with the arrangement. It said that Martin's Brandon became a sanctuary for debtors, runaways, and "others of evil fame." When officials came to serve warrants on his land, Martin threatened "to lay them neck and heels" in the stocks.

Lord De La Warr, portrayed by Jim Boyer, with Martin.

Another charter, "the Greate Charter," established, among other things, the first representative assembly in English America, the Virginia House of Burgesses. When it met for the first time in 1619, Martin's Brandon sent two representatives, Thomas Davis and Robert Stacy. The burgesses from the other plantations were not inclined to allow Martin's representatives a say in creating laws that would not apply to the master and residents of Martin's fiefdom. They excluded Davis and Stacy and told Martin that, if he wished his burgesses seated, he must give up his extraordinary rights. Martin refused, saying, "I hold my patent for my service don, which now newe or late comer can merit or challenge."

Now the burgesses went further. They petitioned the company in London to revoke the patent. It had never been approved by a full Quarter Court of the Company, which was required, and contravened the Greate Charter, which disallowed all grants of special privileges. Martin went to England in the fall of 1621 to fight for his patent. The Virginia Company turned down his petition to retain his privileges but offered him a new grant, equal to those held by others in Virginia.

While Martin was in England, the Indians attacked the English settlements scattered up and down the James, killing about 350 colonists, among them seven at Martin's Brandon. Martin stayed in England and fought on. He called on his influential friends and family to support him, challenging the company while offering it a treatise on retaliation: "The Manner Howe to Bring the Indians into Subiection without makinge an utter exterpation of them together with the reasons." His advice was to burn their villages, keep them from planting corn, and disrupt their trade. Martin hoped that would persuade the surviving Native Americans to become willing workers for the colonists. Offered the same day as his Indian plan, Martin's "The manner how

A portion of Martin's Brandon on the James, with an eighteenth-century
home. On this land, Martin sought to become a law unto himself.

Virginia, if his Majesty and his Councill and company agree, may be made a Royall plantation for God's glory, his Majesty's and Royall Progeny's ever happiness, and the companies exceeding good, and all this land shall receice daily profit thereby" called on Charles I to take title to the colony, which Charles did in 1625.

Late in 1623, however, Martin accepted the inevitable. He surrendered his old patent, took the new, and returned to Virginia in 1624 with clear claim to Martin's Brandon. His reign as Virginia's first feudal lord was over.

In his remaining years, Martin obtained a seat on the governor's council but was soon suspended for divisive activities. During his last days, a series of legal actions occupied his time and energy. Martin sued and was sued in return by business partners, debtors, contractors, merchants, and ship captains. He won some lawsuits and lost others before his death in 1632 at his Martin's Brandon. His grandson inherited the plantation.

Brandon remains a working farm today, although no longer owned by the Martin family. That might have disappointed Martin. He fought hard for that land, fought Indians, fellow colonists, and the Virginia Company. In the end, he survived them all. Martin was among the first Englishmen to set foot in Virginia, and when he died, the last of the original Jamestown colonists still living in the Old Dominion.

So why has the story of his life, filled with daring and intrigue, and populated with well-known characters, been neglected? First and probably most important, Martin did not write his own chronicle, and few of his letters survive. We rely mostly on the accounts of Smith and official records for information about the Jamestown settlement. The early days of the colony were contentious. Martin changed sides frequently, perhaps winning for himself a measure of authority, but no friends to chronicle his adventures.

Martin's story also lacks a single compelling dramatic focus. There is no tale of an Indian maiden saving his life like Smith's, nor was he the first admiral to lead settlers to Virginia like Newport. He was not credited with bringing tobacco to the colonies like John Rolfe. The most important event in Martin's life was an attempt to use his influence to escape authority and create his own fiefdom, and even that failed. Not the stuff of American heroes.

Still Martin was one of the men who made America. He may not have been a star, but he had staying power. He was audacious, argumentative, enterprising, acquisitive, persistent, self-serving, innovative, and litigious. He wanted everything he believed he had earned. He wanted the government to support him but not to restrict him. All in all, not a bad description of the American character.

Pocahontas's London Christmas

Beans, Peas, and Sea-Coal; or, Who Killed Pocahontas?

IVOR NOËL HUME

The most recent representation of the legend of Pocahontas is Terrence Malick's film *The New World,* which has King James I inviting the young Indian woman and her English husband to England to be royally wined and dined. The truth was different.

One of numerous children born to Powhatan, paramount chief of the Tidewater Virginia Indians, Pocahontas was eleven or twelve when the English settled at Jamestown in 1607. Virtually all we know about her comes from the pen of Captain John Smith, whose grasp on the reins of truth was loose and self-serving. We may be sure, however, that in 1609, after his own people attempted one or more times to assassinate him, Smith was shipped home to England. Pocahontas continued her tribal life and may have been wed to an Indian before the English took her hostage in 1613. She spent a year as a Jamestown prisoner and bargaining chip, being tutored, meanwhile, in English ways and religion. In March 1614, one of her captors, the scholarly John Rolfe, asked Governor Thomas Dale's permission to marry her, and with Dale's blessing and Powhatan's acquiescence, did.

Through the following three years of their marriage, Pocahontas, baptized and renamed Rebecca, lived the life of an English wife and bore a son, Thomas. Who suggested sending the Rolfes to London as samples of the fruits of colonization we do not know. But there is no doubting it was not the king or that the Virginia Company, which owned and financed the colony, saw the promotional potential and made the preparations.

Writing from London on June 22, 1616, Virginia Company investor John Chamberlain wrote:

In Terrence Malick's film *The New World*, Pocahontas appears with King James and Queen Anne. Whether they met is arguable.

Sir Thomas Dale is arrived from Virginia and brought with him some ten or twelve old and younge of that countrie, among whom the most remarquable person is Poca-huntas (daughter of Powatan a kinge or cacique of that countrie) married to one Rolfe an English man: I hear not of any other riches or matter of worth, but only of some quantitie of sassafras, tobacco, pitch, and clap-board, things of no great value.

The ship *Treasurer* reached Plymouth about June 3 and was greeted by Devonshire's vice admiral, Sir Lewis Stukely. Disembarking, along with Dale, Captain Samuel Argall, and other notable colonists, were Rolfe, his wife, and her entourage of young Indian women, along with her kinsman Tomocomo, or Uttamatomakkin. Powhatan sent him as his daughter's guardian and as a reporter of everything he saw and heard. Tomocomo's instructions included counting all the English, but having no better system, he began to notch a tally stick—discarding it soon after setting foot on the crowded Plymouth quay.

Although Pocahontas adapted well to English life, her Indian attendants lacked her indoctrination and surrounded her with their shared native traditions. Tomocomo, who personified her father, took a dislike to everything English and became a strong and outspoken critic of the life his kinswoman was required to lead. The situation was no better for John Rolfe, who found himself living in close proximity to a cluster of unacculturated Indians booked by the Virginia Company into the Belle Sauvage Inn at the bottom of London's Ludgate Hill.

Though the principal entry into the city was from the south across London Bridge, a secondary entrance serving the west ran via Westminster along the Thames's north bank, and it is likely Dale's coaches and carts took that route down Fleet Street, stopping in the shadow of the city walls at Ludgate. To get there, travelers crossed a stone bridge across Fleet River, by that time known as Fleet Ditch.

Roman and later London stood on two hills divided by the River Walbrook. On the westerly hill stood the cathedral of St. Paul, beyond which the ground sloped steeply down Ludgate Hill to the Fleet, which ran into the Thames outside the city wall and was a centuries' old dump for every kind of garbage. Butchers tossed their offal in, tanners disposed of their waste, as did humans of theirs through the privies flanking and overhanging the narrow river's fetid banks. The carcasses of dogs, rats, and other animals lay rotting in its mud, their remains exposed in the summer when the flow of rainwater abated. For anyone born amid the fresh, flowing waters of Tidewater Virginia, the stench of the Fleet Ditch should have been a shock, and Pocahontas, her lodgings at the Belle Sauvage, was yards from it.

The inn was maybe 200 years old. By 1453 it was known as "Savages-ynn alias vocat le belle on the Hope," but by 1525 it was the Belle Sauvage, and so it remained until destroyed in London's Great Fire of 1666. No descriptions of the building survive, but maps show it occupied considerable space, with a yard facing Fleet Prison. Nineteen years before Pocahontas and her group arrived, a petition had been submitted to Lord Burghley to have the waters around the prison cleaned up, saying that "the place is a congregation of unwholesome smells of the town."

To the south of the Belle Sauvage stood the Blackfriars Playhouse, whose actors lodged at the inn, with fencers, acrobats, and the masters of performing animals—among them a silver-shoed horse capable of answering questions by stamping its feet. Plays were performed on a wooden platform in the yard, where at a performance of Marlowe's *Dr. Faustus* the Devil was said to have materialized. The Belle Sauvage yard, a stop for coaches entering and leaving the city, was a haunt of thieves and con men preying on passengers. The Belle Sauvage compound was noisy, dangerous, and evil smelling, unfit for a gentleman and his family.

Whether the Virginia Company chose the Belle Sauvage as a mark of disdain that Rolfe had wed an Indian or because it seemed a good place to house a bunch of natural Virginians is debatable.

In his 1625 play *The Staple of News,* Ben Jonson had the character Pennyboy say that a tavern was unfit for a princess.

Captain Smith's *Generall Historie of Virginia, New-England, and the Summer Isles,* coupled with a promotional letter addressed to Queen Anne, tells us virtually all we know about Pocahontas in London. From Smith we learn that she was invited to 1616's most prestigious

George Braun and Frans Hogenberg's early seventeenth-century view of London.

royal party, at Christmastide, a Twelfth Day masque the king and queen gave at Whitehall. The event has been portrayed as Pocahontas's being granted a royal audience. Not so.

A masque, or mask, was more or less as it sounds, an entertainment featuring a masked ball in which the rich and aristocratic players performed masked or with their faces blackened. The latter was said to have been the brainchild of the queen, who in 1605 required her ladies to dance as "blackamoors" in Jonson's *Masque of Blackness*. The effect was considered so droll it contin-

ued through later masques, wherein guests dressed as something they were not—duchesses as their servants, dukes as commoners, rich merchants as paupers. All elitist turnabout fun, but baffling to guests outside the "in" crowd. The 1616/17 entertainment was written as *Christmas, his Masque* by Jonson, with sets and costumes by architect Inigo Jones. January 18, Chamberlain, presumably there, wrote: "The Virginian woman Poca-huntas, with her father counsaillor Hath ben with the king and graciously used, and both she and her assistant well placed at the maske."

The "father counsaillor" and "her assistant" were almost certainly one and the same, namely Tomocomo. We may wonder whether John Rolfe was not invited or declined to attend. Either way, Pocahontas was the star, and Tomocomo in his paint and feathers provided courtiers with a reminder of the princess's nativity.

At some point in the London visit, Smith saw Tomocomo and mentioned that Tomocomo had met the king. But Tomocomo "denied ever to have seene the King, till by circumstances he was satisfied he had: Then he replyed very sadly, You gave Powhatan a white Dog, which Powhatan fed as himselfe, but your King gave me nothing, and I am better than your white Dog."

How could Tomocomo have met the king without knowing it? The answer may be the Twelfth Night Mask ritual. In the 1616 extravaganza, Jonson introduced the character Baby-Cake attended by "an usher bearing a great cake with a bean and a pease" concealed inside. When the cake was cut, the person who drew the bean became king for the night, and he or she who drew the pea became queen. They were the night's master and mistress of the revels.

One may wonder what Tomocomo made of this apparent lunacy, and whether his introduction was to the Bean King and Pea Queen rather than to England's crowned heads. It would explain why he got no gifts from their Twelfth Night majesties.

At some time in 1616, Pocahontas sat for a portrait drawing by young Simon van de Passe, which was hurriedly engraved to be sold in the streets. In it she appears hollow cheeked and heavy eyed. Although the engraving is dated to 1616, the English used the old Julian calendar, which did not begin the new year until March 25. Thus, on February 22, when the gossipy and never-kind Chamberlain sent a copy to a friend, the engraving could have been hot off the press. Wrote Chamberlain:

> Here is a fine picture of no fayre Lady and yet with her tricking up and high stile and titles you might thincke her and her worshipfull husband to be somebody, yf you do not know that the poore companie of Virginia out of theyre povertie are faine to allow her fowre pound a weeke for her maintenance.

The portrait was less than flattering. Before the end of 1624 the picture was reengraved to make the Indian Princesss look more English. Smith did not intend there to be an image of Pocahontas in his *Generall Historie,* but the publisher added to the first edition, published in 1624, two copies of a portrait of the Duchess of Richmond, to whom Smith had dedicated his book, as well as two portraits of Rebecca Rolfe. The first was Van de Passe's and the second an uncredited and softer version—the one used in most subsequent books about Smith.

If, as seems likely, the Van de Passe engraving was published after the Twelfth Night mask, it could suggest Pocahontas was ailing. Chamberlain wrote January 18 that she was planning to return to Virginia "yf the wind wuld come about to send them away." The wind, however, was slow to favor, and she was to die at Gravesend about March 20, just as Samuel Argall, captaining the *George,* was to sail. Buried the next day in the church of St. George at Gravesend—destroyed by fire in 1727—her bereaved husband and son, Thomas, reboarded the ship. The boy was ill, as were his Indian nurses, and reluctantly his father took them ashore at Plymouth and left them in Stukely's custody. Thomas returned to Virginia about 1635, when he was twenty and his father dead.

So what killed Pocahontas? We know that before Christmas, perhaps in late summer, she was at the Thamesside village of Branford, now Brentford, abutting Syon House, the home of the Earl of Northumberland, where his wife played hostess to men involved in colonizing Virginia. There Smith had his long-delayed meeting with Pocahontas, who, he said, was accompanied by "divers of my friends." It was not a Hollywood reunion.

Some historians conclude the Rolfes moved to Branford to escape the possibility of sickness in London. It seems more likely they were there briefly to visit the Duchess of Northumberland and never vacated their Belle Sauvage lodgings.

Behind the inn ran Seacoal Lane, so named because limemakers had burned coal there. By the end of the sixteenth century, coal was much used in industrial work, and the smoke from it and from wood burned in domestic fires hung over the city and settled as smog into the low-lying areas—of which Ludgate was the lowest. The odors from the rancid Fleet Ditch were held down by the sulphur-dioxide–laden smog hanging over the Belle

Sauvage yard. Forty-five years later diarist John Evelyn was still asking:

> And what is all this, but the Hellish and Dismal Cloud of SEA-COALE? which is not onely perpetually imminent over her head . . . her Inhabitants breathe nothing but an impure and thick Mist, accompanied with a fuliginous and filthy vapour . . . corrupting the lungs and disordering the entire habit of their Bodies; so that Catharrs, Phthisicks, Coughs and Consumptions, rage more in this one City than in the whole Earth besides.

A case can be made that the penny-pinching Virginia Company killed Pocahontas by housing her for nigh on seven months at the Belle Sauvage—and that the evidence of it is writ large in the Van de Passe engraving. The mortality bill for one August week in 1665 listed 126 deaths from consumption. One of Pocahontas's women, left behind to be Christianized by the Virginia Company, was later reported to be "very weake of a Consumpcon, att m^r Goughs in the Black Friers." Like the Belle Sauvage, the Black Friars lay beside the Fleet Ditch at the bottom of Ludgate Hill. It is hard not to see the disease's wasting weakness in the face of the twenty-one-year-old Pocahontas.

Much more pleasing to the Anglo-American eye is the well-known painting derived from the Van de Passe engraving, in which she appears healthy and well able to pass for an English lady. Under it is written "Matoaks als Rebecka daughter to the mighty Prince Powhatan Emperour of Attanoughkomouck als Virginia converted and baptized in the Christian faith, and Wife to the wor^{ll} Mr Tho: Rolff." The inscription was appended to the two engravings, but there Pocahontas's husband's first name was John.

No one has established the portrait's date, but having the long "Tho Rolff" inscription under it—something rarely appended to contemporary family portraits—suggests it, or another from which it was copied, was painted for promotion, perhaps by a tavern sign painter to hang in the Belle Sauvage as a reminder of its celebrated lodger.

But, as the inn burned in the 1666 fire, we may ask how the painting escaped the flames. The first documentation was not until 1882, when the painting's owner, the Rolfe-family-related Hastings Elwin of Booton Hall in Norfolk, wrote that the portrait had been handed down to him by his grandfather, who, in turn, had been given it by a Mrs. Zuccelli. Elwin thought it possible that her husband had been the painter, but no artist of that name has been identified.

The painting likely was copied from the second Anglicized engraving, but though the face is well done, the treatment of the clothing is hurried and unconvincing. The value of the Booton Hall portrait is in colors, which may or may not have been right, and on which most subsequent copiers relied. In 1993, New York artist the Reverend Richard Tinker combined the original engraving with the colors derived from the painting, more accurately, I think, reconstructing Pocahontas's appearance when she sat for Van de Passe two months or so before her death.

There are unanswered questions about the Rolfes' stay at the Belle Sauvage, but a case can be made that the death of Powhatan's dearest daughter can be laid at the Virginia Company of London's door in the clouds of all-pervading coal-laden smog. Of its dangers I can attest, nearly having been asphyxiated in the Great London Smog of December 1952, when in four days close to 4,000 died of sulphur-dioxide poisoning.

Footprints on the Past

Tracking the First English-American Shoemakers

When the first Virginia Company colonist set foot on the Jamestown shore, he left in the sand the impression of a shoe. At a glance, the fact looks too pedestrian to be worth putting down, but look again. When civilization gains fresh ground, it goes about the business shod, and shoeprints are the marks it makes on the landscapes of discovery. We speak of exploration in such phrases as "the first to set foot on," "the first to step on," "the first to walk on." From the banks of the James River to the mares of the moon, the impressions of men's small steps are of the tread of their shoes on new soil.

The one at Jamestown was, most likely, of a hand-sewn leather example of English-made footgear. It was as high tech for 1607, perhaps, as Neil Armstrong's machine-stitched, rubber and Teflon-coated nylon boot was for 1969. No one in Virginia that May 14 recorded for posterity the first colonist's footfall, or his name, or what he said, but he probably wore a pair of black, low-cut, well-tanned shoes, studded perhaps with hobnails. Those shoes and the pairs on the feet of the other 104 settlers were essential to set on foot such an enterprise as a trading colony.

Captain John Smith wrote that twenty-four tradesmen and others arrived with him that spring. He didn't say whether among them there were shoemakers, but shoemakers were needed, and sooner rather than later.

We can be almost certain shoemakers arrived as early as 1610. Maybe earlier. In any event, shoemakers invested money in the Jamestown venture at least as early as 1609, as did their guild, and shoemaking was among the industries the Virginia Company of London worked to establish before the firm collapsed in 1624.

Author and shoemaker D.A. Saguto poses on the Jamestown shore wearing shoes he copied from a circa-1606 pair made in Watford, England.

Organized much like a seventeenth-century army unit, the expedition had a hierarchy of ranks. Like Smith, some of the settlers had fought in the Low Countries. Centuries later, an English general was asked what equipment was most important to a soldier. He said, "First, a good, serviceable pair of shoes; second, another good serviceable pair of shoes; and third, a pair of half soles."

The earliest surviving list of recommended apparel for the would-be English Virginian was written for servants going to Smythe's Plantation in 1618. On it are three pairs of shoes and repair supplies—soles, thread, awls, pitch, and rosin—worth 1½ times all other articles of regular clothing combined.

In the twelve months after Jamestown's founding, two ships from England called on the settlement. Among the passengers in the first were jewelers, refiners, goldsmiths, six tailors, a blacksmith, and 120 others. Whether there was a shoemaker in this lot either, we can't say. Yet it is as likely as not, and, if six tailors landed, it is reasonable to think shoemakers could not be far behind. Fourteen more unidentified tradesmen were aboard the second vessel. Still no shoemakers named, but in the Spanish archives is information that, by early 1609, the company was recruiting them.

A letter from the Spanish ambassador in England to his King Philip enclosed a transcript of an English document circulated to encourage tradesmen to enlist for a Virginia voyage. Shoemaking is among the fifteen trades named. According to the ambassador, the Virginia Company offered all a bounty to go.

Among the new shareholders when the king of England rechartered the Virginia Company in 1609 were shoemakers William Brown and Robert Barker. Whether any shoemaker, at the encouragement of such associates, accepted the bounty and traveled to Virginia the record doesn't say. If he did, he likely regretted it.

That October, the Starving Time began. Governor George Percy wrote, "All was fishe thatt Came to Nett to satisfye Crewell hunger, as to eate Bootes shoes or any other leather some Colde come by." The settlers partook of cats, rats, mice, and human corpses—which makes shoe leather sound almost palatable.

That June, the new governor, Thomas West, Lord De La Warr, arrived. According to the company, De La

Gazing into the river from Jamestown Island, Captain John Smith wears a
pair of boots that foppishly contrast with the footwear he probably wore.

Warr brought 150 men from nine occupations, including tanners and shoemakers. Thus, we can be sure the first shoemaker reached Jamestown no later than June 10, 1610, when De La Warr landed.

That year, and again in 1611, the company also sent over "For the Colony in Virginia Britannia Lawes Divine, Morall and Martiall," which reduced Virginia to martial law. The penalty for stealing any commodities from the company store, among them shoes, was death. That provision suggests, as has been supposed, ready-made footwear was being stocked at Jamestown by then.

In January 1611, the company printed a broadside giving notice "to so many honest and industrious men, as Carpenters, Smiths, Coopers, Fishermen, Tanners, Shoemakers, Shipwrights, Brickmen, Gardeners, Husbandmen, and labouring men of all sorts . . . upon such termes as their qualitie and fitnesse shall deserve" to apply to emigrate to Virginia. A more detailed, but undated list numbers men in sixty-six trades and professions. Included were two tanners, two last-makers, two shoemakers, and an unspecified number of leather dressers. Last-makers carved the wooden forms, or lasts, over which the shoemakers made shoes.

In 1616, settler John Rolfe wrote that "smithes, carpenters, shoemakers, tailors, tanners &c. doe worke in their professions for the colony, and mayntayne themselves with food and apparrell."

The first Virginia shoemaker whose name comes down to us was Christopher Nelme of Bristol, England. Nelme had a three-year contract—two years' wages paid in advance—and a bounty of seventy acres of land. He sailed September 15, 1619, on the *Margaret* with a cargo of shoe thread, hobnails, and another form of long, thin, headless, sole-protecting nails aptly named sparrowbills. Awls for stitching, "clowt" leather for resoling worn shoes, and 200 pairs of ready-made shoes were on the manifest, too. Nelme did not long survive; the muster roll for colonists sent in the *Margaret* was annotated by December 1620, when he was marked as dead. His wife, still at home in Bristol, was to be paid his third year's wages.

Other shoemakers in other colonies, such as Thomas Beard and Isaac Rickman, who landed in Massachusetts in 1629, have been given first-American shoemakers' honors. They arrived ten years after Nelme,

A seventeenth-century engraving from John Smith's *Generall Historie* depicting the capture of Captain Smith by Virginia Indians in 1607. The open-sided shoes resemble archaeological finds on the Jamestown site.

however, and, for all we know, there may have been shoemakers among the Spanish tradesmen who paraded in 1571 at the Santa Elena settlement, now South Carolina's Parris Island.

In July 1620, the Virginia Company published another plea for shoemakers, tanners, and leather dressers, among thirty-four tradesmen to go to Virginia, and ready-made imports seemed to continue strong. Nevertheless, in 1625, after the company charter was recalled, a faction of the firm wrote: "There is most extreme want of hose, shooes, & all apparrell, even to a dangerous empeachement of their healthes." The following year the Virginia General Assembly prohibited shoemakers, among others, from using "their science or trades at home or abroad for any strangers or foreigners without the consent of the Governor and Council." The implication is that their goods were too badly needed at home. The General Court also prohibited Virginians from forestalling the market in such badly needed imported goods as shoes.

"Cordwainer" is a formal title for shoemaker. It derives from the medieval legal designation for workers in cordwain leather produced at Cordoba, Spain. The term was used by such guilds as the Worshipful Company of Cordwainers in London. The largest consumer of leather in the city, the Worshipful Company controlled all the London leather trades. It was, as well, among the shareholders of the Virginia Company.

When Captain Smith published his *Generall Historie of Virginia, New-England, and the Summer Isles* in 1624, he attempted to list all of the investors and dedicated thirty copies to London's trades guilds. His list overlooked the cordwainers, but of these thirty books, only its dedicated copy of the *Generall Historie* survives. Smith's handwritten inscription says, in part:

Worthie Gentlemen,
Not only in regard to your Courtisie and Love, Butt also of the Continuall use I have had of your Labours . . . I salute you. . . . for want of Shooes among the Oyster Banks wee tore our hatts and Clothes and those being worne, wee tied the Barkes of trees about our Feete to keepe them from being Cutt by the shelles amongst which we must goe or starve, yett how many thousand of Shooes hath been transported to these plantations, how many soldiers, Marriners and Saylers have bin and are likely to be encased thereby, what vent your Commodities have had and still have, and how many Shipps and men of all Faculties have bin and are yearlie imployed I leave to your own Judgements, and yett by reason of ill managding, the Returns have neither answered the generall Expectations, nor my desire.

These do not read like the words of a member of the cordwainers' company. But outside of St. Mary-le-Bow church, Cheapside—the shoemaking district of medieval London—stands a bronze statue of Smith erected in 1960 by the Jamestown Foundation (precursor to the Jamestown-Yorktown Foundation) to mark the 350th anniversary of his return from the New World. It is a version of the statue that stands on the shoreline of Jamestown Island, in which Smith, doubtfully complete in swaggering boots, gazes out over the James. The London copy is inscribed: "Captain John Smith, Citizen and Cordwainer, 1580–1631." Nearly obscured by trees and pigeons in an out-of-the-way corner of the bustling city, the statue stands at the top of what was the old Cordwanestrate, or Cordwainer Street.

When archaeologist John L. Cotter investigated Jamestown Island in the 1950s, he recovered about seventy-five shoe and leather fragments from three abandoned wells. They suggest the kind of shoes Smith—as well as his fellow colonists—more likely wore, the kind he sports in seventeenth-century engravings.

Some of the well shafts were lined with barrels to support their soft walls, and all were used as seventeenth-century trash pits. Two of them are about fifty yards from the James River beach. The other was on the island's eastern end.

In Well 20, as it is identified, about 100 feet to the east of a structure Cotter provisionally dubbed the First State House, most of the fragments were of men's shoes, reflecting the predominantly male population of early Jamestown. The oldest, or first, things discarded down the well were forty-nine shoe and leather fragments preserved in the waterlogged bottom layers of soil. The styles dated solidly to the first half of the seventeenth century. It was, in any case, as good a neighborhood as Jamestown offered at the time, and some of the shoes were high fashion. They incorporated a relatively new fad, heels, stylish in England since about 1590. This well also produced such newer artifacts as broken clay tobacco pipes, a liquor bottle, some local and some English pottery, all 1620–50.

In barrel-lined Well 21, about 400 feet east, Cotter found the remains of a man's shoe bottom with a wooden heel inside a leather heel cover. The shaft yielded ten more shoe fragments, as well as a sword hilt, a halberd—the iron head of an axe-like polearm—a delft jar, and more clay pipe fragments. The shoe with the covered wooden heel was the sort of footwear proper to gentlemen, of which, Smith said, the colony had an overplus.

An example of the style can be seen in a 1618 portrait of a member of England's Sackville family—a clan that, coincidentally, invested in the Virginia Company. It was an open-sided tie shoe. The ties were concealed beneath decorative, frilly shoe roses, and there were large rounded holes in either side of the uppers.

Similar shoes with these holes in the sides, some larger, some smaller, were worn universally. Depending on the wearer, the design might be less elegant, and the leather might be less costly.

All shoes found at Jamestown were, where style could be deduced, open-sided. In any case, the open-side fashion was generally abandoned later in the 1600s. The holes allowed sand, water, mud, and muck to accumulate inside.

Among the archaeological artifacts recovered at Martin's Hundred, downriver from Jamestown, was a small, rusted, master shoemaker's knife of late-medieval form. At the same site, in the 1970s, archaeologist Ivor Noël Hume led a team of Colonial Williamsburg archaeologists who found the remains of homes, forts, storehouses, and more. From a 1622 grave, they recovered a clod of earth containing the remains of a human foot and its shoe. Two shoe experts consulted about the shoe with Ivor and Audrey Noël Hume in May 1987. Initial X-rays, the recovery of the nails in the laboratory, scrutiny, correspondence, and research revealed the remains of a leather shoe that had been reinforced with hobnails. Shorter-shanked nails had their points properly clinched so as not to gouge the wearer's foot, and multiple rows of slightly longer-shanked hobnails reinforced the outside edge of the heel from wear. In the ship with Nelme were 2,000 sparrow bills and 1,000 three-penny hobnails.

The National Park Service, which has custody of Jamestown Island, began in 1987 to reassess, recatalogue, and earmark thousands of the island's seventeenth-century artifacts, including shoes, for further conservation. Local archaeologists, specialists, and scholars from other institutions participated.

The newest shoe, or, less likely, a man's boot, may date to between the late 1660s and 1680. It had a three-

Perhaps the oldest-style, complete, English example so far discovered in North America, this child's shoe was found in a well on Virginia's Eastern Shore and may have been made locally.

inch-high tapering leather heel built up from dozens of thin layers, or lifts of scrap leather called jumps, into what might be the style the English called the Polony, or Polish-style, heel. This example was roughly octagonal in cross-section and crudely reinforced with two rose-head carpentry nails about three and three-eighths inches long. They were driven all the way through the heel from inside the boot or shoe, exposing the nail heads under the wearer's heel.

The sole had a fashionable square toe of the Restoration period, nearly three inches broad, which had come loose in places and been hastily tacked back on with a few hobnails, small nails usually with a prominent head used off and on in thicker-soled utilitarian footwear since the days of Imperial Rome. They, too, were hammered in from the inside, rather than from the outside as usual, which may have made the shoes unwearable. The wrong nails used for the wrong job, the wrong way, imply that the wearer, not a shoemaker, might have tried to mend the sole. Hobnails were added to the bottoms to protect leather soles from wear and tear and enhance traction on slippery ground.

The thick leather upper had a high, blocked toe shape that overhung the sole at the corners and probably dragged on the ground.

This shoe or boot, parts from five other shoes, and pieces of unidentifiable leather were recovered from another well near the Travis Graveyard, a few miles from

Also found was a well-worn woman's shoe with a wooden heel covered in leather. By this date, these covered, shaped wooden heels were predominantly for women's shoes. Men preferred straighter-sided, layered leather heels. The toe of this shoe was forked, a style known in England from 1612 or so. The sole ended in two pointed, horn-like shapes that flared out to either side at the corners of what would otherwise be a square toe.

Among other shoe fragments recovered were three probably made by one Virginia artisan. They were roughly sewn and showed tool marks made by the same square-hole punch. Besides the shoes and shoe fragments, there were scraps and trimmings of leather, attesting to shoemaking or shoe repair nearby.

Before 1649, Captain Samuel Matthews, a planter for more than thirty years, had set up an industrial estate on his Warwick County plantation, Matthews Manor, near what is now Denbigh at Newport News. He employed eight shoemakers to manufacture shoes from leather produced in his tannery.

After 1650, as population expanded and a more stable society developed, shoemakers, tanners, and other tradespeople began to emerge as important elements in Virginia society as well as the colonial economy. In 1660, the General Assembly enacted laws to control Virginia's budding shoe trade. One ordered each of Virginia's seventeen counties either to erect or to designate existing operations to operate at county expense as "one or more tanhouses, and . . . provide tanners, curryers and shoemakers, to tanne, curry, and make the hides of the country into leather and shoes." Between 1653 and 1658, licenses in England were granted to export more than 45,600 pairs of shoes to Virginia, setting up a competitive economic environment between locally produced and imported goods that vexed the colonies until the Revolution.

By the 1770s, the shoemaking business, represented by the Shoemaker's Shop on Williamsburg's Duke of Gloucester Street, had become one of the two or three largest shopkeeping occupations in Virginia. Despite a halting start, step by step, it became one of the leading industries in the United States.

Jamestown proper. Most of the Jamestown shoes identified belong to the colony's first twenty years and come from the New Towne area just east of the 1607 fort site.

In the summer of 1987, eight seventeenth-century well shafts—some reinforced by wooden boxes sunk into the sand, others barrel lined like the ones at Jamestown—were excavated on Virginia's Eastern Shore. The site, named Church Neck Wells, is on Nassawadox Creek in Northampton County. The wells were on a parcel of land patented in 1638 by Stephen Carleton.

The artifacts dated to between 1670 and 1700. Eight to ten shoes were recovered, including a complete child's shoe—at this writing, in 2000, still by far the best-preserved, complete English shoe of its style excavated in North America. It had been altered with a slit down the front to accommodate a growing foot.

"accepte our poore indevour"

beseeched the first burgesses, as government
by legislature was born in the New World

Was it a hot, hazy day that Friday, the 20th day of July in 1619? Was it one of those steam-bath Peninsula days when the usual thunderstorm comes rip-roaring out of the southwest hell-bent for the Chesapeake, dragging its torrential skirts across the Tidewater but leaving the rest of the afternoon just as hot and humid as before?

What was it like on the birthday of government by legislature in the Americas?

For one thing, there was a church in what was then James Towne, a rough-hewn village on a swampy peninsula now linked to land by only a causeway; we know it today as Jamestown Island. This sturdy wooden sanctuary was the town's third since sea-weary settlers waded ashore on May 14, 1607, and set about building a colony.

There was a bustle of activity, too. Gentlemen of substance had swelled somewhat the population of this little city of a few hundred souls, straggling in from the nearby plantations and the far fringes of civilization a few miles beyond. Planters and townsmen traded nods as the little church drew them all to its door like filings to a magnet.

Inside, the rustle of seat-taking and the murmur of last-minute small talk fell away to a hush as the governor, Sir George Yeardley, stepped into "The Quire" and settled in the seat he warmed every Sabbath. But this was not the Lord's Day; this was a day to debate and petition and resolve. And so, as was the custom in the House of Commons back in England, the men all kept their hats on and referred to themselves as "burgesses."

John Pory, secretary of the colony, had already been named speaker—probably by the governor—and had planned out the whole ceremony and coached each delegate in what to do. He took his seat in front of the governor and watched the governor's council take seats along the sides.

Representation of the 1619 General Assembly painted by Jack Clifton in 1969, displayed at the Capitol in Richmond.

The Reverend Richard Buck intoned a prayer. At the "Amen," the burgesses entered the cramped little nave, the main body of the church, where worshippers sat of a Sabbath. One by one as their names were called, they took an oath of fealty to the crown and the Church of England, then joined the governor and council in the choir. To get there, they had to pass by the railing that separated the choir from the nave. None was officially a burgess until he had symbolically "passed the bar."

Thus the first session of the first representative legislature in the New World began.

Well, not quite. Controversy erupted even before all the delegates sat down. When Captain John Warde's name was called, Speaker Pory objected because Warde didn't hold his land by proper patent and thus he and his second, Lieutenant John Gibbes, could not qualify as burgesses. Warde and Gibbes passed the bar before the day was out, seated by unanimous vote because Warde

had been a hard-working planter and loyal colonist; because the assembly was supposed to include two burgesses from each plantation; and because he vowed to correct the glitch before the meeting next year. Which he did.

More controversy: Governor Yeardley challenged Captain John Martin's two burgesses, Robert Stacy and Thomas Davis, on the grounds that the 1617 patent for Martin's Brandon plantation exempted him "from any commaunde of the Colony, excepte it be in ayding and assisting the same agst any forren or domestical Enemy." Why should his burgesses be allowed to make laws he didn't have to obey?

Besides, the cantankerous Captain Martin was no paragon of loyalty to the colony. He'd squabbled with another planter over cattle, and his people had ruffled some Indian feathers; wasn't there enough trouble with the Indians already? Martin's burgesses were sent packing.

Thus, right from the start, the infant legislature made it clear that it expected to be taken seriously. Allegiance to the crown, the church, and the company was all well and good, but allegiance to the colony was essential.

And what did the crown and the company think of all this? How had they permitted, indeed encouraged, such a dilution of their own power?

It's tempting to imagine this as a noble experiment, the first brick in the grand design of a lofty temple of liberty. And indeed, as things turned out over the next few centuries, it was that. But it was also a necessary business decision forced by an ugly fact: The company was tearing itself apart by factional infighting and was going broke.

And no wonder. From the start, it had been underfunded and overconfident for the kind of enterprise it launched. Chartered in 1606, the Virginia Company of London wooed investors with the same high hopes as earlier companies: to find gold, to discover a sea lane to the treasures of the Orient, to "recover out of the armes of the Divell a number of poore and miserable souls, wrapt up in death, in almost invincible ignorance."

But wise men now chose wiser goals. The cure for gold fever was a healthy dose of reality, and by this time the golden fantasy no longer glittered in the sober gaze of men like Sir Edwin Sandys. One of the chief architects of the company's destiny, this far-seeing shareholder perhaps more than any other had influenced king and company to let the governed share in governing.

The Virginia Company was a new kind of business enterprise, for it sought its fortune not by a sudden bonanza—though that was always a heady possibility—but by trading and the patient exploitation of natural resources. Compared to finding El Dorado or the Northwest Passage, it was a plodding process that involved setting up an outpost in the wilderness thousands of miles away and then waiting for crops to grow, or mines to be dug, or industries to develop.

With no real precedent for such a venture, the company sent over shiploads of colonists—some of them criminals whose brawn was deemed too valuable to waste by execution; some of them gentlemen exempted from manual labor; some of them brash adventurers with little taste for the trades. Poorly provisioned, the colonists were expected to feed, shelter, and defend themselves while shipping back to the company an endless bounty of furs, fish, whatever.

The colonists tried splitting logs into clapboards for England's carpenters, but when Indians nearly overran their puny palisade of brush, the loggers quickly turned to fort-building instead. They tried glassmaking, but that failed. They tried making tar and silk, burning lime, smelting iron, but each dream went up in smoke.

Then came the dream that was supposed to go up in smoke: tobacco. Colonists used the "golden weed" as money. Barrels of it thudded into the holds of ships bound for England. Soldiers of fortune began to sink roots as planters, clearing woodlands for croplands that in time would grow into some of the great plantations along the James River shores.

Too late; the Virginia Company was mortally wounded from within and up to its taffrails in financial obligations. From the start, it had managed its colony through a resident governor and council subservient to the company's stockholders in London. But as the company weakened, so did its council's credibility among the colonists.

Well, they weren't the best of colonists in the first place. "Lascivious sonnes, masters of bad servants, and wives of ill husbands," the company once called them. Small wonder they muttered of splintering the colony and quitting this "paradise" for good.

Some had already tried. When the new governor, Sir Thomas Gates, arrived at James Towne in 1610, he had expected a warm welcome from industrious colonists dwelling in a well-ordered settlement. Instead he found a dilapidated slum peopled by ragtag malcontents fed up with mosquitoes, Indians, hunger, disease, bad water, the hot and humid summers, a horrendous death rate, and neglect by the company that was supposed to be supporting and supplying them.

Soon after, Lord De La Warr sailed up the James River from England and met Gates and four sorry shiploads of colonists sailing down the river for Newfoundland. They had even wanted to burn the ramshackle settlement behind them, but Gates, at Martin's insistence, had dissuaded them, for "we know not but that as homeless men as ourselves may come and inhabit here."

It was a prescient move, for by nightfall the deserters were back in the dilapidated village themselves, ordered to return by Lord De La Warr. After a tongue-lashing for their "many vanities and their idleness," De La Warr reorganized the colonists and set them to repairing, replanting, and restoring the colony they had sought to abandon. He soon had to leave it himself, desperately ill with one of the diseases that had decimated the colony and helped dishearten its people.

Gates, and especially his successor, Sir Thomas Dale, ruled the colony with iron discipline under the "Lawes Divine, Morall and Martiall." Miscreants were flogged or strung up by their thumbs with weights on their feet. Defiance could mean death. It was martial law with a vengeance.

Harsh discipline was probably necessary for that group in that circumstance. And such punishments were certainly not unknown back home in England. And they certainly were not unknown to Governor Yeardley, when he stepped aboard a ship in London in January 1619, with a pivotal document from the company under his arm: the Charter of Grants and Liberties.

It was a wordy treatise, this so-called "Great Charter," for it had much to set aright in the tangled affairs of the colony: the granting of lands, the collection of taxes and quit-rents, the treatment of Indians, and myriad other loose ends not the least of which was placating a restive group of colonists tired of the lash and the pillory.

When he got to James Towne, Yeardley proclaimed that "those cruell lawes" were abrogated and announced that, so the colonists "might have a hande in the governinge of themselves, it was granted that a generall assemblie should be helde yearly once, whereat were to be present the Govr and Counsell with two Burgesses freely to be elected by the inhabitants thereof."

How elected? By show of hands, perhaps, or "by the major part of voices," as in 1624. And by which inhabitants? Certainly not the women, children, or convicts. Males over sixteen were obliged to "pay into the hands . . . of the burgess one pound of the best tobacco . . . to be distributed to the speaker" for the assembly's expenses. So it seems likely that they were the voters whose hands or voices sent twenty-two men to the colony's capital that hot July to hammer out "what-

soever lawes and orders should by them be thought good and proffittable for our subsistence."

The newborn legislature proved a precocious youngster. Despite the numbing heat, the illness of several burgesses, and the death of one in mid-session, the fledgling assembly formed committees, drew up proposals to the company for changes in the colony's charter, passed laws on everything from morals to a dress code, weighed entreaties from the colonists—even one from Powhatan chieftain Opechancanough—petitioned for its acts to take immediate effect without waiting for the company's approval, asked the company's permission to disapprove any laws it sent over, reconvened on its closing day to review and reaffirm its works—and did it all and more in a scant six days!

The burgesses even apologized to the company for their "poore indevour" and asked it "to supporte the weakness of this little flocke." In 1621 the company agreed that "no orders shall bind the colony unless they be ratified in the general assembly." This was England's first successful colony, and the idea was beginning to jell that the best way to run it from the far side of an ocean might be to let it help run itself.

It was an idea whose time had not yet come. Despite the counsel of men like Sandys, many on both sides of the ocean deemed the idea untested, the time unripe, the colony unready.

Then, suddenly, the colony was almost undone. On March 22, 1622, Indians stormed more than thirty plantations, burning and massacring at will, and left Virginia reeling "in great amazement and ruine." Dismay and confusion followed the "deadly stroake." For that year and the next, history is unsure that the burgesses even met. Probably the governor and council alone ruled "the stragglinge and woefull inhabitants, soe dismembered" by the devastating attack.

Not until 1624 does the record show that the burgesses again formally assembled at James Towne. This time they had to face a royal inquiry into just what was going on in the colony and its moribund parent. It would be the last assembly under the Virginia Company.

Scarcely a face reappeared from that first assembly of five years before. John Pory was there, but now the former speaker, who had since returned to England, was

The speaker of the House of Burgesses, portrayed here by Wayne Moss, was always a man of experience, means, and stature in the colony. Presiding over the meetings, he commanded order and decorum as much through the personal respect due him as through the high station and powers of his office. He could—and did—have burgesses like Thomas Jefferson taken into custody for nonattendance, and his word was law within the hall of the House. The last speaker, Williamsburg's Peyton Randolph, was the first president of the Continental Congress.

▶ The ceremonial mace of the House of Burgesses symbolized the power and might it exercised by the right of the king's grant of the Virginia charters. Placed on the central table in front of the speaker of the House when the assembly was in session, it was borne in and out of the chamber by the clerk, portrayed here by David DeSimone.

The interpreters who appear in the House of Burgesses reenactment photographs are as follows: Willie Balderson, John Barrows, Stan Beadle, Dan Bjick, Phillip Bond, Charles Bush, Robert Campbell, Bob Chandler, David DeSimone, Bill Ferguson, Ryan Fletcher, Jack Flintom, Stephen Furey-Moore, John Greenman, John Hamant, Art Hopper, Mark Howell, Carson Hudson, Don Kline, John Labanish, Bob Lawler, Russ Lawson, Jim Loba, Harriott Lomax, John Lowe, Jim McDonald, Wayne Moss, Charlie Red, Mark Sowell, Peter Stinely, Louis Vosteen, Robb Warren, Bill Weldon, Tim Wilson, and Garland Wood.

Evocative tableau in the Hall of the House of Burgesses animates Williamsburg's past. Front and center is black-robed George Wythe—impersonated by Don Kline—who served for many years as clerk.

The royal governor, portrayed here by John Hamant, was first among
equals when the governor's council gathered on the second floor of the
Capitol in what was quite literally the Virginia General Assembly's upper
chamber.

back in the colony as one of the king's five inquisitors. So the burgesses rejected their old colleague's request to sign papers critical of the company. And when the burgesses refused to hand over some of the assembly's important papers—its own courier would deliver them to England, thank you—Pory had to bribe the clerk, Edward Sharpless, to get them.

For that, the hapless Sharpless nearly went earless. The governor and council clapped him in the pillory with his ears nailed to it, after which he was supposed to leave without them. "Why?" growled John Martin, as crusty now as five years before. "For disclosinge of the Secretts and Councell of the Governor and Counceill," replied the council. To which Martin hoped aloud "to see some of them sitt there them selves shortly and doubted not but some of them would wish his eares one againe shortly."

Sharpless kept his ears, forfeiting only a piece of one of them. But the incident only added to the growing wrangle between colony, company, and crown. And two of the three were about to lose.

By the time John Pory got back to England, the Virginia Company was history. And so, for the moment, was the colony's right to an assembly of burgesses. With the company gone, the king and his council ruled alone. The burgesses begged leave to continue their assembly, "then wch nothing can more conduce to our satisfaction or the publique utilitie," but their plea fell on deaf ears. Indeed, on dead ears: on March 27, 1625, King James died.

Most of the colony's rights and privileges were continued by his son, Charles I, and for this the colonists were much relieved. But to assemble as burgesses, to enact laws, to administer, to govern? The new monarch soon disposed of that question. "The Government of the Colonie of Virginia," he proclaimed, "shall immediately depend upon Our Selfe."

The colonists had a loophole: they could convene to handle a special circumstance if need be—the approval of a tobacco contract, the construction of a palisade. They began meeting occasionally, then annually; they even enacted laws without the king's say-so. They weren't being sneaky; they were simply handling local problems locally. And if the king knew—and surely he did—he didn't seem to mind. Why should he? For fifteen years after the company's demise, he dithered over just what form of local government the colony should have. If the colonists chose to fill the vacuum with assemblies like the ones held before, perhaps it pleased the crown to let them do it and see how it went.

At last the breakthrough came. In 1639 the king instructed his governor, Sir Francis Wyatt, to formally initiate a system of annual assemblies. To the next governor, Sir William Berkeley, the king repeated the mandate. From then on, the assembly of burgesses stood on the solid bedrock of royal approval.

The colonists had kept it alive through fifteen years of neglect by king and council. Now the colonists would enjoy the fruits of self-government and pass to their American posterity from Ottawa to Buenos Aires the grand idea of a representative legislature. A year before the Pilgrims landed at Plymouth, the people of Virginia had begun to work out the basic equation of checks and balances that today apportions political power between the legislative, the executive, and the judicial.

It's one of history's little jokes that an achievement that changed the world took place on a piece of land that has fewer inhabitants now than it did after the first colonists settled there. The little wooden church, the triangular stockade, the slapdash stick-and-mud huts that served the first adventurers as homes and shops and storerooms—if we would glimpse any, we must dig and deduce, for not a trace of them remains above ground. No great city juts from the brushy woods that overgrow the island today.

But then, none ever did. James Towne, James Citty, Jamestown—by whatever name, the colony's first capital never mustered more than 500 residents, never reared more than a sprinkle of brick buildings, and never let its townspeople forget that they were living on the edge of noxious swampland.

When the new statehouse—the town's fourth—burned in 1698, Jamestown's prospects turned to ashes with it. The burgesses voted to move the capital to Middle Plantation, seven miles inland, and rename that little settlement Williamsburg for "our most gratious and glorious King William." The colonists left behind a small village that had been England's toehold in the New World and the colony's capital for almost a century. Now, bereft of its heart and role, plucky little James Towne slowly nodded off and died in its sleep.

Remembering what happened to those first four statehouses, Williamsburg's planners built an imposing new Capitol with no fireplaces to warm it, no candles to light it, and no smoking within the chilly chambers of the court, the council room, and the assembly hall. But who could legislate in the dark, or debate with teeth chattering, or regulate the planting of tobacco without pulling a pipeful? House rules of a later year said you couldn't even chew the stuff if the speaker was in his seat!

The burgesses soon forgot their fears. Cheery fireplaces and proper chimneys were added to the building. Candleglow lit it bright—and raging flames lit it even brighter as it burned to the ground in 1747.

This is the building re-created in present-day Williamsburg, as naked of chimneys as the original.

Other walls arose to echo the thunderclap rhetoric of burgess Patrick Henry. Other rippled panes illumined the page as burgess Thomas Jefferson scratched his notes and memos. But the assembly was still called the House of Burgesses, as it had come to be known in James Towne. And, like its earliest prototype in the small wooden church, the House of Burgesses in the 1770s was again reinventing government.

As that crucial decade dawned, the government of the Virginia colony bore a strong family resemblance to its sire of 1619: a governor, his council, and duly elected burgesses. Jefferson was one of them, and although rumors of revolt hung heavy in the air, he was still referring to the colonies as "British America."

He insisted, as had the first burgesses, that those who lived in a colony knew best how to run it. Indeed, it was their right to run it, and neither Parliament nor governor could say them nay. If they didn't allow a legislature to meet, he argued, then the people could do it anyway "to unlimited extent, either assembling together in person, sending deputies, or in any other way they may think proper." So when Virginia's last royal governor, Lord Dunmore, declared the House of Burgesses dissolved in 1774, nearly every town and county in the Virginia colony formed a committee to take over many of the functions of local government and joined hands to thwart the governor and revive the boycott of imports from England.

They also continued to send their representatives to a legislative assembly. But after convening for the last

Young Virginia gentlemen closely studied and carefully practiced the arts of oratory as they prepared to take their parts in the life of the colony. But it was a gift that came naturally to Patrick Henry, portrayed here by interpreter Bill Weldon. The power of persuasion, however, was not confined to men who could speak on their feet. Thomas Jefferson considered himself so poor a public speaker that he seldom addressed the House and, as president, preferred to submit his addresses to Congress in writing.

time in May 1776, it never again would be known as the House of Burgesses. Just as well, perhaps, for the name was never quite accurate anyway. "Burgess" sprouts from Latin roots: "Burgensis" meant a freeman "from a city." Actually, the Virginia House of Burgesses had reflected county representation since 1634.

During the Revolution the capital of Virginia pulled up stakes one final time, as the seat of government—state government now—shifted upriver to Richmond. The ancient assembly of burgesses was reborn as the lower house in the commonwealth's legislature, its members representing the local jurisdictions much the same as the original burgesses had represented each "corporation"—borough, hundred, and plantation—in the infant colony.

A semblance of the old governor's council lingered in the upper house, for it, too, was smaller than its counterbalance; and it, too, tended to draw its members from the aristocracy—not the favorites of a distant king but the bluebloods of the great plantations.

The two houses shared the right to elect a governor. They also shared—and still share—a new name that echoed the old: the Virginia General Assembly.

It's a different assembly from the one that met at Williamsburg. Persons of varied roots occupy its seats today, and the voters who elect them elect the governor as well. But, like legislatures throughout the Americas and beyond, the Virginia General Assembly can trace its form and function to a meeting four centuries ago of a score of men sweltering in a little wooden church in the wilderness.

Historical Rivalry

JAMES AXTELL

Virginia's Jamestown was the continent's first permanent English settlement. So how is it that Massachusett's Plymouth has precedence in the minds of so many Americans?

The site of the first permanent settlement in English America has an enduring image problem and a bit of an inferiority issue. Until the relatively recent rediscovery of the site of the original fort by William Kelso's intrepid band of archaeologists and its newsworthy finds, Jamestown has played second fiddle to the Plymouth Colony throughout the nation's postrevolutionary history.

Despite a thirteen-year age advantage, Jamestown has not secured the prime place in the American public's minds or hearts. School and college textbooks are not to blame: whatever else is wrong with them, their chronologies still assign precedence to 1607 Jamestown over 1620 Plymouth and the 1630 Massachusetts Bay Colony. Even the uneven quality of teaching and learning in our academies, as measured by standardized exit exams or jaw-dropping media polls, cannot explain why Jamestown is consistently rated the runner-up among early colonial icons. Something else is at work.

The question is twofold: Why does Plymouth command our national attention and affection? And why doesn't Jamestown?

Before we tackle those questions, we should recognize three other candidates for the "founding colony" prize, none of which ever wins enough primary votes to get on the ballot. The Spanish were in Florida early in the sixteenth century, first hoping to find more gold than Caribbean riverbeds and placer mines yielded and, when that proved

Jamestown and Plymouth vie for primacy in America's recollection of its history, Plymouth usually winning despite Jamestown's precedence. D. A. Saguto's Virginia soldier and Mike Durling's Massachusetts Pilgrim cold-shoulder each other.

◄ ▼ The ruins of Jamestown's brick church and Plymouth Rock are rival relics of settlement. The rock's authenticity is suspect.

elusive, to secure the Florida Strait for its returning treasure fleets from Central America and Havana. The murderous expulsion of an erstwhile colony of French Protestant "heretics" led to the founding of St. Augustine in 1565, which in turn gave Spain claim to at least chronological priority in the memory of all the Americas.

Another claimant is the short-lived English colony—or, more accurately, colonies—on Roanoke Island in the mid-1580s. Walter Ralegh's plan to plant a fortified privateering base just behind the Outer Banks was aimed at the Spanish *flotas,* which sailed on the Gulf Stream past Florida before heading home. Beset by poor planning, ferocious storms, and worse Indian relations, Roanoke can only make claim on the public memory for its unwelcome gift of "Virginia"—for the "Virgin Queen," Elizabeth I—to the proud colony of North Carolina and its mysterious but understandable disappearance. No one remembers the local Indian chiefs (in part because the leading one changed his name in medias res), the English military commander of the first colony, the largely absentee governor of the second, or the meaning of the letters "CRO" carved on the deserted fort.

Spain has another candidate, nearly as early as Jamestown, but because 1610's Santa Fe was founded in distant, dusty New Mexico, it has much less notice and only regional affection. The reason Hispanic places like St. Augustine and Santa Fe can't compete with the Anglo likes of Jamestown and Plymouth is that the Spanish carry some burden of the Black Legend, the largely Protestant and intensely English attribution of preternatural cruelty, greed, and bloodthirst to Europe's sixteenth-century heavyweight. Envying Spain's success in becoming rich and carving out a global empire, the English had to believe in their own religious purity and colonial altruism. When Great Britain and later the new United States were able to reduce Spain to impotence in eastern North America, nationalistic historians on the winning side, as is their wont, effectively wrote the losers out of the story, except as a moral foil.

Jamestown suffers from some of the bad press that Roanoke and the Spanish presidios get. Its goals were unworthy of the new nation's self-image, its early years were disastrous, its racial and ethnic record was shameful, and it barely survived into the eighteenth century.

As a creature of the Virginia Company of London, the joint-stock enterprise that sponsored the settlement, Jamestown was dominated by aggressive young men on the make. It attained none of its redeeming religious goals or moral schemes: profit for investors was its reason for being and martial law was often its mode of government. With an Anglican church and minister, it earned no historical credit as a refuge from religious persecution or bastion of tolerance. Gold lust and tobacco fever have never seemed worthy goads to colony or nation building, at least in retrospect.

Nor were the colony's early years filled with inspiring triumphs over adversity. Because it was built on a salty malarial swamp of an island, in the middle of one of the most powerful Indian confederacies in eastern America—the Powhatan—Jamestown lost more settlers than it sustained. Poor planning, inadequate supplies, and self-aggrandizing leaders caused widespread mortality during the infamous Starving Time. Ham-handed relations with the Powhatan's bellicose tribes led to wholesale death, particularly during the equally infamous native uprising of 1622, in which a third of the colonists were killed. The royal takeover of the colony two years later certified the company's failure to cope with American challenges. Another surprise attack in 1644, which killed more than five hundred Virginians, was more than enough to destroy the illusion of repaired Anglo-Indian relations.

Long before the Time-Warner film *The New World,* Jamestown provided the public with one icon of benign race relations. Americans feeling guilty about the nation's treatment of its native peoples embraced a fanciful image of Princess Pocahontas's romance with Captain John Smith, her willing conversion to Christianity, and her happy marriage to tobacco planter and widower John Rolfe. It mattered not that a bachelor-soldier in his thirties like Smith was an unlikely love interest for an Indian girl not yet in her teens, that she was kidnapped by the English and forcibly converted by an Anglican minister to whose house she was committed, and that her much older farmer-husband said he married her not for "carnall affection" but for the good of the plantation, England's honor, his own salvation, and the conversion of "an unbeleeving creature" to the true faith.

A re-creation of Jamestown's fort trails a dismal, distant second to the *Mayflower* as symbol of America's founding.

Jamestown has a better claim to iconic status on political grounds. In 1619, Virginia established an elected House of Burgesses to balance the near-dictatorial power of the governor and his council. This timid move toward representative democracy—only white, male heads of property-owning households could vote or have office—might have been more memorable had the assembly not first met in a daub-and-wattle church long since vanished, making pilgrimages less feasible.

Equally inconvenient is the colony's long and sordid history of black slavery, also begun in 1619 when a Dutch ship sold some of its African cargo as servants to labor-starved planters unable to obtain willing workers from the pugnacious Powhatans. When the town burned for the third time in 1693 and the colonial capital moved to Williamsburg six years later, visitors were left with one less reason to put the original settlement on their vacation itineraries.

When the National Park Service declared Jamestown a historic site in 1930, conducted archaeological excavations in 1934, and created a museum for the colony's 350th anniversary, the town consisted of remnants of house foundations and the tower ruins of the fourth—and first brick—church, burned during Bacon's Rebellion in 1676. Since it was believed—mistakenly—that the original fort site had eroded into the James River, the town's remains had the barest of interest for visitors; a fresh-built museum did little better.

To confound visitors more, and also in 1957, the state built an unfocused hodgepodge of a museum and replicas of the original fort and ships a short distance away on the mainland and called it Jamestown Festival Park—now Jamestown Settlement. This gave visitors a more accurate image of the founding English colony, but it was not on the original site and contained no authentic artifacts or monuments of iconic status.

Both sites, moreover, had to contend with the larger, more visitor-friendly, more patriotically oriented Rockefeller restoration of the colonial capital at Williamsburg, with its aesthetically pleasing Governor's Palace and historically charged Capitol not far from the College of William and Mary's restored Wren Building. Five miles from Jamestown, the Revolution at Williamsburg trumped the founding in America's memory.

Carmella Pocahontas Richardson, thirteen, portraying Pocahontas, and twenty-something Richard Peeling, as John Smith, are the same relative ages as their historical counterparts.

All of these circumstances allowed Plymouth to lay first claim on the public's attention, despite two minor similarities to its southern rivals. Like Roanoke, Plymouth might have been located in "Virginia." The Pilgrims had permission from the Virginia Company to settle within its chartered territory as far as forty-one degrees north. They were headed for the mouth of the Hudson River when they tangled with the sandy shoals of Cape Cod and chose to head north to a hospitable beach and a well-watered, partially cleared site soon to be christened "Plimoth."

Like Jamestown, the Plimoth colony lost half its population during its first year. Its settlers had arrived after a two-month voyage and weeks on the Cape in the teeth of a New England winter, without housing or adequate food and supplies. But unlike the Virginians, they never thought of leaving or made the attempt. They came and continued to come in families, headed by God-fearing patriarchs. And they were determined to raise their children in a purified Calvinist faith, separated from what they saw as England's social and ecclesiastical corruption and from the alien and worldly customs of the Dutch cities to which many of them had fled years before.

But Plymouth's other advantages were more numerous and lodged it indelibly in the new nation's mythic past. In addition to its religious mission and family orientation, Plymouth has at least half a dozen features that maintain its iconic lead over Jamestown. The first is the vessel of transfer. The Pilgrims came in the storied *Mayflower,* a single ship whose botanical name has graced a replica and is the instantly recognizable title of a current bestseller. The first Virginians made their passage in three unprepossessing craft, whose names are obscure even in Virginia households. When my teenage son worked as a Jamestown Settlement interpreter onboard the replica flagship *Susan Constant,* he was frequently asked whether the smaller *Godspeed* and *Discovery* were the *Niña* and the *Pinta.*

The *Mayflower* also lent its name to the compact that the passengers, lying off Cape Cod on November 11, 1620, drew up to govern themselves. Pledging "all due submission and obedience" to King James I, the forty-one adult male signers constituted themselves "a Civil

Body Politic" for the making and execution of laws for "the general good of the Colony." In all regards but one, this was an unexceptional document. Puritan church covenants were similar, and the Virginia Company had voted shortly after the Pilgrims left to allow leaders of "Particular Plantations" with their "gravest" advisors to establish laws and order until "a form of Government" could be "settled for them" in London. But the Pilgrims exercised an unusual degree of what their leader William Bradford called "liberty" because they had slipped beyond Virginia's patent into New England, "which belonged to another government, with which the Virginia Company had nothing to do." Virginia's installation of an elected assembly the year before required no such derring-do.

When the *Mayflower* moved to Plymouth and some of its male passengers disembarked, they allegedly set foot on a 200-ton boulder, set incongruously on the otherwise sand beach. There is no contemporary evidence for such an improbable landing—only the say-so of a ninety-five-year-old descendant of one of the founders—but the rocky advent has been immortalized in picture and verse ever since. As fixed as the rock is in America's iconology, it moved around as much as the Pilgrims themselves and wound up twenty times smaller than it began. Sliced like a bagel in 1774 for removal to Liberty Tree Square, the mobile top half accidentally split in two half a century later before the whole was mortared back together and enshrined in a variety of monumental cages on the waterfront. There it reigns today, greatly diminished by waves, weather, and the incessant demands of modern pilgrims for souvenirs and talismans of America's most famous arrival.

Compared with Jamestown's relations with its native neighbors, Plymouth's were a picnic. They did not begin that way on the Cape, where the hungry newcomers dug up Indian graves for keepsakes and caches of seed corn and helped themselves to choice items from abandoned wigwams. But they also carefully covered the graves and made restitution in trade goods as soon as they could. The presence of two English-speaking Indians, Samoset and Squanto, proved heaven-sent as the "Saints" navigated the tricky shoals of native politics and diplomacy. As every American schoolchild learns,

Jamestown still yields discoveries, and modern archaeology has reconstructed much about the early days of English settlement, but Jamestown
has not yet replaced Plymouth in the American imagination as birthplace
of the nation.

Squanto also taught them how to plant Indian corn with fish fertilizer and other American secrets of survival.

The following autumn, at an unknown date, the Pilgrims invited the Wampanoag sachem Massasoit and some of his people to a traditional English harvest festival. Fortunately, the Indians contributed five deer to the three-day celebration; the hosts had not reckoned on feeding the ninety men the chief brought with him. This equally iconic celebration of the First Thanksgiving—despite Virginia's claim of priority at Berkeley Plantation in 1619—was given lasting authority by President Abraham Lincoln during the Civil War when he declared Thanksgiving a national holiday. Countless artists have done the rest.

If Plymouth's historical assets were not enough to put it permanently ahead of Jamestown, it also enjoyed superior publicity. From the Revolution to late in the nineteenth century, New England was the arbiter, standard, and primary source of American culture. Its poets, novelists, orators, historians, and textbook writers saw to it that Plymouth became and remained America's "first" and best-known colony. Plymouth's last two centennials especially were grand occasions for reconfirming its place in the nation's memory. And when the outdoor history museum Plimoth Plantation was mounted in 1947, a decade before the re-creation at Jamestown, the New Englanders' lead was nigh insurmountable.

It remains to be seen whether the archaeological discoveries at the original fort and the rebuilt ships, reconfigured fort, and enlarged museum at Jamestown during its fourth centennial will give upstart Plymouth a run for its money.

"the tyme appointed"

MARY MILEY THEOBALD

The morning of March 22, 1622, Virginia's Powhatan Indian alliance executed a well-conceived and coordinated attack on English settlements spread more than fifty miles up and down the James River. Warriors from perhaps a dozen of the thirty-two affiliated tribes—Quiyoughcohannocks, Warraskoyacks, Weanocks, Appomatucks, Arrohatecks, and others—fell on men, women, and children in their homes and in their fields, burning houses and barns, killing livestock, mutilating the bodies of their victims. Planned by the Pamunkey headman Opechancanough, kinsman of the now-deceased paramount chieftain Powhatan, the offensive slew about 350 whites, a sixth of the total in the fifteen-year-old colony.

From modern Richmond to Hampton Roads, the onslaught devastated Jamestown's outlying plantations, but it failed of its purpose: stopping the relentless encroachment of the English. Settlers kept coming, expropriating native lands, killing Indians who got in the way, and twenty-two years later, Opechancanough organized a second attempt. About five hundred English died this time, but by 1644 there were so many colonists that the impact was not as severe, and a wave of retaliation reduced the Indian threat in Tidewater almost to a memory. A question lingered, however, one yet to be answered to everyone's satisfaction: How had Opechancanough synchronized the strikes of widely dispersed tribes against scattered targets across so many square miles?

Opechancanough, who became the leading chief—*werowance* was the Indians' word for headman—after Powhatan's death in 1618, kept in regular contact with the tribes of his realm, just as Powhatan had. Every Indian village was on or near the water and could be reached easily by canoe as well as by runners with memorized messages. But it's

A member of deceased artist Theodore de Bry's family in Strasbourg published this fanciful illustration of the first uprising. It depicted Jamestown,
in the background, as a fortified, moated village.

a safe bet those messages didn't command the warriors to "rise up at 8:00 A.M. on Friday, March 22." How did Opechancanough choose the date? What sort of calendar did the Indians use that allowed them to make simultaneous attacks?

Although our knowledge of the seventeenth-century Powhatans is sketchy—coming to us primarily through European observers during the early years of contact—it has been supplemented by archaeologists and anthropologists. Those who study the Virginia Indians agree that planning for the violence of 1622 had been under way for months, even years. Initially, the plan was keyed to the death ceremony for Powhatan, a ritual at which the tribes could gather for the raids.

Powhatan's body had been stored in a shrine at Uttamussack beside the Pamunkey River, in today's King William County. Dead *werowances* were not entombed until a few years had passed and the body had decomposed, so it was not until 1621 that, as an Englishman put it, the "takinge upp of Powhatans bones" would occur.

But that summer Opechancanough made a mistake. He misjudged the loyalty of Esmy Shichans, the ruler of the Accomacks and the Occohannocks on the Eastern Shore—the peninsula across the Chesapeake Bay from Tidewater. Esmy Shichans had drifted away from Powhatan influence into a more comfortable relationship with the English. George Percy, the son of an English earl and twice governor of the Virginia colony, wrote that Opechancanough

This representation of Opechancanough, from Smith's 1624 *Generall Historie,* is an adaptation of John White's 1580s watercolor of an Indian warrior.

> made strenuous efforts to obtain from another Indian king, whose land was very fertile in poisonous herbs, a large quantity of poison with the intention to therewith exterminate the English, but neither presents nor threats could induce this King to accede to the demands.

The herb was probably water hemlock, or *Cicuta maculata,* a lethal plant abundant on the Eastern Shore. Esmy Shichans refused to send the poison and alerted Jamestown. Opechancanough could do nothing but deny the plot and bide his time until the colonists had let down their guard.

Some English chroniclers believed that the attack of 1622 was a response to the killing of Nemattanow, an important *werowance,* or perhaps a shaman, known to the English as Jack of the Feather. Wrote Percy: "He used to come into the felde all covered over with feathers and Swans wings fastened unto his showlders as thowghe he meante to flye." Nemattanow said magic made him immune to English bullets. That may have made him a little too bold in his dealings with the colonists. When he returned alone from a trading trip wearing the hat of the colonist who had accompanied him, Nemattanow was suspected of murder. He was seized by servants of the missing man and shot.

"This occurence enraged King Opechankenough so that they say he swore to revenge the death of this Indian

Historians once thought, but now doubt, that the murder of shaman Jack of the Feather triggered 1622's uprising. His appearance could have resembled this North Carolina native's, captured in the 1580s by John White.

upon the English on the first favorable opportunity," Percy said. That echoes the belief of others, but he thought there was more to it than simple revenge for a single death:

> My opinion is that their heathen priests, who are the tools of the devil, were constantly working upon the credulity and ignorance of this people to make them believe that the English had come to exterminate them in the same way as the Spaniard had done in other parts of the West Indies, and to prevent this the murderous attack was decided upon and brought into execution.

Although Percy scoffs at the idea that the English intended to exterminate the Virginia Indians, time would tell a different story.

Historians generally agree that the murder of Nemattanow was not the cause of the 1622 attack. It had been planned for early spring, long before Nemat-

tanow's death. Food supplies were always lowest in the spring, but that year, Opechancanough knew, the English were desperately short of sustenance. Early spring was a good time to strike: Indian families, which dispersed each winter, were out of the reach of English retaliation, and planting time had not come. If the English were pushed back to Jamestown, the fields they had seized from the Indians could be reclaimed and sown in time for the growing season.

Thus Opechancanough timed his raid. He sent word of his plan by way of messengers on foot or by canoe. There was probably no village that lay farther than one day's travel from his central seat near modern West Point, at the head of the York River. The protocol was described by colonist William Strachey in an early account of Jamestown:

> When they intend any warrs . . . a Weroance or some lusty fellow is appointed Captayne over a Nation or Regiment to be

A modern artist's conception, accurately informed by archaeology and research, of the 1622 attack on Martin's Hundred, seven miles below Jamestown. At least seventy-three people died there, more than at any other plantation.

led forth, and when they would presse a number of Soldiers to be ready by a daie, an officer is dispatcht away, who coming into the Townes, or otherwise meeting such whome he hath order to warne, he strykes them over the back a sound blow with a bastinado, and byds them be ready to serve the great king, and tells them the Randivous, from whence they dare not at the tyme appointed be absent.

Anthropologist Helen Rountree speculates that the "officer" would have directed warriors to the nearest Eng-

lish outpost: in this case, men from the Warraskoyack villages would be sent to attack Martin's Hundred, and Nansemond warriors would have been dispatched to settlements in what is now Newport News and Hampton.

"The tyme appointed" for the spring raid could have been the next day—indeed, historians know of an instance in which a messenger arrived in the evening to tell his brother to join the raid planned for the next morning. According to seventeenth-century chronicler Edward Waterhouse, Chanco, a Christianized Indian

▲ Painted to suggest a scene of the attack at Martin's Hundred in 1622, this illustration must approximate dramas played out at farms and homes scattered across Virginia's Tidewater that year, and again in 1644.

◀ Warned of the impending assault in 1622, the soldiers of the fort at Jamestown—represented here by Colonial Williamsburg's Willie Balderson—stood to their guard and warded off the attack.

boy living with colonist Edward Pace across the river from Jamestown, was

> urged by another Indian his Brother (who came the night before and lay with him) to kill Pace, (so commanded by their King as he declared) . . . telling further that by such houre in the morning a number would come from divers places to finish the Execution.

But most warriors would have required more than one night to prepare for the raid: to go through prewar rituals, stock up on arrows, and travel to the target. How did Opechancanough coordinate them?

More than one historian has suggested that the attacks were timed to coincide with the Christian Holy Week, thinking that the 1622 raid was on Good Friday. Eminent colonist George Thorpe had often conferred with Opechancanough on matters of religion, trying to convert the old chief to Christianity, and presumably would have shared with him the details of Easter and the resurrection. The Powhatans had a predilection for blending irony and warfare; these are Indians who killed colonists for stealing corn by stuffing corn down their throats. It is possible Opechancanough planned the attack for Good Friday to emphasize a rejection of the foreigner's religion.

Easter, however, does not cooperate with this theory, falling as it does on April 21 in 1622, weeks after the massacre. Easter came closer to the attack date in 1644—on the Thursday before Easter Sunday—but a raid timed for Maundy Thursday stretches credulity.

A late-nineteenth-century error moved the attack of 1644 back one day—to Good Friday—and confused that with the date of the 1622 attack. Memorable and catchy, the mistake persists in textbooks and on Internet sites despite the efforts of historians to correct it. Although no major religious holiday coincided with either attack, both did occur during the Easter season. Anthropologist Frederic Gleach believes the timing was intentional.

Could the raids of 1622 and 1644 have been coordinated with some celestial event? According to NASA charts, there were no solar or lunar eclipses within a month of either raid. Nor does the vernal equinox coincide with either date. In the Northern Hemisphere, the first day of spring falls near—but not on—the attack dates, coming two days before the 1622 raid and a month before 1644's.

Like most agrarian societies, the Powhatans recognized lunar months. "They reckon their time, by dayes and moons and years," wrote a clergyman in 1689, and lunar quarters were probably used as time markers by the Powhatans, as they were by the neighboring Delawares. Examining the phases of the moon for the dates in question—dates that require adjusting from the Julian calendar that English colonists used to today's modified Gregorian calendar used by NASA—an intriguing coincidence comes to light. The 1622 attack came one day shy of the third-quarter moon. So did the attack of 1644.

It could be just the one-in-twenty-eight chance of two events falling on the same day of the lunar month. More likely, the first date had no particular import, but Opechancanough patterned the 1644 surprise attack after 1622's, using the same lunar date that brought him success the first time. It seems unlikely that something so important would be timed solely by a visual sighting of the moon. What if spring rain clouds obscured the moon for a week? But the Powhatans were perfectly capable of counting the days between quarter moons. According to Captain John Smith, they had a numbering system that used specific numbers from one to ten, after which "they count no more but by tennes" to reach one hundred. When necessary, they used devices such as notched sticks and knotted string to track larger numbers. The notched stick method would not have been necessary for small numbers such as the number of days to count before launching the attack.

It is also possible that the day before the third quarter of the moon had some specific connotation. Queries of today's Virginia Indian leaders received the polite reply that discussing this sort of spiritual cultural knowledge is inappropriate outside the Indian community.

However he managed it, Opechancanough twice set the date for a massive assault on multiple English settlements and twice sent word to his people. Everyone got the message. No one attacked a day early or a day late.

How Was "the tyme appointed"?

ANTHONY AVENI

I magine living without watches or calendars. How would you know when your bills were due or when to plan periodic visits to your dentist or physician? For most cultures that thrived before the invention of the mechanical clock the time to stop work was reckoned by whether you could see heads on a coin, and lunchtime was determined by raising your hand skyward to see whether the sun had reached its highest point. Longer-term intervals were counted off on notched sticks, and by the lost art of moon watching.

The neat thing about the moon is that anyone who pays attention to it can easily discern changes in its face from day to day. The moon begins its month-long cycle as a thin "first crescent," visible in the west shortly after sunset. Within a week it moves farther from the setting sun as it waxes to a D-shaped first quarter seen high on the meridian. Then it bulges through the waxing gibbous phase as it grows to a full moon. Rising directly opposite the setting sun, it takes over the duties of lighting the sky all night in the sun's absence. That seven-day period from quarter to full correlates perfectly with our week, a convenient timing device in agrarian societies because that's just about the time it takes to pick vegetables, carry them to a regional market, dispense them before they spoil, and get back to the fields after a day of rest to repeat the market cycle.

During the last two weeks of the 29½-day lunar cycle, the process takes place in reverse, as the moon transforms itself through waning gibbous to last quarter and finally to the thinnest of crescents seen hovering over the predawn sun before it disappears for a day or two. The British term "fortnight," which stands for two weeks or fourteen nights, may have been a spin-off of the early relationship between the week and the month—an

Virginia's Powhatan Indians, here represented by Jerry Fortune of the Rappahannock tribe, made the heavens their calendar.

interval that divides the month into its pair of familiar half cycles from new to full and from full to new moon. Then it happens all over again. Little wonder lunar mythologies all over the world characterize the man in the moon as a nocturnal hero who waxes to maturity, only to be eaten away in old age by the devil of darkness. Though his feeble remnant falls from the sky, his son soon rises anew to avenge the death of his father.

In low-tech societies, the month-to-month intervals are convenient for reckoning major changes in the environment, such as when the rains come and go, when the bear hibernates, when the salmon spawn or the geese go away, when the mulberries are ripe or the nuts ready to crush to make flour, when the corn should be planted and harvested. All of these events and activities functioned as names of months in the orally transmitted calendars of Native Americans. Harvest, the first, and Hunter's, the second, full moons following the autumn equinox on September 22 or 23 are familiar northeast native survivals.

The Powhatan Indians, as Virginia's band of Algonquians are known, were no exception.

Edward Waterhouse, in the 1623 Virginia Company of London tract *A Declaration of the State of the Colony and Affaires in Virginia,* described the Powhatans as "naked, tanned, deformed, savages . . . no other than wild beasts," and "worse then their old Deuill which they worship." The Powhatans, to the contrary, were skilled lunar timekeepers. These farming hunter-gatherers, who lived in a land of rivers, bays, and estuaries, grew corn and vegetables in summer, took game in winter, and fished during spring. They reckoned a "moon of stags," a "corn moon," and a first and second "moon of cohonks"—the Algonquian word sounds just like the call of the geese, the sound from which the word derives. Moreover, they tallied their moons by knots on strings and notched sticks.

Any effective lunar calendar must be in sync with the seasonal or solar year, which the crop cycle follows. But as nature would have it, the moon and sun have trouble living together in harmony. Our years of 365+ days can accommodate twelve lunar cycles, or 354 days, with a shortfall of eleven days, or thirteen with an overrun of eighteen, that is to say, 383 days. Our Roman

forebears, who bequeathed us the calendar we use, force-fitted the two cycles together. They artificially length-ened the months to thirty and thirty-one days, a most unnatural choice for attentive sky watchers, which the Romans decidedly were not. Another solution for keep-ing seasonal time by the moon would be to keep succes-sive twelve-month years, inserting a thirteenth month into the year cycle when necessary to make up for lost time, as we do with our Leap Year. Many Native Ameri-can tribes, likely including the Powhatans, did just that.

Some were more precise with their lunar reckoning. We know the Delaware named the phases of the same moon; for example, the new moon, likely the first visible crescent; the round or full moon; and the half round, or probably last quarter, moon. The intervals between the directly visible phases—ranging from a few to several days—proved convenient in day-to-day practical opera-tions. Think of how often in a given day you refer to activities that will take place "after the weekend," "early next week," or "in a few weeks."

"Little Corn," "Great Corn," "Turkey," "Cold Meal," and "Deer" are a long way from our abstract Janu-ary, February, March, and April, but what we learn from Native American timekeeping is that the names given to time periods represent "lived time"—the activity itself. And in any successful society such activity would necessar-ily include scheduling the conduct of war.

One of the most revealing discoveries about the recently deciphered inscriptions of the ancient Maya of Yucatan is that they undertook their raids in neighboring cities when the maize was already in the ground, that is, after the intensive labor associated with sowing the crop following the rains had already been dispensed with. We know this because hieroglyphs and imagery pertaining to warfare have been correlated with the appearance of the planet Venus at specific times in the seasonal year. The Maya were conducting real "Star Wars."

As we learn from the previous chapter, "the tyme appointed," by Mary Miley Theobald, although there were undoubtedly some profoundly political causes, such as loss of land, dissatisfaction over English policies, avenging recent wrongs, and so forth, the crucial ques-tion of the proximate cause or causes remains unsettled. Timing of the end-of-winter attack is another issue, and

▲ The sophisticated use Indians made of natural resources, suggested by the interpretations of Henricus Historical Park and Pete McKee, embraced the sky.

◀ The moon passes through a cycle of illumination, known as a lunation, in 29½ days. This composite of twenty-four digital photos, shot by António Cidadão through a reflecting telescope in his home rooftop observatory in Oeiras, Portugal, tracks a lunation.

The Virginia Company of London emphasized the naturalism of Eiasuntomino on a 1615 broadside promoting a fund-raising lottery for Jamestown.

Matahan, also portrayed on the Virginia Company of London broadside, lived in adaptive harmony with the rhythms of nature's seasons.

this is where the moon enters our story. Early spring would have been an illogical time for the Powhatans to rise against an adversary.

John Smith tells us that May was the main corn—along with pumpkin and melon—planting month, with some early planting in April and later planting in June. Each crop was reaped four months later. These crucial Nepinough, or corn-earing, months were the busiest time in the agricultural cycle; it would have been important to the natives to recoup the fields after an attack by the middle of May to allow enough time to perform

these vital activities. Though the record is sparse, given what we know of their methods for keeping time, it is not at all implausible that the Powhatans would have conducted star—or moon—wars of their own. What little we do know of the celestial circumstances surrounding the Powhatan coups of 1622 and 1644 points to it.

On the eve of the March 22, 1622, attack, calculations reveal that the moon was in its third quarter phase and that it rose in the south-southeast in the constellation of Sagittarius about an hour past midnight. The moon presented almost precisely the same aspect the night before the April 18, 1644, attack: third quarter, rising, this time in Capricorn, in the same direction, also about one hour after midnight. Successful attacks require not only good timing but advance planning. Waterhouse's account of the first uprising says, "Several days before this bloodthirsty people put their plan into execution they led some of our people through very dangerous woods," and, "On Friday before the day appointed by them for the attack they visited, entirely unharmed, some of our people in their dwellings."

If Opechancanough, who masterminded both attacks, wanted to plan them on these dates, the most obvious way to convey his intent to his cohorts would have been to set the lunar clock by counting days from the first visible crescent. For more effective long-range planning the Powhatans, an association of scattered tribes, could have synchronized the strikes to take place on a particular moon in the cycle, provided they shared an intertribal calendar—another not unlikely assumption.

For the 1622 attack, in the latitude of Virginia, the first visible crescent occurred March 1; for the 1644 episode it happened March 28—in both cases twenty-one days, or three-quarters of a lunar cycle, before history records the dramatic results.

Why, then, did the two attacks occur a month apart—one in March, the other in April—as reckoned by our calendar? Here we need to call to mind two facts we have already learned about native timekeeping: first, the moon always takes precedence; and second, there can be twelve or thirteen moon cycles in a lunar year. Suppose, for example, that we count moons from the December solstice, which is December 21, the day when the sun rises and sets farthest to the south.

Suppose Year One—or better, "Sun One"—ends with the completion of the twelfth moon, eleven days short of the winter solstice of Year Two. Then the first moon of Year Two will begin with the observation of the first crescent around December 10. If Sun Two also contains twelve moons, then the first moon of Sun Three will begin about November 30. Clearly, the next year cycle, or Sun Four, would be a most convenient one in which to insert a thirteenth moon.

Now, if we were to count to the last quarter from the first crescent of Moon One of Sun One, we would

The moon was in its third quarter in March 1622 and April 1644 when Virginia's Native Americans attacked European intruders.

arrive at December 21 + twenty-one days, or January 11. But if we performed the same operation, in say Sun Three, we would land on December 21 (November 30 + twenty-one days). From this hypothetical example it is easy to see that, with a casual system for intercalating months, identical dates in the Powhatan moon calendar could correspond to dates up to a month apart in our sun or seasonal calendar.

The historical record conflicts on whether Opechancanough took Easter into account when planning the attacks. What makes this difficult to corroborate in real time is that Easter is computed in such a wide variety of ways that reckoning when it was celebrated is difficult. Incidentally, there is a touch of irony in the fact that our way of calculating Easter depends on the Jewish lunar calendar, and, like dates set in the Powhatan lunar calendar, it, too, is a movable holiday—it floats in the seasonal calendar.

To make matters more difficult, because the events under consideration occurred in the century following major corrections of the Western calendar, there has been considerable confusion over whether dates reported by Virginia's earliest historians are given in the Julian, or Old Style, calendar in use in Roman Catholic Europe before 1582 or the Gregorian, New Style, calendar

A Native American who some historians think could have been Opechancanough led attacks on Spanish missionaries near Yorktown in 1571 during a first quarter moon. These engravings, published in 1675 at Prague by Melchior Küssell, are conjectural.

adopted since. The two calendars differed by eleven days at that time, but the computation of Easter yields dates up to a month apart. Thus, in 1622 Easter Sunday, Old Style, fell on April 21, but it occurred on March 27, New Style. Could it be that those who noted that the attack took place around the Easter holiday were referring the Old Style March 22 date to the New Style celebration of Easter, five days before which it took place?

By striking coincidence both versions of Easter fell on exactly the same dates in 1644, the year of the second uprising. But this time if we wish to juxtapose it with the Paschal holiday, as some historical accounts require, we must assume that the record refers to the Old Style Easter date. In that case the attack would have taken place three days before Easter. Unfortunately no 1644 almanacs seem to survive, but an extrapolation of an Anglican common prayer book dated 1641 suggests that the April, Old Style, date is indeed the most likely one to have been recognized in the colonies.

Last, and not often considered in the problem of whether the Powhatan coups were celestially timed, there are the circumstances of the attack on the mission of the Jesuits, who first attempted to establish permanent settlements in Virginia. It happened on the eve of the feast of Purification, or Candlemas, which was February 2, in the year 1571. What transpired in the sky the night before?

A quarter moon, this time first quarter, rode high in the sky at sunset, illuminating the landscape until midnight. Might this signal a tradition of strikes on the enemy at quarter moons coinciding with key points in their holiday cycle? Only our lack of knowledge of Powhatan religious and social customs prevents us from speculating further.

Chanco's Reward

DENNIS MONTGOMERY

Virginia Route 10—the "Colonial Trail," as the highway is more imaginatively named—bends through the history of the south shore of the James. About three miles west of Surry, it slides past highway marker No. 224 K, a reminder of the Native American who saved seventeenth-century Jamestown, and likely the colony of Virginia. Despite this signal service, the first account of the young man's kindness neglected to give his name, and, before the English were done, ingratitude was a proper noun for his reward.

Raised in 1928 where Route 618 strikes the Trail, the sign is headlined "Pace's Paines." It reads:

> This place, seven miles north, was settled by Richard Pace in 1620. On the night before the Indian massacre of March 22, 1622, an Indian, Chanco, revealed the plot to Pace, who reached Jamestown in time to save the settlers in that vicinity.

Even now Chanco's name is mentioned but in passing.

The object of the uprising, masterminded by the Powhatan headman Opechancanough, was, it appears, to kill every English settler. If Jamestown, struggling Virginia's single town, had been overrun, the countryside's survivors might well have quit the colony.

What was Pace's Paines, the archaeologists believe, rests beneath a pasture at Mount Pleasant Farm. Not much to look at, but there is another monument to see further down Route 10. A boulder planted in the Surry County Courthouse lawn in 1929 gives Chanco credit due. It says:

▲ Pace rowed this reach of river to warn the fort at Jamestown of the pending assault, putting defenders on their guard in time to prevent attack.

▶ Archaeologists think what remains of Pace's Paines is beneath a cow pasture where today peacocks sometimes prowl.

In Memory of
Chanco
The Indian who lived with Richard Pace at Pace's Paines in this
county and who on the night before the massacre of March 22,
1622, informed Pace of Opechancanough's plot and thus saved
the Jamestown colony.

But marker and monument tell a disjointed story and ignore its ignominious sequel.

The tale is best begun in the 373-year-old *A Relation of the Barbarous Massacre in the time of peace and League treacherously executed by the Native Infidels.* Collected out of Virginia reports and letters, this London tract reaches Pace's Paines about a quarter the way through. It says:

> The slaughter had been universal if God had not put it in to the heart of an Indian belonging to one Perry to disclose it, who living in the house of one Pace, was urged by another Indian, his Brother (who came the night before and lay with him) to kill Pace . . . as he would kill Perry, telling him further that by such an hour in the morning a number would come from diverse places to finish the Execution, who failed not at the time. Perry's Indian rose out of his bed and reveals it to Pace, that used him as a son, and thus the rest of the Colony had warning given them, by this means was saved.
>
> . . . Pace upon this discovery, securing his house, before day rowed over the river to James City (in that place near three miles in breadth) and gave notice thereof to the Governor, by which means they were prevented there, and at such other Plantations as was possible for a timely intelligence to be given. For where they saw us standing upon our Guard, at the sight of a Piece they all ran away.

In the language of the day, Jamestown was "James City," and "piece" was another name for a firearm. Notice that Perry's Indian is named not at all.

The Indians still killed about 350 English and kidnapped a score of others. In the aftermath, Pace took refuge at Jamestown. Chanco, who must have had no choice, returned to his tribe.

In a bloody campaign of reprisals, the English that year slew more Indians, according to a colonist, than they had since the settlers landed fifteen years before. They torched crops and villages and drove the famished naturals far into the forest.

Chanco resurfaced, and his name first was recorded in April 1623 as a go-between in an Indian bid for peace. According to the English, he said "that blood enough had already been shed on both sides, that many of his People were starved by our taking Away their Corn and burning their houses."

In exchange for allowing the Indians to return to their villages, "they would send home our People . . . whom they saved alive since the massacre, and would suffer us to plant quietly in all places."

The English told Chanco his people would be allowed to plant if they returned the hostages. Interpreter Robert Poole went with him to deliver the response, an offer the English had no intention of honoring anyway. To London they reported:

> If they send home our people and grow secure upon the treaty, we shall have the better Advantage both to surprise them and to cut down their Corn by knowing where they plant, which otherwise they will plant in such corners, as it will not be possible for us to find out.

A week later, dressed like an Indian queen, a Mrs. Boyse, the most important English hostage, came in. Poole, however, had made threatening speeches, and before they freed the others, the Indians wanted reassurances from another Englishman.

The governor spurned the request and sent Chanco back alone, "suffering him to carry certain bonds from the friends of the prisoners," that is to say, private ransoms, for their return.

When the hostages reached Jamestown, English attacks on the Indians resumed with sharpened ferocity. They had made Chanco, Jamestown's savior, the tool of their duplicity and revenge.

Doctor John Pott

First Citizen of Williamsburg

One of the first tasks of developing a subdivision is to name its streets. If that subdivision should happen to be in Williamsburg, what could be more appropriate than naming one of them for the first man to build a home within its modern boundaries? It helps, too, if the honoree did something memorable—like inventing the safety pin or finding a cure for a dire disease. Someone like Dr. John Pott, whose fame rests on less laudable medical achievements. The man for whom John Pott Drive is named was instrumental in causing the deaths of more than 600 Virginia colonists and 200 Indians.

In the days between 1607 and 1625, when the Old Dominion was a project of the Virginia Company of London, its principal operatives were the governor, lieutenant governor, treasurer, secretary, and the physician general, all appointed by the company's courts and committees in London. Choosing the right physician to send to Virginia was no easy decision, but in 1621 the company's London physician, Dr. Theodore Gulstone, pronounced Galstone, knew the very man. Dr. John Pott, he said, was a master of arts and "well practised in Chirurgerie and Phisique, and expert also in Distillinge of waters and that hee had many other ingenious devices."

Though at that court session the officers were advised the company's stock was "utterly exhausted," they recognized that their medical man on call in Virginia had to be well supplied. They also knew that a successful doctor should be a happy doctor, and so it was ordered that "hee should be entertayned and for his better content" provided with a house. He should also be supplied with a chest of medicines to the value of £20 sterling and £10 worth of "Books of Phisique which would always belonge unto the Company" and which Gulstone would choose.

Pott's wife could travel over at company expense, and so could her maid. If a couple of surgeons could be found, their passages also would be paid. Although Pott was said to be well practiced in surgery, in seventeenth-century England there was an educational and hierarchical gulf between physicians and surgeons. Physicians needed a university degree, as Pott had from Cambridge, but surgeons needed only a command of anatomy and to be handy with a saw. Surgeons did the cutting while physicians did the cauterizing and stitching, although in extremis either could do the job. Pott accepted the post in July 1621, regardless of whether the surgeons were forthcoming. Although not mentioned in his terms of appointment, he was also supplied with apothecary Joseph Fitch, for whom the company put out £6 for "furnishinge himself with aparrell & necessaries for his voyage." Not only that, the new doctor was to be given the use of twenty company tenants already in Virginia.

All in all, Pott was onto a good thing. Furthermore, when he arrived he would automatically be appointed to the council at Jamestown, assuring him of a position of respect and importance. Just to be on the safe side, however, he also took with him a goodly supply of liquor, a popular commodity in the Virginia country. He sailed with his wife, Elizabeth, aboard the ship *George* in the summer of 1621, but apparently without her maid. Three male servants, however, came on other vessels, Richard Townshend, nineteen, and Thomas Wilson, twenty-seven, on the company's chartered ship *Abigail,* and Osmond Smith, seventeen, on the *Bona Nova*. Also sailing aboard the *Abigail* were seven more men, twenty to thirty-three, who were to work for the doctor on company acres on the mainland west of Jamestown Island.

At the outset, all went relatively well. Pott got his company house on the Back Street at Jamestown and three acres. The town was growing, not exactly to city standards, but prospering just the same. Tobacco had become the staple export and, by the pound, the most common means of exchange. Therefore, using his men on the mainland—or, as it was called, the Maine—the good doctor also became a tobacco and corn planter and enjoyed such good things as colonial life afforded. But he seems to have shared his good life with the wrong people. In a letter to an influential company member in London,

Secretary George Sandys said, "What a pittifull Councellour have wee in your Doctour!" Sandys said that at first Pott "kept Companie too much with the Inferiours, who hung upon him while his good liquor lasted."

Nine months later the good times came to a terrifying halt. On March 22, 1622, the Indian Opechancanough launched a colony-wide assault on the plantations, killing about 350 people, among them, six members of the council and Pott's apothecary, Fitch. Although there is no record of the doctor's work in the immediate aftermath of the attack, he must have been kept busy patching up the wounded.

When the company in London learned of the disaster, its immediate response was to blame the vengeance of God as a punishment for assorted transgressions. Among the remedies proposed were the prompt redress of the "two enormous excesses of apparell and drinkeing, which had brought the name of Virginia to the detestation of all good mindes." This, to say the least, was not a helpful response. Its mailing was delayed while cooler heads gave heed to the plight of the survivors and sent back the *Abigail* with fresh faces to replace the colonists lost to Indian wrath.

These people were sponsored by the owners of the private, as opposed to company, plantations and were destined to be distributed throughout the colony. Also aboard was Pott's maid, Susan Blackwood. Much more important, however, was the occupant of the aft cabin. She was Lady Margaret, wife to Governor Sir Francis Wyatt, and it is from a letter written by her that we learn about the horrors of the voyage and its aftermath.

> Our Shipp was so pesterd with people & goods that we were so full of infection that after a while we saw little but throwing folkes over boord. . . . Few else are left alive that came in that Shipp. . . . This was our fortune at the Sea, and the land little better.

The *Abigail* dropped anchor at Jamestown just before Christmas in 1622, nine months after the Indian attack. The surviving colonists were in desperate need of food and the arrival of the relief ship was a moment for rejoicing, or so they thought. Ever since the Black Death had ravaged Europe in the fourteenth century, there had been outbreaks of contagious diseases collectively defined as plague. Now a plague ship had arrived in the James River, and the responsibility of what to do about it fell squarely on the shoulders of the colony's medical officer.

The obvious course would have been to quarantine everyone aboard until such time as the hardiest survived and could be released. But no hospital had been built, nor was there any housing complex away from Jamestown that was safe from Indian assault. More to the point, the governor's lady and her entourage were aboard, and it would have called for a high degree of courage on Pott's part to order her to stay there. So he didn't.

The *Abigail*'s sick and dying were permitted to disembark and sent on their way to their plantations, taking the plague with them. It was akin to firing a poisoned shotgun into the colony, and by doing nothing, Doctor Pott pulled the trigger. During the next three months more than 600 died, twice the number killed by the Indians.

Within three days of Lady Wyatt's arrival she, too, fell sick and was removed along with the governor to Daniel Gookin's large plantation at modern Newport News. She found that most of Gookin's men had been killed and his plantation "ready to fall to decay." Nevertheless, the healthful air encouraged her recovery by the end of March. Secretary Sandys put it down to her "being of so chearefull a disposeition, which is in this Countrie an Antidote against all diseases."

The *Abigail* was supposed to have carried supplies of flour and seed corn, but they were not ready when ship's Captain Samuel Each was ready to sail. He had refused to wait any longer and so left those essentials to follow on a second ship, the *Seaflower*. Instead, he carried crates of armor that the sick and disenchanted colonists allowed to remain at the river's edge for two weeks while the tides flowed over them.

Through the winter of 1622–23, waiting for the arrival of the *Seaflower* became the last hope for many colonists. In April, she blew up at anchor at Bermuda.

The winter was bad for colonists and Indians, and in the spring the Native American leader Opechancanough sent a deputation to Martin's Hundred to parley with the English. He proposed a cessation of hostilities and assurances of safety for the Indians return-

ing to villages along the York River that they had vacated in the face of retaliation from the English. In return, Opechancanough would release twenty women he had prisoner.

Neither side bargained in good faith. March 22, exactly a year after the attack, twelve soldiers led by Captain Robert Tucker went to treat with the Indians of the Potomac region, taking with them a butt of sack carefully enhanced by Pott, who, you will remember, was so "expert also in Distillinge of waters and . . . many other ingenious devices."

On arrival, the warriors and kings of several tribes assembled to hear speeches from both sides. Colonist Robert Bennett described what happened next.

> Soe Capten Tucker begane and our interpreter tasted before the kinge would tacke yt, but not of the same. Soe thene the kinge with the kinge of Cheskacke sonnes and all the great men weare drunk . . . how manye we canot wryte of but yt is thought some tooe hundred weare poysned.

The completeness of this victory was marred only by Opechancanough's failure to respond to his invitation to attend. There was solace, however, in being able to report that on the way home fifty more Indians were killed and, to prove it, Tucker's men "brought hom parte of ther heades." Although scalping was steeped in Indian religious lore, the English had no such excuse—nor did Pott for his role in what is among the most despicable acts in the annals of English-American history. Later, when a commission was being assembled to investigate conditions in the colony, the Earl of Warwick ordered Pott's name stricken from the list because he was "the pysoner of the salvages thear."

Pott's activities in the years that followed are remembered largely for his appearances as a defendant in court proceedings. Historian Richard L. Morton described him as "happy-go-lucky, jovial, and indispensable," but the evidence given by those who worked for him and took him to trial leaves a different impression.

In 1623, following the parley with Opechancanough's delegation at Martin's Hundred at which the release of women hostages was discussed, Pott paid two pounds of beads to secure freedom for Jane, widow of

▲ Interpreter Alex Clark as Pott mixes the poison that later would be used to murder 200 Indians.

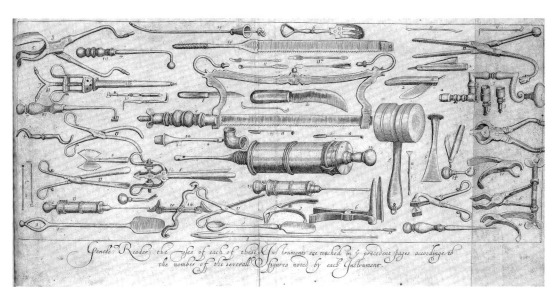

◀ Contents of a surgeon's chest from John Woodall's 1617 *Surgions Mate*. Woodall sent one of the chests to Jamestown in 1609.

released her, saying that her servitude at the hands of Pott "differeth not from her slavery with the Indians."

Two years later, Pott's apprentice Townshend told the General Court that he had been bound to the doctor to learn "the art of an Apothecarye" but was receiving no such instruction. The court ruled that Pott should get on with the teaching "by all convenient wayes & means," and if he did not Pott should pay Townshend for his services to the end of his indenture. Also in 1626, another apprentice, Randall Holt, appealed against his indenture and was ordered to continue another year, at the end of which Pott was to give him a new suit "from head to foote" and three barrels of corn. The young man married an heiress, acquired property, served in the 1629 General Assembly, and became a member of the council in 1642. Meanwhile, Pott continued to get himself into trouble and eventually into jail.

In 1625, he instructed his men to shoot four hogs that he said had invaded his cornfield. He also said he had no idea to whom the hogs belonged. In those days a hog was an important family asset and if killed still belonged to the owner. Pott, however, had the carcasses taken to his house and prepared them to be eaten. A Jamestown resident, one Mrs. Blaney, went to court on a claim that one of the hogs was hers and that she confronted Dr. Pott, who refused to accept that it was. Mrs. Blaney said the confrontation was so traumatic that she miscarried, and she blamed Pott for it. The court ruled that her accusation was too "Barbarows to Imagine." The doctor was not responsible for the miscarriage, and the damage to his corn equaled the value of the hogs. Nevertheless, the judges ruled that his "killing and eating of them without a legall order was irregular and Liable to Censure."

The year 1625 was a time for trauma of a different kind. King Charles I had determined that the Virginia Company's charter should be revoked and that Virginia should become a crown colony. During the governorship of Sir George Yeardley, Pott had been reinstated to the council, and so, on Yeardley's death in 1627, he was elevated to acting governor pending the arrival of the king's appointee, Sir John Harvey.

While he waited, Governor Pott was granted 200 acres in what was to become Middle Plantation, and eventually part of Williamsburg.

Mrs. Blaney, portrayed by Allison Harcourt, sued Pott over a pig he had shot. He said it had wandered into his cornfield.

Ralph Dickenson, killed in the Indian uprising at Martin's Hundred. He had been working out a seven years' indenture at the time of his death, and Pott insisted that the widowed Jane should work for him not only to repay him for the beads but to fulfill her late husband's remaining years of indenture. When her case was heard in March 1624, she said she had already "served teen months, tow much for two pound of beads." The court agreed and

The mound marks a boundary of what is thought to be Pott's land on
Jamestown Island, given to him by the Virginia Company.

Pott's memory is preserved in the church at Jamestown.

the governor had him arrested and jailed. At Pott's trial July 9, 1630, a jury of thirteen men, three of whom had been his fellow councilors, convicted him of horse stealing and had his estate confiscated. His wife, Elizabeth, sailed for England to petition the king for his release and the righting of the wrongs done him.

Harvey was playing a power game. Having destroyed Pott, he wrote to the king recommending that the doctor be pardoned, as "he is the only Physician in the Colonie, and skilled in the Epidemicall diseases of the planters." Harvey demonstrated that, having used his power to take away, he also could restore, thus bringing his people to "holding a better respect to the Governor than hitherto they have done."

Virginians watched his exertions of power with increasing dismay, and in the winter of 1634–35 the aggrieved Pott entered the political fray by traveling from plantation to plantation circulating a petition calling, in effect, for Harvey's recall.

When the governor heard, he again had Pott arrested, and Pott, in turn, promptly lodged an appeal to the king. Harvey called a meeting of the council only to be accused of suspected treason against his majesty, whereupon, at a signal from Pott, forty musketeers made their presence felt.

The outcome was that Harvey was sent back to England to face the council's charges and so, too, was Pott, who was to stand trial to support his appeal against several allegedly capital crimes. Governor and doctor sailed aboard the same ship—but probably had little to say to each other.

When the ship docked at Plymouth, however, Harvey had a great deal to say, and said it first. Pott was arrested as the principal author and agent of "the late mutiny and rebellion." Harvey was cleared and returned to his governorship, and the case against Pott seems to have been dropped. He returned to Virginia and died there in 1642, leaving behind a chronicle of misadventure and murder, and the distinction of having been among the first Americans to try to recall an unpopular governor.

Harvey arrived in the spring of 1630 and immediately decided to demonstrate his authority by humiliating the always vulnerable Pott, whom he charged with "pardoninge wilfull Murther, markinge other mens Cattel for his owne, and killing up their hoggs." Pending his trial, Harvey ordered him confined to his plantation. When the doctor defied him and went to Elizabeth City,

"the unfortunate Accident"

DENNIS MONTGOMERY

Jamestown's fourth statehouse burned. But where remains a riddle.

No accident in Williamsburg's history is as pivotal—or obscure—as a fire 300 years ago that destroyed a building in Jamestown. All that was recorded of the blaze can be transcribed in a handful of paragraphs. The dwelling was of a design so undistinguished that its remains seem until lately to have gone unrecognized. A two-story pile of native brick, the edifice was, however, central to Virginia's history at the turn of the seventeenth century. It was the colony's statehouse.

The last in a series of statehouses on damp and mosquito-plagued Jamestown Island, it had sheltered the General Assembly for fourteen years. The men who ran the colony seized its loss late in October 1698 as the opportunity to move the seat of government seven miles inland to Middle Plantation, which they renamed Williamsburg.

Abandoned by the government and eventually by its tavernkeepers, tradesmen, and merchants, England's first permanent American settlement faded away. When the twentieth century began, nearly all Jamestown had been buried by the plow, and the loss of early records clouded even the written recollections of its seventeenth-century houses, streets, and public buildings.

Historians know the last statehouse—the word "capitol" wasn't statutory until Williamsburg—was among tattered Jamestown's better buildings. The term "statehouse," however, is to modem ears more impressive than could have been this edifice.

The foundations of the Ludwell Statehouse Group—the series of rectangles in the lower center beside the river—are now interpreted as the "traditional site" of the last Jamestown statehouses. The new rival location, Structure 112, is near the top of the picture in the trees to the left of the Jamestown Monument obelisk and just beyond the triangular-roofed Visitor Center.

Based on the archaeological investigations of Structure 112 and a knowledge of seventeenth-century architecture, artist Sidney King in 1957 painted this conception of the last house on the site, when it was thought to have been a mansion. Archaeologists covered the excavation with earth and sand after they completed their investigations. The site today provides shade for Jamestown Island picnickers.

A few deeds, journals, contracts, letters, and artifacts offered clues to its location, but the certain whereabouts of so historically significant a structure have remained a riddle.

Colonial Williamsburg Foundation historians have helped to puzzle out what they think is a likely answer. Carl Lounsbury says, "Any new interpretation of the statehouses of Jamestown must start with a fundamental question: What constituted a statehouse?" It was not necessarily, as he put it in a 1994 presentation, "a publicly owned building where the judicial, legislative, and administrative bodies of the provincial government deliberated, maintained their offices, and housed public records."

In the ninety years Jamestown was the capital, the burgesses gathered in the settlement's church, its private homes, and public taverns, as well as in buildings purchased or constructed for their use. "Even a rented building might be considered a statehouse if the court and assembly met in the same structure," Lounsbury says. That makes it risky to number statehouses or to translate the documents to what stands on the ground.

By the late 1630s, Virginia's general court met in Governor John Harvey's home, which may have been several yards northeast of today's Jamestown Monument. There lies Structure 112, an accretion of footings from three seventeenth-century buildings, the first a frame house dating perhaps to 1623.

Historians supposed the burgesses also met at Harvey's house and called it the First Statehouse. But Lounsbury says it was in Harvey's day described as the courthouse, and there is no evidence lawmakers ever used it. They may have continued at the church for a time and later rented quarters.

In 1641, the colony bought Harvey's house and gave it to his successor Governor William Berkeley. Between March 1655 and June 1656, it burned. Investigators concluded that the government purchased a dwelling to take its place—a Second Statehouse—on the ridge west of the church, and that about 1670 it, too, burned.

But reanalysis of the documents tells historical archivist Martha W. McCartney that in 1655 and 1656 the burgesses rented space among the three units of a row house Berkeley built on that ridge in the 1640s and, Lounsbury says, "may have moved the council, general court, and perhaps the assembly to one or more of those buildings." Berkeley sold all three, one of them described as "the former statehouse," to tavernkeeper Thomas Woodhouse in 1656. Its foundations are at the center of what now remain of five common-walled, two-story brick houses called the Ludwell Statehouse Group.

The burgesses must have left Woodhouse's by 1660, when the council paid Thomas Hunt for the use of his place by the General Assembly. A push to buy or build a statehouse began in 1661, and two years later this question was put to the burgesses: "Since the charge the country is yearly at for houses for the quarter courts and assemblys to sit in would in two or 3 years defray the purchase of a State House. Whether it were not more profitable to purchase for that purpose then continue for ever at the expence, accompanied with the dishonor of all our laws being made and our judgments given in alehouses." The upshot was the Third Statehouse, purpose-built "to accommodate the affairs of the country."

In 1900, Colonel Samuel Yonge of the United States Engineer Department began a systematic survey of archaeological Jamestown, and he unearthed a five-unit row house on the first ridge west of the church. Yonge theorized the Third Statehouse was built on those foundations in 1665. By his interpretation of the ground and the documents, the burgesses met in the easternmost unit of what he dubbed the Ludwell Statehouse Group.

Today's research again departs from Yonge's deductions. The date, form, dimensions, and location of the Third Statehouse are in dispute.

But on some facts there is agreement: The building stood until 1676, when rebel Nathaniel Bacon's troops captured and torched Jamestown. The government returned to makeshift accommodations until the Fourth Statehouse, built on the foundations of third, opened in 1686. The colony's secretary set up an office on the ground floor, and to safeguard his records, his windows were shuttered and barred. This structure served until the 1698 fire destroyed it during the waning days of Governor Edmund Andros's administration.

When Bacon undid with the torch what progress had been made in sixty-nine years, Jamestown, by a contemporary account, had but sixteen or eighteen dwellings, most of brick "faire and large; and in them a dozen families (for all the houses are not inhabited) getting their livings by keeping of ordinaries at extraordinarie rates." Yonge wrote, "The town, even though measured by what would appear to be a standard of its time, was small, poor, and insignificant."

The city burned the first time in 1608, when it was still a wooden fort. The Bacon's Rebellion blaze was not the next nor the last noteworthy conflagration, but it may have done the most damage to Jamestown's future. In his 1705 *The History and Present State of Virginia,* Virginia's Robert Beverley wrote, "This unhappy town did never after arrive at the perfection it then had."

The fullest account of the statehouse fire in 1698 is an entry in *The Executive Journals of the Council of Virginia,* which say, "His excellency taking into serious Consideration the unfortunate Accident which this day happened to the State House by being burnt down & the public Records & Papers of this Countrey (there kept) which were forced to be hurryed out & thrown into Heaps & desiring the Opinion of the Councill what present Care should be taken thereof likewise called into the Councill Chamber such of the noted Gentlemen of this Countrey as were present in Town."

Beverley says some "conveniences" built for the safety of the colony's records were lost, suggesting some documents were, too. But he seems to say the statehouse's foundations were saved. He wrote that Governor

Andros "made several offers to rebuild the State-House in the same Place, and had his government continued by Six Months longer, 'tis probable he would have effected it after such a manner, as might have been least burdensome to the People."

But former Governor Francis Nicholson returned the next month to resume command. Nicholson was fresh from Annapolis, where he had designed and built a new capital for Maryland, just as he would for Virginia. The impact on Jamestown was profound. Six years later, Beverley said, Jamestown "is almost deserted by the Wild Project of Governour Nicholson who procured that the Assembly and General Court should be removed thence to *Williamsburg*."

Writing in 1724, colonist Hugh Jones mentions the burning of another public building in the statehouse fire, a prison. There is no reported evidence for a prison on the Ludwell Statehouse ridge. But in a 1993 archaeology article, Colonial Williamsburg's Kathleen Bragdon, Edward Chappell, and Willie Graham say that near Structure 112 stood "a public lock up or armory."

Did Yonge put his third and fourth statehouses in the right place on the ridge to the west? Not in the light of recent findings. Lounsbury says that rereading and mapping seventeenth-century deeds show "many of Yonge's speculations about the location of various land-holdings are no longer valid."

That's not to say that Yonge's contributions to Jamestown archaeology were for naught. Lounsbury says the discovery of the Ludwell Statehouse Group was "among the most important fragments of the town's storied past unearthed by Yonge."

Reinvestigating Yonge's Ludwell Statehouse Group in 1955, archaeologist Louis R. Caywood uncovered five burials beneath its cellars. Colleagues John L. Cotter and Dr. Joel L. Shiner found seventy more and opened ten of what are believed to total 300 unmarked graves on the ridge. The dead were buried helter-skelter, without coffins, perhaps hastily, maybe during the Starving Time in the winter of 1609–10. It is likely the oldest graveyard at Jamestown. A tall wooden cross now fronts the site.

But it looks as if Yonge was mistaken about the statehouses. The archaeologists found the Ludwell Statehouse Group burned. Lounsbury says there is no evidence the easternmost unit ever was rebuilt, "which calls into question whether it could ever have been the home of the 1660s and 1680s statehouse."

Signs are that the statehouse Bacon's men destroyed and the government reconstructed is Structure 112. Its foundations, Lounsbury says, supported "a large building which has clear indications of being rebuilt or altered several times over a long occupancy throughout the seventeenth century." The evidence is clear the second of the three buildings on the site burned, and the third closely followed its footprint. "Of all the structures in town," Lounsbury says, "it is the most likely candidate to have been the brick structure erected in the mid 1660s to 'accommodate the affairs of the country.'"

He writes, "Besides its scale and construction material, the meager artifactual evidence which survives from the site can be associated with government activities. A plaster fragment of a leopard's head hints that a coat of arms decorated a wall, and archaeologists recently found shutter hinges and iron bars that may have come from the secretary's office windows."

But, Lounsbury asks, "If Yonge's statehouse thesis has begun to crumble in the face of new investigations, what shall replace it? Like Yonge, until systematic reevaluation of the documentary and archaeological evidence is completed and new excavations undertaken, we can only offer the most tenuous outline of public building in the seventeenth-century capital and only hope that it does not become accepted without the necessary testing. Keeping in mind that we too must weave a plausible theory from the thinnest of evidence, I propose a slightly different scenario. After leaving the church in the 1630s, the general court and perhaps the house of burgesses met in John Harvey's building which just possibly may be Structure 112."

Governor Berkeley, who gave the government use of the property in 1641, still owned it when, by 1670, the Third Statehouse was built. Lounsbury reasons the assembly, general court, and secretary probably returned to this site, though the council mostly met elsewhere. Berkeley, who gave the government the use of the Harvey house, owned the Structure 112 site until his death in 1677. It passed to Berkeley's widow, Lady Francis, who married the wealthy Colonel Phillip Ludwell, the contractor for the Third Statehouse.

Beneath the brick-capped foundations of the Ludwell Statehouse Group
are the graves of as many as 300 Jamestown settlers. The cemetery,
marked by the modern wooden cross in the background, may be the
island's oldest.

"One thread that binds this theory together," Lounsbury writes, "is the presence of important people associated with the land on which these buildings sat: first Governor Harvey, then Governor Berkeley and finally Phillip Ludwell. . . . In an era when private gain and public weal was often confused if not synonymous, this should not be too surprising."

Lounsbury concludes: "This scenario still does not refute all the documentary evidence which suggests that the Ludwell Statehouse Group may have served some government function in the last years of the seventeenth century. We still need to know what this building was. If it were the last statehouse, then the spaces occupied by the secretary and the burgesses were far larger than they would be in the first Capitol in Williamsburg. . . . Yet these foundations have a public scale to them. If the structure were a dwelling, it would have been one of the most spacious ones built in the colony in the late seventeenth century. . . . In the end, I leave it to the archaeologists to discover its true nature."

The evidence, however, is strong enough that the Ludwell Statehouse Group site is now interpreted only as the "traditional site" of the statehouse.

Williamsburg's "serene and temperate aire, drye and champaign land" and Jamestown's fens and damps are commonly noticed as reasons for moving Virginia's government. But the College of William and Mary and Nicholson's ambition probably had as much to do with it.

Nicholson had been lieutenant governor from June 1690 to September 1692, when Andros relieved him.

Before that departure, he contributed £150 toward founding the college. A trustee, he returned for board meetings as well as to meddle in Andros's affairs, and he replaced Sir Edmund within days of the statehouse fire. Nicholson must have seen the opportunity to add Virginia's government to the new college's town.

The first meeting of the assembly after his return was April 27, 1699. The chief order of business was to adjourn to Middle Plantation and reconvene. On May 3, Nicholson recommended "a pile of buildings Erected so soon as possible" more commodious than Jamestown's statehouse.

On the 28th, the clerk of the House reported: "A Message from his Excellency in writing by Mr. *Harrison* was read at the Table as followeth. . . . 'You having desired me to continue my Favour in generall to this his Majesties Colony and Dominion of Virginia but particularly to the Colledge is another very great Obligation upon me for my Using all lawfull Wayes and Meanes for the Promoteing and Supporting the Good of them, and therefore I do now cordially recomend to you the Placeing of yor publick Building (wch *God* willing you are designed to have) somewhere at Middle Plantation nigh his Majesties Royall Colledg of *William and Mary* which I think will tend to *Gods* Glory, his Majesties Service, and the Welfare and Prosperity of yor Country in generall and of the Colledge in particular.'"

June 7 the General Assembly passed *An Act Directing the Building of the Capitoll and the City of Williamsburgh*. Nicholson assented the 8th.

Jamestown Rediscovered

Archaeologists Unearth More of the Storied Settlement's Past

The archaeologist directing the rediscovery of Jamestown spread a half-dozen dirty coin-like counters in the palm of his hand and counted his blessings. "There's more here than I ever dreamed of," he said. As he spoke, William Kelso looked over the patches of earth scraped smooth to expose the stains and artifacts that mark the long-forgotten activities of the men and women who settled and struggled at England's first permanent New World settlement. "We could go on forever," Kelso said.

Kelso is in charge of the painstaking, time-consuming reinvestigation of the original settlement on Jamestown Island. He leads the Jamestown Rediscovery project, mounted by the Association for the Preservation of Virginia Antiquities, now known as APVA Preservation Virginia.

APVA owns 22½ acres of what was a James River isthmus when the English dropped anchor in 1607, and on that ground the settlers enclosed their communal hold on Virginia within a triangle of freshly cut tree trunks stuck deep in the clay-tough ground.

The palisade was a bulwark against the Spanish, who never sailed deep enough into Hampton Roads to challenge the settlers, and the Powhatan Indians, who came by land and canoe out of curiosity, friendship, and, later, retaliatory anger. The earth-fast timbers, when they rotted or the English pulled them down, left a row of dark circular stains—footprints, archaeologists call them—in the soil. Kelso uncovered them in 1996 hard by the island's southerly shore. It was a sensational contradiction of the long-lived assumption that the James had washed all the fort site away.

Kelso was finding all sorts and manner of seventeenth-century artifacts undisturbed beneath the zone of soil plowed during the eighteenth and nineteenth centuries, when

Archaeologist William Kelso, in the excavated cellar house of circa 1610, displays some of the jetons uncovered nearby.

Archaeologists from the College of William and Mary and the Colonial Williamsburg Foundation had made a broad archaeological assessment of Jamestown Island beyond the fort. Their exploratory work had been done for the National Park Service and was a follow-up to archaeological explorations made before the Jamestown Festival of 1957.

The growth of Jamestown as the colony's capital and principal port had been the special study of Audrey Horning, an archaeologist with the foundation. A review of the island's documentary history aimed at finding the boundary lines of private property had been undertaken for the park service by independent scholar Martha W. McCartney.

Each object the archaeologists uncovered—be it a mysterious sliver of something unidentified or a drinking jug miraculously intact—was tagged, cleaned, and studied. Each was a clue to understanding the suffering and success of the people who lived in a company town administered by English entrepreneurs.

The coin-like counters Kelso admired were jetons—tokens merchants used to make quick monetary calculations. In a sense, Kelso said, these copper discs functioned much like an abacus and were piled in stacks on a board ruled much like a checkerboard. "They were just laying there scattered about, a dozen or so of them, by the brick foundation of something—we don't know what, yet—just east of the fort," he said.

Kelso displayed the jetons for a gaggle of tourists who paused on the path beside his workplace. "Look, they have designs engraved on them. This one has the alphabet on it, but a few letters—vowels mostly—are missing. And there are two *Z*s. The extra *Z* is probably the mark of the maker. And here, on this one, is an engraving of a man at a counting table using jetons. This is remarkable stuff. Really neat."

And it is meaningful stuff, too.

Kelso's archaeology reveals that the Jamestown settlers were industrious. In his writings, Captain John Smith complained about lazy gentlemen and laggards dependent on corn bartered from the Native Americans. But, to Kelso's mind, the number and variety of artifacts proved that Smith's oft-cited remarks do not fairly characterize all of the Jamestown adventurers. Half of the first 104 men and boys aboard the *Susan Constant,*

the island was farmed. The quantity of bits and pieces of metal, pottery, bones—scraps and fragments of man's presence and handiwork—had been uncovered in a third of an acre where Kelso and company began digging in 1994. Their goal was to sift through 2½ acres more before the 2007 commemoration of Jamestown's 400th anniversary.

Godspeed, and *Discovery* were artisans, craftsmen, and tradesmen, although few were farmers.

"Look," he said to emphasize his point. "It was an experiment just to sail across the ocean in 1607. It was an experiment to learn to live so far from home. They had to experience being here to know what to do, and what not to do. Hey, it was an experiment, and they succeeded. And the artifacts tell us this."

The artifacts are evidence that:

The colonists fashioned copper jewelry, which was, along with Dutch and Venetian beads, the coin of the wilderness. They made bricks. They experimented with making glass. They made lead shot for their muskets. They made tools and implements from spare armor. They cleared perhaps as much as forty acres of forest and planted crops.

They attempted to raise horses, cows, hogs, goats, sheep, and chickens. They cut down trees to extend the palisades and cut timber for homebuilding. Their first commercial export was a shipload of clapboard.

They hunted deer and wild turkeys. They fished for sturgeon, caught turtles, and dredged for oysters and clams. They gathered fuel. They collected sassafras. They explored the waterways of Tidewater.

They dug wells, clay pits, trenches, and cellars for the gunpowder magazine. They stood watch and manned blockhouses near the fort. They built huts, houses, and a church. They had to rebuild nearly everything after a fire in January 1608. They cared for the sick and buried the dead.

"There was a lot of activity going on. No doubt about that," Kelso said. "Look, in the end, at least some of them succeeded. They survived. They survived hard times—and that took a lot of work. Sure, there were idle gentlemen and ineffective leaders. And, sure, the adventurers didn't find gold and failed to make a profit for the Virginia Company, but Jamestown was not, as one historian put it, 'a fiasco.'" He refers to Edmund S. Morgan, professor emeritus at Yale.

"Jamestown was permanent—except, of course, for about thirty hours, which doesn't trouble me," Kelso said.

The colonists, frustrated and weary, out of food, and many sick, left June 7, 1610, intending to return to England. That does not signal failure to Kelso. The

▲ A model of a settler's head gazes past a resin casting of a skull and skeleton discovered inside the fort.

▶ In the afternoon shadows, the cellar house excavation looks like a footprint in the earth scraped smooth by APVA archaeologists. The toes are steps to what might have been a storeroom, used in 1610 as a trash pit. The trench to the left of the cellar marks an extension of the palisade of James Fort.

Ernelyn Marx works in the excavation.

refugee colonists who lived through the stark winter of 1609–10 were not resupplied until the arrival on May 23 of the company's acting governor, Thomas Gates. Shipwrecked in Bermuda the previous July, he came in two small makeshift vessels with 135 people marooned with him for the past eight months.

Gates considered the situation at Jamestown too dire and frail to recover and ordered its abandonment. They sailed away June 7, but the ships were met the next day off Mulberry Island and turned back by the arriving Thomas West, Lord De La Warr, who came with a load of supplies, 150 fresh settlers, and a commission to succeed Gates.

The number of people who began and survived the winter of 1609–10 at Jamestown is uncertain. Smith said there were "not past sixtie men, women and children" at Jamestown left alive, but some had run away to England or the Indians, and some encamped downstream. Nevertheless, it is sure that those months would always be known as the Starving Time.

Some English were reduced to cannibalism and eating snakes. They were victims of a drought so severe that crops planted by settlers and natives withered, and forage was scarce. At the fort, where the river was salty, there was little potable water.

Dennis Blanton, former director of the William and Mary Center for Archaeological Research, and climatologists at the University of Arkansas discovered the evidence of the drought while studying the growth rings of ancient cypress trees in Tidewater. They concluded that extraordinary conditions would have made life difficult between 1606 and 1612. They also noticed that the most extreme drought in 800 years hampered settlers on Roanoke Island and likely contributed to the failure of the Lost Colony in 1587.

When Lord De La Warr, Gates, the Jamestown refugees, and the new settlers from England dropped anchor at Jamestown on what, by their calendar, was June 10, 1610, the settlement was, as Kelso puts it, "a mess." During the Starving Time, the palisades and many dwellings had fallen into disrepair, and the settlers didn't bother to fix up the place they were about to leave.

"We know that Gates ordered buried some armament because there was no room for it aboard ship. The departing colonists left behind broken equipment and things that would be useless on their sea journey. I imagine," Kelso said, "there was a lot of stuff scattered about when De La Warr set the sailors to unload ships and the landmen to cleanse the town." And De La Warr dispatched George Somers to return to Bermuda for food supplies.

"There was, at Jamestown, a general housecleaning," Kelso said. Gates and De La Warr imposed military law and required everyone to pitch in and put the settlement in order. They collected trash and unwanted items and tossed them into a cellar just beyond the fort's eastern palisade.

Nick Luccketti, former director of field projects for the Jamestown Rediscovery, points out that the cellar hole is about twenty-five feet, north to south, fourteen feet wide, and seven feet deep. Dirt steps lead to a dirt floor. At the end opposite the steps, there is an extension of the cellar, another compartment dug later. Postholes for the structure over the cellar had been located. There was a clear mark of a barrel that sat on the floor and of a fire that had been built on the floor.

"It is obvious this cellar hole was filled at one time with stuff from the fort, and everything in it dates from 1610 or before," Luccketti said. "We found in this hole in the ground lots of copper, weapons, sections of breastplates, pike heads, helmets, a sword pommel, pieces of cut-up and refashioned armor, pieces of muskets and crossbows, English and Dutch coins, animal bones, broken delftware, glass trading beads, clay pipestems."

The material is similar to a cache of pre-1610 artifacts found in a pit within the palisade walls excavated in 1994. Luccketti said that about 100,000 artifacts had been lifted from the cellar hole.

"The number is astounding," Kelso said. "I never thought we'd recover things that are so old in these amounts—much to our delight."

Adjacent to the cellar hole, nearer the riverside and just downstream from the fort's easternmost bulwark, archaeologists in 1998 excavated the brick foundation of what they believed to be a warehouse built in 1644 by John White, a leading merchant and politician. It symbolizes, Kelso said, the evolution of Jamestown from military camp to commercial port. This excavation of a cobblestone foundation, brickwork, and fallen brick had been kept open, protected by an aluminum and fabric dome, so that visitors might get an understanding and appreciation of the knowledge that archaeology yields.

The months spent excavating the depth of White's fifty-by-thirty-foot warehouse and the cellar hole slowed expansion of the horizontal search for additional evidence of the triangular palisade and eastward extensions of it. The digging also delayed the search for evidence of earthfast buildings—structures built on a framework of

Bly Straube, Jamestown Rediscovery curator, admires the patched-together earthenware pieces of a London distilling flask.

poles sunk in the ground—within the fort. The next season of fieldwork was to concentrate on plotted ten-foot grid squares nearer the ruin of a seventeenth-century church tower—the Old Church Tower—and adjacent to the half-exposed brick foundation where Kelso picked up the jetons. "We've got to uncover big spaces before we can understand James Fort," Kelso said.

An earth fortification built in 1861 by slaves for a garrison of Confederate soldiers—Fort Pocahontas—masked the promise of undisturbed ground directly beneath the high dirt mound. It proved to be archaeo-logically rich.

Artifacts uncovered at Jamestown illustrate not only what the settlers did but what they looked like. Kelso had uncovered from within James Fort the skeletons of two early settlers—a man, who was assigned the archae-ologist's toe-tag of JR102C, and a woman, JR156C. Remarkable as it may seem, Kelso has a good idea, with the help of a sculptor-anthropologist using computer imaging, of their facial appearance.

"This is where science and history get personal," Kelso said. "When you actually can see the features of the earliest settlers, Jamestown becomes not just a place, but more a gathering of brave and rugged people."

The Jamestown artifacts were studied, preserved, and stored in a climate-controlled laboratory added to the Yeardley House, a caretaker's house. The Yeardley House also had been restored and refurbished for offices—a $500,000 project. Built for the 1907 anniversary of Jamestown, it was named for Sir George Yeardley, who succeeded Lord De La Warr as governor, and built, it is said, to resemble Sir Walter Ralegh's home in England.

From her sunlit office in the Yeardley House, cura-tor Bly Straube identified the objects that Kelso and his crew had uncovered. She was, in Kelso's judgment, "the authority on early seventeenth-century artifacts found in the United States."

In metal cabinet drawers were stored the mundane things like arrowheads and musket balls and unexpected things that surprise, delight, and mystify, such as an engraved silver pick used to scrape and scoop wax out of ears. Straube held up it to show that it is in the shape of a mythological sea rhinoceros, an example of elegance in the wilds.

Also among the finds were two religious medallions, one with images of Mary with the Child Jesus. "These are Catholic medallions, perhaps indicating that the English were tolerant in that they permitted Catholic sailors or artisans to wear them," Straube said.

Straube is fond of showing off pieces of Spanish olive jars—a few glued together almost complete. "These were the barrels of the time, in which wine and vinegar, beans and nuts were shipped," she said.

There were many other objects not of English ori-gin. There was a German distilling vessel, French wine flasks, and Chinese wine cups. In addition, there were Dutch and Venetian beads—"the blue ones were favored," she said.

The armor and weapons are English, and because the English emptied their storerooms to outfit the colonists, Straube had examples of breastplates, sword handles, and other military equipment that are not found in English museums.

Photographs and narrative descriptions of Straube's inventory were posted on the Internet so the Jamestown artifacts could be studied and analyzed by any scholar or student sitting at a computer.

Among those who had become intrigued with the archaeological work at Jamestown were Roxanne Gilmore, wife of former Virginia Governor James Gilmore and an archaeologist herself; Jeannie Baliles, wife of former Governor Gerald Baliles; and crime nov-elist Patricia Cornwell. Each participated in the dig and together, along with Kelso, visited museums and conser-vation laboratories in England and Ireland.

Archaeologists like Kelso, Luccketti, and Roxanne Gilmore were interested in solving the mysteries of Jamestown, mysteries of historic importance—and they were up against a 2007 deadline.

Meanwhile, APVA and the National Park Service were developing a master plan for the presentation of Jamestown during the quadricentennial year. Prelimi-nary ideas for the erection of a new visitor center on the island were being reviewed by the public and interested agencies. The former visitor center, dedicated in 1957, was wiped away by a hurricane.

Just how the remains of James Fort—covered for protection after their exposure—were to be interpreted for the commemoration had not been decided. First, Kelso needed to find more evidence of the inland pal-isades and the structures that were within them.

The surprises kept turning up—not only rare finds but a sheer volume of mundane shards of glass, ceramics, and other materials—all offering the prospect of learn-ing much more about the Jamestown settlement.

As the archaeological study progressed, the eastern and western palisades of James Fort were located and marked with "curtains" of upright split posts. Areas within and just outside the fort's walls were excavated. Evidence of a mud-and-stud barracks and a gentleman's quarters were found inside the eastern palisade, and stone foundations of two substantial buildings flanking the interior of the western wall were uncovered. Signs of four crude lean-to buildings were also identified.

Kelso garnered a flurry of international publicity when he attempted to identify conclusively skeletal remains as those of Captain Bartholomew Gosnold, one the colony's initial councilors. A DNA match in England could not be made.

Far more than a million artifacts have been retrieved. Trash pits and two abandoned wells yielded significant finds. Among them were Elizabethan-era body armor known as a coat of jacks, an exceptionally fine pewter flagon, hoes and other tools, and evidence of Native Americans living in the fort. Also of interest were pieces of bone from butchered wild and domestic animals.

The brackish muck in a well at the northern bulwark, which Kelso believes is the first dug on the island, has preserved masses of organic matter—insects, green leaves, twigs, seeds, and even pollen. Laboratory analysis of faunal artifacts is providing evidence of diet, which is of particular interest for the early years of hunger and disease. Innovative testing techniques on submerged oyster shells may disclose the quality of air and water at the time when Europeans first had an impact on the native ecosystem. Kelso is exuberant about the potential of these environmental findings.

Remarkably, this well was discovered under a collapsed fireplace that is believed to have been built in 1617 when an extension was added to a long building likely used by officials. Among the debris in the well was found a 1602 Irish halfpenny and a German stoneware jug circa 1608.

The well itself is unusual for its circumference and construction. The shaft is lined by a six-foot-square timber frame fashioned much like a log cabin and strengthened with vertical posts at the four corners. Should it be possible to lift the well lining intact from the ground and infuse it with preservative chemicals, it would become the second structure to survive seventeenth-century Jamestown—the other being the nearby brick church tower of 1647. Whether such a retrieval is possible is, for the time being, speculative.

Kelso has three remaining goals to keep him and his team in the field. He wants to discover the sites of the first English church and the original storehouse and to commemorate the early burial ground of the fort's soldiers. These graves should be honored, Kelso believes, as America's first military cemetery.

An interpretative display of the archaeological work under the auspices of APVA—including Gosnold's bones—is presented in a $4.9 million Archaearium. The Archaearium (pronounced "ar-kee-AIR-ee-um"), an invented word meaning place of origin, overlooks the James Fort site on the island renamed "Historic Jamestowne," so as to distinguish it from Jamestown Settlement, the state park upstream.

About the Contributors

Anthony Aveni is the Russell Colgate Distinguished University Professor of Astronomy, Anthropology, and Native American Studies at Colgate University. Among his recent works is a children's book, *The First Americans,* which won the 2006 Golden Spur Award for Juvenile Nonfiction and was a top ten selection by the International Reading Association.

James Axtell is the Kenan Professor of Humanities at the College of William and Mary. A member of the American Academy of Arts and Sciences, he is the author or editor of seventeen books on the history of colonial Indian-European relations and the history of education.

Allan C. Fisher Jr. was a *National Geographic* editor and the author of *America's Inland Waterway.*

Andrew Gardner writes and directs television documentaries, including *Gospel of Liberty,* which portrays George Whitfield and the aftermath of the Great Awakening in colonial Virginia.

Charles M. Holloway served as special assistant to the U.S. commissioner of education and as director of information and corporate communications at the College Board. He also was director of university communications at the College of William and Mary and has published two books.

Bruce P. Lenman is a Fellow of the Royal Society of Edinburgh, emeritus professor of history at the University of St. Andrews, and honorary professor at the University of Dundee. He has authored a dozen books in the fields of Scottish history and early-modern European overseas expansion. He lives in Stirling just under the rock crowned by the castle where James was baptized in 1567.

Michael Lombardi is an independent writer, producer, and director. He was previously director of operations and executive producer of Colonial Williamsburg Productions.

Will Molineux has been a reporter for the *Virginia Gazette,* the *Richmond News Leader,* and the *Daily Press;* Williamsburg bureau manager for the *Daily Press;* and editor of the *Daily Press* editorial page. He has also edited pictorial books on Williamsburg and Jamestown.

Dennis Montgomery began his career as a writer and editor with the Associated Press in 1968. His work with *Colonial Williamsburg,* the journal of the Colonial Williamsburg Foundation, began twenty-three years later and led him to the magazine's helm in 1998.

Paul C. Nagel devoted the first half of his career to university life, including four years as director of the Virginia Historical Society. Since 1985, he has written exclusively for the general reader, including several books about the Adamses of Massachusetts and another about Virginia's Lees.

Mark Nicholls is a fellow, a tutor, and the librarian at St. John's College, Cambridge, whose teaching and research interests lie in Tudor and Stuart government and politics. His books include *Investigating Gunpowder Plot* and *The History of the Modern British Isles, 1529–1603,* the first volume in the Blackwell History of Modern Britain series.

Ivor Noël Hume came to Colonial Williamsburg from London's Guildhall Museum in 1957 to head the foundation's Department of Archaeology. In 1992, he was made Officer of the British Empire by Queen Elizabeth II. He is the author of fifteen books and made two prizewinning television films for Colonial Williamsburg. His play on the life of Captain John Smith was presented at the Kimball Theatre in Williamsburg as a contribution to Virginia's 400th anniversary commemoration.

David Robinson is a retired *National Geographic* book editor. He has authored several books and nearly a hundred articles for a variety of publications.

D. A. Saguto has headed Colonial Williamsburg's shoemaking program since 1990. He is a fourth-generation artisan, as well as a lecturer, author, and consultant who has researched and taught traditional shoemaking in North America and Europe. He has designed and installed six historical shoemaking exhibits for the Smithsonian Institution in Washington, D. C.

Mary Miley Theobald taught museum studies and American history at Virginia Commonwealth University and now writes books and articles, most on history and travel topics. Her books include *Williamsburg Christmas* and *Colonial Williamsburg: The First 75 Years,* which was nominated for a Library of Virginia Literary Award.

Dr. Lewis Wright is a retired neurosurgeon. He has studied the life of the Reverend Robert Hunt for several decades.

Index